INTELLECTUAL FREEDOM MANUAL

INTELLECTUAL FREEDOM MANUAL

ELEVENTH EDITION

Compiled by the Office for Intellectual Freedom of the American Library Association

Erin Jones, Editor

ALA Editions
CHICAGO | 2026

ERIN JONES is the equitable libraries division director for Alameda County Library in California. She is a fierce advocate for intellectual freedom and privacy. Jones previously led the Privacy Subcommittee of ALA's Intellectual Freedom Committee and co-led the teams that developed Article VII of the *Library Bill of Rights* and the Core Values of Librarianship. She currently serves as a trustee for the LeRoy C. Merritt Humanitarian Fund. Her work has been honored with the California Library Association's Zoia Horn Award in both 2016 and 2021. She is also a coeditor of the *Ultimate Privacy Field Guide* (2022).

THE OFFICE FOR INTELLECTUAL FREEDOM is charged with implementing ALA policies concerning the concept of intellectual freedom as embodied in the *Library Bill of Rights,* ALA's basic policy on free access to libraries and library materials. The goal of the office is to educate library workers and the general public about the nature and importance of intellectual freedom in libraries.

ISBNs
979-8-89255-278-3 (paper)
979-8-89255-298-1 (PDF)
979-8-89255-299-8 (ePub)

Library of Congress Cataloging-in-Publication Data
Names: Jones, Erin (Librarian), Editor | American Library Association. Office for Intellectual Freedom
Title: Intellectual freedom manual / compiled by the Office for Intellectual Freedom of the American Library Association ; Erin Jones, editor.
Description: Chicago : Eleventh edition. | ALA Editions, 2026. |Includes bibliographical references and index.
Identifiers: LCCN 2025048348 (print) | ISBN 9798892552783 paperback
Subjects: Libraries—Censorship—United States—Handbooks, manuals, etc | Intellectual freedom—United States—Handbooks, manuals, etc
Classification: LCC Z711.4 .I57 2026 (print)
LC record available at https://lccn.loc.gov/2025048348

Book design by Alejandra Diaz in the Source Serif, Lato and Aleo typefaces.

♾ This paper meets the requirements of ANSI/NISO Z39.48-1992 (Permanence of Paper).

Printed in the United States of America

30 29 28 27 26 5 4 3 2 1

ALA Editions purchases fund advocacy, awareness, and accreditation programs for library professionals worldwide.

For John Spears, whose unwavering belief in intellectual freedom shaped this work. His passion for amplifying every voice and ensuring access for all is reflected in these pages.

5
Actions to Protect Intellectual Freedom in Your Library

1. **Create a culture** that supports intellectual freedom by regularly talking about it with users, coworkers, employees, administrators, legislators, governing bodies, friends, and family members. Don't wait for a crisis to educate others about the library profession's principles. Meet with other organizations and people in your community to form partnerships around common interests.
2. **Develop written policies** that support intellectual freedom in the following areas:
   - collection development;
   - resource reconsideration;
   - internet use;
   - meeting rooms;
   - displays and exhibit spaces;
   - privacy and confidentiality; and
   - user behavior.
3. **Formally adopt these core ALA statements** as policy for your library:
   - *Libraries: An American Value*
   - *Library Bill of Rights*
   - *Code of Ethics of the American Library Association*
   - *The Freedom to Read* statement

   Post the *Library Bill of Rights* where all users can see it; in buildings and on the library website.
4. **Train all staff regularly on intellectual freedom.** Use this manual to help them understand library values and what to do if someone challenges a resource or service.
5. **Ask for help** if you need it. If you're facing a challenge or concern and need help, contact your state intellectual freedom committee or ALA's Office for Intellectual Freedom at oif@ala.org or (312) 280-4221.

Contents

PART II: INTELLECTUAL FREEDOM TOPICS AND BEST PRACTICES

Acknowledgments

Special thanks to:

- The staff of the ALA Office for Intellectual Freedom, especially Eric Stroshane, for his guidance as the liaison to the editor.
- All the contributors who shared their time, expertise, and personal stories.
- The members of the Intellectual Freedom Committee, its Privacy Subcommittee, and the Committee on Professional Ethics for reviewing and updating policies and documents.
- Julie Oborny for helping ensure that all the interpretations were written in clear, plain language.
- Trina Magi and Martin Garnar for generously sharing their process and materials from editing the 10th edition of this manual.
- Deb Sica for approving my role as editor of the manual and for supporting me day-to-day, especially when things got intense.
- Rachel Chance, senior editor at ALA Editions, for always being available, answering every call, and helping guide this project to the finish line.

Introduction

Intellectual freedom begins with access. Without access, people cannot explore the topics and ideas that matter to them. Access means more than physically reaching a resource, it also means being able to understand it. If you walk into a library to find information on a topic, but every book is written in a language you don't speak, do you truly have access? Do you have intellectual freedom?

As library workers, we are responsible for providing access to the widest possible range of materials, so every member of the community can find the information they need in a way they can understand. Our own professional documents should follow the same principle.

Since 1974, the *Intellectual Freedom Manual* has been the essential reference for library workers seeking guidance on intellectual freedom topics. Past editions have served the profession well, especially those in library school or academia. This edition builds on that strong foundation while expanding its reach. It is written to be accessible to everyone, from the library volunteer to the director.

This edition applies the principles of plain language, making policies clear and easy to understand. The entire manual is written at or below a 12th grade reading level, making it a practical guide for real-world use. When a library worker faces a challenging intellectual freedom issue, they won't need to wade through dense language to get the answers they need.

To most people, policies feel dry and stiff. They're something libraries need, but often dread enforcing or explaining. Yet policy is the foundation of our work. It shapes culture, protects staff and users, and impacts real people. That's why this manual includes stories from individuals whose lives have been shaped by intellectual freedom. The policies your library adopts and enforces have real-world effects on your staff and your community.

This edition also brings in a wider range of voices. With twenty-three contributors, it reflects a broad spectrum of experiences. We made a deliberate effort to center and uplift the voices of BIPOC and LGBTQIA+ people, who are often the targets of censorship efforts. You'll find contributions from people working in libraries directly and indirectly, as well as passionate library advocates. The authors come from red states, blue states, tribal communities, rural towns, and major cities. Intellectual freedom isn't a partisan value—it's a cornerstone of democracy.

Inclusion matters. That's why this manual uses the term "library worker" rather than "librarian." Library workers include everyone who helps make the library run; from the facilities driver moving materials, to the finance officer balancing the budget, to the trustee voting on policy.

What follows is a brief guide to the contents of this manual and how you can use it to support intellectual freedom in libraries. It offers practical information to help you build the skills to lead from any role and ensure that everyone in your community has the right to access information.

> A note on terminology: This manual acknowledges that the legal term "child pornography" appears in U.S. federal law. However, the term "child sexual abuse material" (CSAM) is more accurate, as it focuses on the abuse and exploitation involved and centers the harm done to the child. Many organizations, including the U.S. Department of Justice, have called for a shift to CSAM. This manual uses that term whenever possible.

YOUR GUIDE TO WHAT'S INSIDE

This manual is divided into three parts. The table of contents and index can help you quickly find the information you need to address a specific topic or concern in your library.

Throughout the manual, you'll find short personal stories that bring policy issues to life, as well as essays from legal professionals sharing their insights on how the law impacts intellectual freedom. Each chapter begins with an overview that explains the big ideas and offers reflection questions.

Part I: Intellectual Freedom and Libraries

This section introduces what intellectual freedom is and why it matters. It also includes the core intellectual freedom documents of the American Library Association (ALA). Following those documents are policy worksheets that libraries can use to draft or revise their own intellectual freedom policies.

Part II: Intellectual Freedom Topics and Best Practices

This section includes nine chapters focused on key intellectual freedom topics:

- Access
- Censorship
- Children and youth
- Collection development
- Copyright
- Meeting rooms, exhibit spaces, and programming
- Politics, religion, and free expression
- Privacy
- Requests from law enforcement

Part III: Advocacy and Assistance

This final section offers practical guidance on advocating for intellectual freedom, getting help, lobbying, and working with your elected officials.

Appendixes

There are also two appendixes:

1. *Glossary of Terms:* Definitions of key terms used in the manual
2. *For Further Reading:* A selected bibliography for those who want to explore intellectual freedom topics more deeply

How to Use the Manual

- Refer to the manual when writing library policies.
  - Use "Creating Intellectual Freedom Policies for Your Library" (part I, chapter 3) to guide you in creating solid intellectual freedom policies.
- Turn to it for guidance when a question or problem emerges.
  - Consult the relevant chapter in "Intellectual Freedom Topics and Best Practices" (part II).
  - Review the tips in "Advocating and Lobbying for Intellectual Freedom" (part III, chapter 13).
  - Use the resources found in "Where to Get Help and Get Involved" (part III, chapter 14) for additional help.
- Use it to orient new employees, volunteers, and trustees.
  - Ask them to read "Why Intellectual Freedom Matters" (Prologue) and "What Is Intellectual Freedom?" (part I, chapter 1) and "Core Intellectual Freedom Documents of the American Library Association" (part I, chapter 2).
- Use it for professional development.
  - Have library staff, volunteers, and trustees read chapters in "Intellectual Freedom Topics and Best Practices" (part II). Then, schedule times to discuss the "Reflection Questions" at the beginning of each chapter.
- Use it as a textbook in library and information science courses.
  - Use the "Reflection Questions" at the beginning of each chapter in "Intellectual Freedom Topics and Best Practices" (part II) as writing prompts or to start class discussions
- Connect with other library workers and promote intellectual freedom.
  - Read "Where to Get Help and Get Involved" (part III, chapter 14) to learn about organizations, committees, programs, and awards that focus on intellectual freedom.

This edition of the *Intellectual Freedom Manual* is built on the idea of access. It uses clear, inclusive language so every library worker can understand the issues and take action. We all have a role in protecting intellectual freedom and making sure everyone in our community can find the information they need. Use this manual to learn how you can help keep libraries a trusted source of information and a key part of a strong democracy.

Note: We acknowledge the use of ChatGPT for grammar checks and plain language suggestions. All recommendations were carefully reviewed, with final decisions made by human editors.

Prologue

Why Intellectual Freedom Matters

Becky Calzada

Ideas can be fragile. They need our support, our encouragement, and our protection. And maybe even more importantly, they need our belief and attention.

—Kobi Yamada, author of *What Do You Do with an Idea?*

WHY MAKE TIME TO READ THIS BOOK?

To all library workers—front-line stewards of truth, curiosity, and access—this is a call to action. At a time when books are being pulled from shelves, when marginalized voices are being silenced, and when democratic institutions face mounting pressure, your role has never been more critical. You are more than information providers. You are defenders of one of the most powerful ideals in any free society: *intellectual freedom.*

This is not just a lofty principle. Intellectual freedom is the foundation upon which libraries—and our democracy—stand. When we protect the right to seek, receive, and share ideas without restriction, we are protecting the core values of democratic participation, free expression, and human dignity.

INTELLECTUAL FREEDOM: A CORE LIBRARY VALUE

From the first lending library established back in 1731 in Philadelphia by Benjamin Franklin to the digital repositories of today, libraries have always stood for the freedom to access information. Intellectual freedom is not simply one of the American Library Association's *core values*—it is the one that makes all the others possible. It asserts that every person has the right to seek information, explore ideas, form opinions, and share these without fear of suppression.

When library workers champion intellectual freedom, we affirm our belief that every individual has the right to seek, read, think, and question on their own terms. We affirm that the library is a sanctuary for voluntary inquiry, a space where ideas—no matter how new, radical, or uncomfortable—can live and breathe.

INTELLECTUAL FREEDOM AND DEMOCRACY

A democracy is only as strong as its citizens' ability to think independently, to challenge long held beliefs, and to participate in the shaping of society. Intellectual freedom is the beating heart of this process. It empowers people with access to the full spectrum of thought—from classic texts to emerging voices, from long-standing debates to radical reimaginings.

Without it, civic engagement becomes hollow. Discourse narrows. Creativity wanes. In its absence, democracy withers.

INTELLECTUAL FREEDOM AND THE PURPOSE OF LIBRARIES

Libraries are not neutral spaces—they are purposeful ones. Their purpose is to cultivate a culture of lifelong learning and free inquiry. They are sanctuaries for independent thought, designed to uplift every voice and invite every question. To protect intellectual freedom is to uphold this mission. It is to guarantee that anyone who walks through our doors can explore information without gatekeeping, coercion, or censorship.

WHY THIS MANUAL, AND WHY NOW?

Since 2021, libraries have found themselves on the front lines of a renewed and relentless culture war. There is an orchestrated drive to restrict access to information, to erase diverse perspectives, and to narrow the lens of acceptable thought. Books are challenged. Programs are scrutinized. Staff are threatened. What is under attack is not just content, but the principle of free access to information itself.

This manual exists because *we must respond*. We must become not only keepers of collections but also advocates—skilled, informed, and unflinching. Intellectual freedom requires us to rise as its guardians, to ensure that the library remains a place where ideas are not feared but fostered.

INVESTING IN OURSELVES, INVESTING IN FREEDOM

Why spend the time reading this book? Why learn and apply its lessons and advice? Because we are the last line of defense. Because every reader who finds themselves in a book, every student who discovers an idea that changes their world, and every voice that dares to speak truth to power depends on us to hold the line.

To protect intellectual freedom is to:

- Promote a *well-informed citizenry* capable of critical thinking and responsible action.
- Uphold the *freedom to think and express,* even when ideas are unpopular or controversial.
- Support *democratic processes* through the open exchange of knowledge.
- Encourage *innovation and creativity* by ensuring that ideas can be explored without limits.
- Defend *human rights* by advocating for the voices and stories of all people, especially those historically marginalized.

PREPARING WITH PURPOSE: THE POWER OF COMMUNICATION AND PROACTIVE LEARNING

Defending intellectual freedom is not just about holding the right beliefs—it's about being able to *articulate, explain,* and *stand up* for those beliefs with clarity and conviction. In an era when the very nature of libraries is being questioned, communication becomes one of our most essential tools.

Honing your communication skills is not optional—it is strategic. Whether you are speaking at a school board meeting, answering a concerned parent, writing a program rationale, or training new staff, your ability to calmly and confidently advocate for intellectual freedom makes a tangible difference.

That's why investing time in this manual matters.

Reading the *Intellectual Freedom Manual* is more than an academic exercise—it is preparation for the real-world challenges that library workers face daily. This manual offers legal grounding, historical context, policy guidance, and the practical tools needed to respond effectively and responsibly. But it is not enough to read it passively. It must be *internalized, discussed, practiced,* and *applied.*

Ask yourself:

- Can I clearly explain why a diverse collection is essential to intellectual freedom?
- Am I prepared to respond to a materials challenge or public criticism with facts, empathy, and authority?
- Do I know our policies and procedures—and how to implement them fairly and consistently?

Proactive preparation is a form of continuous improvement. It ensures that when the moment comes—and it *will* come—you are not scrambling to react. You are already ready.

This manual is your training ground. Your toolkit. Your guide. And by investing time to sharpen your communication and deepen your understanding, you become not just a supporter of intellectual freedom—but a formidable defender of it.

WHAT INTELLECTUAL FREEDOM NEEDS NOW

This moment calls for more than quiet agreement. It calls for bold, persistent, principled action. Intellectual freedom needs:

- A *cadre of informed and skilled advocates* who understand the policies, the principles, and the power of access.
- *Tireless champions* willing to speak out, take action, and educate others.
- A lasting *commitment to resisting censorship* and standing firm in defense of open, informed decision-making.

We must step into this work with clear eyes and steady resolve. Because ideas—fragile, powerful, transformative—depend on us. Because libraries are more than buildings. They are battlegrounds for truth and access to information. And because intellectual freedom, once lost, is not easily regained.

Let this be our rallying cry: We are the defenders of access, the protectors of inquiry, the champions of thought. We are library workers. And we choose to fight for intellectual freedom.

Part I
Intellectual Freedom and Libraries

CHAPTER 1
What Is Intellectual Freedom?

Deborah Caldwell-Stone

Intellectual freedom is a core value of the American Library Association (ALA). It forms the foundation for the principles that guide the practice of modern librarianship.[1] Yet, ALA has not adopted or endorsed an official definition of intellectual freedom.[2]

While no official definition of intellectual freedom exists in ALA's official policy manual, other ALA statements and publications offer several definitions. For example, prior editions of the *Intellectual Freedom Manual* gave this definition:

> Intellectual freedom is the right of every individual to both seek and receive information from all points of view without restriction. It provides free access to all expressions of ideas through which any and all sides of a question, cause or movement may be explored.[3]

Another definition, from the library and information science scholar Eliza Dresang, expands the definition of intellectual freedom to include the individual's right of free expression:

> Intellectual Freedom as a concept in librarianship means freedom to think or believe what one will, freedom to express one's thoughts and beliefs in unrestricted manners and means, and freedom to access information and ideas regardless of their content or the viewpoint of the author or the age, background, or beliefs of the receiver.[4]

Both of these definitions inform ALA's statement on intellectual freedom as a core value:

> Intellectual freedom empowers people to think for themselves and to make informed decisions while respecting each individual's dignity and independence. Library workers encourage people to cultivate curiosity and form ideas by questioning the world and accessing information from diverse viewpoints and formats without restrictions or censorship. The right to

> privacy is a crucial safeguard to this freedom, ensuring everyone has the right to develop their thoughts and opinions free of surveillance.[5]

Intellectual freedom means both the freedom to hold, access, and disseminate ideas, and the creation of the conditions that uphold and defend those freedoms, including the right to privacy. These principles are central to librarianship and all information professions.

INTELLECTUAL FREEDOM IN LIBRARIES

The American Library Association and the International Federation of Library Associations (IFLA) have created statements to help library workers apply intellectual freedom principles in their work. These statements also provide guidance to institutions when including these principles in their mission, policies, and procedures.

- The *Library Bill of Rights* is ALA's basic policy on intellectual freedom. It is partly based on First Amendment principles that support free and open access to information in public libraries. It includes seven articles that guide how libraries provide services to users of all ages. ALA has also developed interpretations that explain how the *Library Bill of Rights* applies to specific library services and practices.
- The *ALA Code of Ethics* includes nine principles that guide library workers in performing their duties. It can also help library workers resolve conflicts that may arise between competing ethical principles.
- *IFLA's "Statement on Libraries and Intellectual Freedom"* affirms IFLA's commitment to uninhibited access to information, freedom of expression, and the privacy of library use.[6]
- *IFLA's "Code of Ethics for Librarians and Other Information Workers"* guides library workers' practice throughout the world. It is a model policy that encourages national and regional library associations to create or revise their own codes of ethical practice.[7]

ALA members support and defend intellectual freedom principles. They do this through multiple groups:

- The Intellectual Freedom Committee and its Privacy Subcommittee monitor developing issues and recommend actions to safeguard the rights of libraries, library users, and library workers.
- The Committee on Professional Ethics maintains and revises the *Code of Ethics* when new issues challenge information professions.
- The Intellectual Freedom Round Table offers a forum for ALA members to get involved in defending intellectual freedom.

ALA also promotes and defends intellectual freedom through its Office for Intellectual Freedom (OIF). Founded in 1969, the mission of the office is to educate library workers and the public about the nature and importance of intellectual freedom in libraries. OIF offers services, programs, publications, and online resources to support this mission. It also provides confidential support to library workers facing challenges to materials or services.

OIF staff also lead and support public awareness programs like Banned Books Week, Right to Read Day, and Unite Against Book Bans, and they maintain ALA's banned books database.

The Freedom to Read Foundation (FTRF) is a separate but closely related organization. ALA members established it to act as the legal defense arm for intellectual freedom in libraries. FTRF goes to court to defend the First Amendment right to receive information and to support libraries' ability to offer any materials they can legally acquire.

A Deeper Understanding

Intellectual freedom is a fundamental human right that belongs to every person. It is more than just freedom of speech or freedom of thought; it also includes respect for each person and their ability to make their own decisions. The Universal Declaration of Human Rights (UDHR), adopted by the United Nations General Assembly in 1948, lists the elements of intellectual freedom recognized as international human rights[8] Article 19 includes the right to seek, receive, and share information and ideas without limitation. The UDHR describes the rights listed in Article 19 as personal rights that all societies and governments must protect.[9]

ALA has incorporated the UDHR into its policies.[10] This was done to:

- describe the rights that library workers seek to protect;
- provide a way to address intellectual freedom issues occurring outside the United States; and
- respond to human rights violations by governments, businesses, and organizations.[11]

In the United States, the rights related to intellectual freedom are protected by the First Amendment. These rights include freedom of speech, freedom of the press, and freedom of belief.[12] Courts in the United States have expanded the rights protected by the First Amendment to make sure that everyone can fully exercise their intellectual freedom. This includes the right to receive information and the right to privacy.

The right to receive information and the right to privacy provide the legal basis for the practice of intellectual freedom in publicly funded libraries. Everyone in the United States—regardless of age—has a First Amendment right to freely access the public library. They also have the right to access and use the library's information resources without censorship.[13]

The duty to protect First Amendment rights applies only to workers in publicly funded libraries. However, all library workers have the ethical responsibility to practice, defend, and advocate for intellectual freedom. Libraries in private schools, universities, and other institutions can adopt the *Library Bill of Rights*, the *Code of Ethics*, and similar statements of principle to support strong intellectual freedom practices in the library. The principles in these statements of professional values, codes of ethics, and law should always be the rule and not the exception. Following that rule is needed now, more than ever.

By promoting the freedom to read, libraries enrich people's lives and support personal growth, lifelong learning, and success in the workplace. Intellectual freedom makes it possible for individuals to discuss the latest bestseller in a library book club or read it privately with nobody looking over their shoulder. Diverse collections give users the opportunity to read widely and critically, and to decide for themselves what to read next. Intellectual freedom gives students access to a full range of ideas in order to understand all sides of an issue—scientific, political, and beyond—to prepare them for college or the workforce. Intellectual freedom empowers people of all ages to make smart decisions and solve real-world problems. Practicing these principles means offering tools and opportunities for civic engagement, including voter registration, health care information, and support for new Americans.

Barriers to Access and Censorship

The practice of intellectual freedom in libraries depends on free access to all expressions of ideas. Barriers to information access can result in censorship and a loss of intellectual freedom. The following are some of the common barriers to information access that all libraries may face:

- Demands to restrict or remove books, art, displays, and other resources
- Demands to cancel a speaker or programs
- Internet filters that block access to online content
- Restrictions on the access and use of the library's public spaces and meeting rooms
- Physical barriers to accessing library spaces (e.g., a building without a wheelchair ramp)
- Costly licenses, fees, or service models that place content out of reach of libraries and users
- Service models or platforms that rely on the collection and use of library users' personal information

Academic Libraries

For many years, academic libraries were mostly free from the intellectual freedom problems seen in school and public libraries. That is no longer true.

Today, academic libraries face growing controversy in a polarized political climate. Challenges to intellectual freedom now come from both progressives and conservatives.

The American Association of University Professors, the Association of College and Research Libraries, and the Office for Intellectual Freedom all report growing and ongoing challenges to intellectual freedom in colleges and universities. These challenges limit academic and intellectual freedom for students, faculty, and library staff:

- *Laws and state actions eliminating diversity, equity, and inclusion (DEI):* State legislatures and the federal government are passing laws that ban DEI programs in higher education or take away funding from schools that continue their support for DEI.
- *Challenges to library collections:* Universities and colleges are being told to remove books that are seen as promoting or discussing:
  - racism;
  - gender identity;
  - sexual orientation;
  - sexuality; and
  - the experiences of marginalized groups.

  Challenges may also come from faculty and staff who ask to remove books because of the reputation of an author or a perceived lack of quality. Alumni and donors may try to use their funding to pressure the library to remove certain books or prevent new ones from being added.
- *Campus protests and free speech zones:* Protests that challenge university and government policy have made college campuses a contested space for free expression. Administrators may try to control protests and controversial speech by creating free speech zones or using other tactics. These actions can chill library programs, instruction, services, and collections. Protests may also happen in the library. When they do, library workers must balance safety and access with the need to protect free expression.
- *De-platforming speakers and policing speech:* In recent years, students, faculty, and community members have asked administrators to include content or trigger warnings in curricula. They have also asked for the cancellation of speakers and programs with content they find disturbing or harmful. This creates a conflict between intellectual freedom values and the rights and needs of diverse and marginalized groups. Library workers must be prepared to navigate this conflict while upholding intellectual freedom in the library.
- *Technology and privacy:* There is now a reliance on online and digital technologies for instruction, access to library resources, and course management. These tools can threaten student privacy if they are used to monitor reading habits and track internet use.

School Libraries

School libraries improve students' lives and support their education. Effective school libraries provide spaces for personalized learning environments and make sure all students can access the resources they need.[14] School librarians foster literacy skills, help students think critically, and encourage students to become lifelong learners. Students do better in school when they have access to a quality school library staffed by a certified, degreed librarian.[15]

Yet school libraries are often misunderstood by administrators, boards, and the public. Some see them only as book warehouses that support classroom instruction. Others view them as luxuries that can be cut when budgets are tight. Like academic libraries, school libraries have become centers of controversy. School librarians now face a growing number of challenges to intellectual freedom and students' access to information:

- *Laws and state actions eliminating diversity, equity, and inclusion (DEI):* State legislatures and local school boards are acting to remove DEI from K–12 schools and their libraries. They are doing this through laws, regulations, and local ordinances. The goal is to limit any study or discussion of divisive topics, such as:
  - racism;
  - gender identity;
  - sexual orientation;
  - sexuality; and
  - the experiences of marginalized groups.

  To do this, state and local lawmakers are passing laws that restrict or remove books addressing these topics from school libraries. Some laws also limit how much school librarians can be involved in selecting or removing books.

- *Organized challenges:* Extremist parental rights groups and other censorship advocates falsely claim that books and resources about "divisive topics" harm students' learning and well-being. This creates fears about student learning and safety. As a result, school libraries are seeing record numbers of demands to remove these books.
- *Internet filters:* The Children's Internet Protection Act (CIPA) requires schools to use internet filters. These filters are meant to block access to illegal, sexually explicit content. However, filters often block students' access to legal and important information. Now, organized parental rights groups are demanding that similar filters be added to school library catalogs and research databases.
- *Ratings systems:* Religious and political groups are creating book ratings systems to label certain titles as "objectionable content." School boards and lawmakers use these ratings to limit access to library books and control what books are added to the school library.

- *Student privacy:* Administrators and parents can now monitor students' reading habits and track their internet use. They do this through digital instruction tools, access to library resources, and course management software. In some states, lawmakers have passed laws to remove reader privacy protections for minors.

Public Libraries

Public libraries are community hubs for access to information, lifelong learning, and civic engagement. They provide books, tools, and technology for learning and sharing ideas. Public libraries make it possible for everyone to learn, find information, enrich their lives, get a job, and take part in elections and community discussions.

Public libraries also level the playing field for immigrants, low-income communities, and marginalized groups by ensuring they have access to the information they want and need. Public libraries show how intellectual freedom can create a more just and equitable society. This may be why public libraries are facing many of the same intellectual freedom challenges as academic and school libraries:

- *Organized challenges:* Extremist parental rights groups and other censorship advocates are demanding that public libraries limit access to books and resources about:
  - racism;
  - gender identity;
  - sexual orientation;
  - sexuality; and
  - the experiences of marginalized groups.

  The groups make these demands without regard for public libraries' responsibilities under the First Amendment and the library profession's commitment to intellectual freedom.

- *Internet filters:* Organized censorship groups are demanding that public libraries remove or limit access to research databases. They falsely claim that these resources contain sexual content that is not suitable for minors.
- *Ratings systems:* Book ratings created by religious and political groups are being used to restrict or remove books and limit future purchases.
- *Meeting rooms and programs:* Many public libraries offer spaces for the community to use for meetings, programs, and public discussion. When controversial speakers and groups use these spaces, people ask the library to cancel the event. Libraries are also pressured to cancel their own programs and displays. For example, some people or groups object to Drag Story Hour and Pride Month displays.

STANDING UP FOR INTELLECTUAL FREEDOM

Libraries, and those who work in libraries, are currently facing an unprecedented campaign of book censorship. This is part of a larger, organized attack on libraries and the profession of librarianship. The number of demands to censor books and other library resources is at an all-time high. From 2021 to 2024, OIF recorded more book challenges than in any other period since it began tracking them in 1990.

These demands to remove and restrict books are not the result of any grassroots movement. Instead, they are driven by a small but vocal and politically powerful minority. They want to remove entire genres and categories of books from library shelves in pursuit of a larger authoritarian campaign to put politics and religion over the well-being and education of young people, and everyone's right to find and access books in the library.

The most insidious attack on libraries and intellectual freedom is the attempt by elected officials to overturn court decisions holding that public libraries are spaces governed by the First Amendment. They argue that libraries and their collections are a vehicle to express their views, so that they can censor library materials and deny people access to the ideas and opinions they don't like. Some courts are rejecting these claims and affirming that libraries belong to the communities they serve, and not to politicians or pressure groups. But other courts are bowing to politicians or pressure groups and accepting the argument that there is no First Amendment right to access books and other materials in public libraries.

These threats to libraries and intellectual freedom are real and growing, challenging the legal foundations that protect the freedom to read in the United States. This situation requires all library workers to uphold the core value of intellectual freedom in libraries by standing behind their professional ethics to defend and advocate for intellectual freedom while building a culture of intellectual freedom in their libraries and communities.

NOTES

1. "Core Values of Librarianship," American Library Association, January 2024, ala.org/advocacy/advocacy/intfreedom/corevalues.
2. J. M. Krug and C. Morgan, *Intellectual Freedom Manual*, Eighth Edition (Chicago: American Library Association, 2010), 12.
3. Candace Morgan, "Glossary," in *Intellectual Freedom Manual*, Tenth Edition (Chicago: American Library Association, 2021), 300.
4. Eliza T. Dresang, "Intellectual Freedom and Libraries: Complexity and Change in the Twenty-First-Century Digital Environment," *Library Quarterly* 76, no. 2 (2006): 169–92.
5. "Core Values of Librarianship," American Library Association.
6. International Federation of Library Associations, "Statement on Libraries and Intellectual Freedom" (1999), repository.ifla.org/handle/20.500.14598/1424.
7. International Federation of Library Associations, "Code of Ethics for Librarians and Other Information Workers" (2012), repository.ifla.org/handle/20.500.14598/1850.
8. United Nations, *Universal Declaration of Human Rights* (1948), un.org/en/about-us/universal-declaration-of-human-rights.
9. United Nations, *Universal Declaration of Human Rights.*
10. "The Universal Right to Free Expression: An Interpretation of the *Library Bill of Rights,"* adopted January 16, 1991, by the ALA Council; amended on July 1, 2014; and May 29, 2025.
11. T. Magi and M. Garnar, eds., *A History of ALA Policy on Intellectual Freedom* (American Library Association, 2015), 242–43.
12. U.S. Const. amend. I.
13. *Kreimer v. Bureau of Police for the town of Morristown, NJ,* 958 F.2d 1242 (3d Cir. 1992).
14. American Association of School Librarians, "The Role of the School Library," ala.org/sites/default/files/aasl/content/advocacy/statements/docs/AASL_Role_of_the_School_Library.pdf.
15. Center for American Progress, "Investing in School Libraries and Librarians to Improve Literacy Outcomes," April 18, 2024; R. Burress, C. Atkins, B. McDonald, and B. Buress, "The Power of Full-Time Certified School Librarians in Missouri: Boosting Student Achievement Across Disciplines," *School Libraries Worldwide*, October 2023, https://journals.library.ualberta.ca/slw/index.php/slw/article/view/8695.

CHAPTER 2
Core Intellectual Freedom Documents of the American Library Association

Library Bill of Rights

Adopted June 19, 1939, by the ALA Council; amended October 14, 1944; June 18, 1948; February 2, 1961; June 27, 1967; January 23, 1980; January 29, 2019. Inclusion of "age" reaffirmed January 23, 1996.

The American Library Association affirms that all libraries are forums for information and ideas, and that the following basic policies should guide their services.

I. Books and other library resources should be provided for the interest, information, and enlightenment of all people of the community the library serves. Materials should not be excluded because of the origin, background, or views of those contributing to their creation.

II. Libraries should provide materials and information presenting all points of view on current and historical issues. Materials should not be proscribed or removed because of partisan or doctrinal disapproval.

III. Libraries should challenge censorship in the fulfillment of their responsibility to provide information and enlightenment.

IV. Libraries should cooperate with all persons and groups concerned with resisting abridgment of free expression and free access to ideas.

V. A person's right to use a library should not be denied or abridged because of origin, age, background, or views.

VI. Libraries which make exhibit spaces and meeting rooms available to the public they serve should make such facilities available on an equitable basis, regardless of the beliefs or affiliations of individuals or groups requesting their use.

VII. All people, regardless of origin, age, background, or views, possess a right to privacy and confidentiality in their library use. Libraries should advocate for, educate about, and protect people's privacy, safeguarding all library use data, including personally identifiable information.

In the *Library Bill of Rights* and all its interpretations:

- Origin means all the traits someone is born into and can't change.
- Age means all the traits that come with a person's stage of life and maturity.
- Background means all the traits that are a result of a person's life experiences.
- Views means all the opinions and beliefs held and expressed by a person.

Note: This definition comes from "Equity, Diversity, Inclusion, and Belonging: An Interpretation of the *Library Bill of Rights*."

In 1993, the ALA Intellectual Freedom Committee first adopted a version of this statement in "Access to Library Resources and Services Regardless of Gender or Sexual Orientation: An Interpretation of the *Library Bill of Rights*" (now titled "Library Access and Representation for All Sexes, Gender Identities and Expressions, and Sexual Orientations: An Interpretation of the *Library Bill of Rights*").

Code of Ethics of the American Library Association

Adopted at the 1939 Midwinter Meeting by the ALA Council; amended June 30, 1981; June 28, 1995; January 22, 2008; and June 29, 2021.

As members of the American Library Association, we recognize the importance of codifying and making known to the profession and to the general public the ethical principles that guide the work of librarians, other professionals providing information services, library trustees and library staffs.

Ethical dilemmas occur when values are in conflict. The American Library Association *Code of Ethics* states the values to which we are committed, and embodies the ethical responsibilities of the profession in this changing information environment.

We significantly influence or control the selection, organization, preservation, and dissemination of information. In a political system grounded in an informed citizenry, we are members of a profession explicitly committed to intellectual freedom and the freedom of access to information. We have a special obligation to ensure the free flow of information and ideas to present and future generations.

The principles of this Code are expressed in broad statements to guide ethical decision making. These statements provide a framework; they cannot and do not dictate conduct to cover particular situations.

1. We provide the highest level of service to all library users through appropriate and usefully organized resources; equitable service policies; equitable access; and accurate, unbiased, and courteous responses to all requests.
2. We uphold the principles of intellectual freedom and resist all efforts to censor library resources.

3. We protect each library user's right to privacy and confidentiality with respect to information sought or received and resources consulted, borrowed, acquired or transmitted.
4. We respect intellectual property rights and advocate balance between the interests of information users and rights holders.
5. We treat co-workers and other colleagues with respect, fairness, and good faith, and advocate conditions of employment that safeguard the rights and welfare of all employees of our institutions.
6. We do not advance private interests at the expense of library users, colleagues, or our employing institutions.
7. We distinguish between our personal convictions and professional duties and do not allow our personal beliefs to interfere with fair representation of the aims of our institutions or the provision of access to their information resources.
8. We strive for excellence in the profession by maintaining and enhancing our own knowledge and skills, by encouraging the professional development of co-workers, and by fostering the aspirations of potential members of the profession.
9. We affirm the inherent dignity and rights of every person. We work to recognize and dismantle systemic and individual biases; to confront inequity and oppression; to enhance diversity and inclusion; and to advance racial and social justice in our libraries, communities, profession, and associations through awareness, advocacy, education, collaboration, services, and allocation of resources and spaces.

Enforcement of the *Code of Ethics* Q&A

Adopted January 2009 by the ALA Committee on Professional Ethics; amended January 28, 2019; and September 24, 2024.

The principles discussed in the American Library Association's (ALA) *Code of Ethics* are broad statements to guide library workers and boards in ethical decision-making. This Q&A is an extension of the Code to further expand and assist in that decision-making.

Why should a library adopt the *Code of Ethics* if it's not enforced, and what can I do to support it?

The *Code of Ethics* helps everyone understand the values and responsibilities of library workers, even if they are not strict rules. It guides our decisions and actions, ensuring we support intellectual freedom and access to information.

You can support the Code by:

- Posting it in your workplace
- Learning about relevant laws and how they might affect ethical behavior
- Encouraging your workplace to adopt it as a policy
- Promoting ethics education

- Personally committing to live by these values and continually reflecting on your own ethical practices

Libraries should make decisions internally on any disciplinary actions for violating the *Code of Ethics.*

Can the *Code of Ethics* be enforced, and are there any consequences for violating it?

The American Library Association does not enforce the *Code of Ethics.* These statements provide a framework; they cannot and do not dictate conduct to cover particular situations.

Libraries are encouraged to adopt the *Code of Ethics* locally. This way, each library can handle enforcement and ensure compliance with local laws.

What is the relationship between the *Code of Ethics* and the *ALA Code of Conduct*?

ALA is a voluntary organization and no library or library employee is required to follow the *Code of Ethics* or any other policies of ALA Council within their local jurisdiction. These policies are best practices, developed and offered as guidance, for their governing agencies in writing their own policies.

ALA has enforceable *Codes of Conduct* for online discussions and meetings/conferences.[1,2] These codes are based on the values in the *Code of Ethics.* Violations of these *Codes of Conduct* can result in removal from meetings, conferences, or online discussion platforms.

Libraries may develop their own codes of conduct or library use policies based on the principles in the *Code of Ethics* and other core documents.

Is there an ethical obligation to speak up and push for changes to policies that are harmful to the public or my profession?

Library workers should feel an ethical obligation to speak up when they see violations of the *Code of Ethics.* Some examples include:

- You are an academic librarian who disagrees with the university's lack of a privacy policy for electronic resources
- You are a children's librarian who disagrees with the library's policy of fines for children
- You are a library director and your trustees disagree with your stance on not having internet filters on computers
- You are a school library worker and your administrator wants you to remove a book without going through the library reconsideration process.

Library workers will need to use their judgment to decide when and how to speak up. Workers denied employment rights while defending the *Code of Ethics* may seek support from the LeRoy C. Merritt Humanitarian Fund.[3]

Where can I find more information?

Additional questions about the *Code of Ethics* can be directed to the Committee on Professional Ethics c/o the ALA Office for Intellectual Freedom by phone at (312) 280-4221 or by email at oif@ala.org.[4]

NOTES

1. American Library Association, "Online Code of Conduct," ALA Connect (website), connect.ala.org/codeofconduct.
2. American Library Association, ALA Virtual Meeting Code of Conduct (website), alaannual.org/general-information/ala-virtual-meeting-code-conduct.
3. American Library Association, LeRoy C. Merritt Humanitarian Fund (website), ala.org/aboutala/affiliates/relatedgroups/merrittfund/merritt humanitarian.
4. American Library Association, Committee on Professional Ethics (website), ala.org/aboutala/committees/ala/ala-profethic; American Library Association, Office for Intellectual Freedom (website), ala.org/aboutala/offices/oif.

The Freedom to Read

Adopted June 25, 1953, by the ALA Council and the Association of American Publishers Freedom to Read Committee; amended January 28, 1972; January 16, 1991; July 12, 2000; and June 30, 2004. (This statement was originally issued in May 1953 by the Westchester Conference of the American Library Association and the American Book Publishers Council, which in 1970 consolidated with the American Educational Publishers Institute to become the Association of American Publishers.)

The freedom to read is essential to our democracy. It is continuously under attack. Private groups and public authorities in various parts of the country are working to remove or limit access to reading materials, to censor content in schools, to label "controversial" views, to distribute lists of "objectionable" books or authors, and to purge libraries. These actions apparently rise from a view that our national tradition of free expression is no longer valid; that censorship and suppression are needed to counter threats to safety or national security, as well as to avoid the subversion of politics and the corruption of morals. We, as individuals devoted to reading and as librarians and publishers responsible for disseminating ideas, wish to assert the public interest in the preservation of the freedom to read.

Most attempts at suppression rest on a denial of the fundamental premise of democracy: that the ordinary individual, by exercising critical judgment, will select the good and reject the bad. We trust Americans to recognize propaganda and misinformation, and to make their own decisions about what they read and believe. We do not believe they are prepared to sacrifice their heritage of a free press in order to be "protected" against what others think may be bad for them. We believe they still favor free enterprise in ideas and expression.

These efforts at suppression are related to a larger pattern of pressures being brought against education, the press, art and images, films, broadcast media, and the Internet. The problem is not only one of actual censorship. The shadow of fear cast by these pressures leads, we suspect, to an even larger voluntary curtailment of expression by those who seek to avoid controversy or unwelcome scrutiny by government officials.

Such pressure toward conformity is perhaps natural to a time of accelerated change. And yet suppression is never more dangerous than in such a time of social tension. Freedom has given the United States the elasticity to endure strain. Freedom keeps open the path of novel and creative solutions, and enables change to come by choice. Every silencing of a heresy, every enforcement of an orthodoxy, diminishes the toughness and resilience of our society and leaves it the less able to deal with controversy and difference.

Now as always in our history, reading is among our greatest freedoms. The freedom to read and write is almost the only means for making generally available ideas or manners of expression that can initially command only a small audience. The written word is the natural medium for the new idea and the untried voice from which come the original contributions to social growth. It is essential to the extended discussion that serious thought requires, and to the accumulation of knowledge and ideas into organized collections.

We believe that free communication is essential to the preservation of a free society and a creative culture. We believe that these pressures toward conformity present the danger of limiting the range and variety of inquiry and expression on which our democracy and our culture depend. We believe that every American community must zealously guard the freedom to publish and to circulate, in order to preserve its own freedom to read. We believe that publishers and librarians have a profound responsibility to give validity to that freedom to read by making it possible for the readers to choose freely from a variety of offerings.

The freedom to read is guaranteed by the Constitution. Those with faith in free people will stand firm on these constitutional guarantees of essential rights and will exercise the responsibilities that accompany these rights.

We therefore affirm these propositions:

1. *It is in the public interest for publishers and librarians to make available the widest diversity of views and expressions, including those that are unorthodox, unpopular, or considered dangerous by the majority.*

Creative thought is by definition new, and what is new is different. The bearer of every new thought is a rebel until that idea is refined and tested. Totalitarian systems attempt to maintain themselves in power by the ruthless suppression of any concept that challenges the established orthodoxy. The power of a democratic system to adapt to change is vastly strengthened by the freedom of its citizens to choose widely from among conflicting opinions offered freely to them. To stifle every nonconformist idea at birth would mark the end of the democratic process. Furthermore, only through the constant activity of weighing and selecting can the democratic mind attain the strength demanded by times like these. We need to know not only what we believe but why we believe it.

2. *Publishers, librarians, and booksellers do not need to endorse every idea or presentation they make available. It would conflict with the public interest for them to establish their own political, moral, or aesthetic views as a standard for determining what should be published or circulated.*

Publishers and librarians serve the educational process by helping to make available knowledge and ideas required for the growth of the mind and the increase of learning. They do not foster education by imposing as mentors the patterns of their own thought. The people should have the freedom to read and consider a broader range of ideas than those that may be held by any single librarian or publisher or government or church. It is wrong that what one can read should be confined to what another thinks proper.

3. *It is contrary to the public interest for publishers or librarians to bar access to writings on the basis of the personal history or political affiliations of the author.*

No art or literature can flourish if it is to be measured by the political views or private lives of its creators. No society of free people can flourish that draws up lists of writers to whom it will not listen, whatever they may have to say.

4. *There is no place in our society for efforts to coerce the taste of others, to confine adults to the reading matter deemed suitable for adolescents, or to inhibit the efforts of writers to achieve artistic expression.*

To some, much of modern expression is shocking. But is not much of life itself shocking? We cut off literature at the source if we prevent writers from dealing with the stuff of life. Parents and teachers have a responsibility to prepare the young to meet the diversity of experiences in life to which they will be exposed, as they have a responsibility to help them learn to think critically for themselves. These are affirmative responsibilities, not to be discharged simply by preventing them from reading works for which they are not yet prepared. In these matters values differ, and values cannot be legislated; nor can machinery be devised that will suit the demands of one group without limiting the freedom of others.

5. *It is not in the public interest to force a reader to accept the prejudgment of a label characterizing any expression or its author as subversive or dangerous.*

The ideal of labeling presupposes the existence of individuals or groups with wisdom to determine by authority what is good or bad for others. It presupposes that individuals must be directed in making up their minds about the ideas they examine. But Americans do not need others to do their thinking for them.

6. *It is the responsibility of publishers and librarians, as guardians of the people's freedom to read, to contest encroachments upon that freedom by individuals or groups seeking to impose their own standards or tastes upon the community at large; and by the government whenever it seeks to reduce or deny public access to public information.*

It is inevitable in the give and take of the democratic process that the political, the moral, or the aesthetic concepts of an individual or group will occasionally collide with those of another individual or group. In a free society individuals are free to determine for themselves what they wish to read, and each group is free to determine what it will recommend to its freely associated members. But no group has the right to take the law into its own hands, and to impose its own concept of politics or morality upon other members of a democratic society. Freedom is no freedom if it is accorded only to the accepted and the inoffensive. Further, democratic societies are more safe, free, and creative when the free flow of public information is not restricted by governmental prerogative or self-censorship.

7. *It is the responsibility of publishers and librarians to give full meaning to the freedom to read by providing books that enrich the quality and diversity of thought and expression. By the exercise of this affirmative responsibility, they can demonstrate that the answer to a "bad" book is a good one, the answer to a "bad" idea is a good one.*

The freedom to read is of little consequence when the reader cannot obtain matter fit for that reader's purpose. What is needed is not only the absence of restraint, but the positive provision of opportunity for the people to read the best that has been thought and said. Books are the major channel by which the intellectual inheritance is handed down, and the principal means of its testing and growth. The defense of the freedom to read requires of all publishers and librarians the utmost of their faculties, and deserves of all Americans the fullest of their support.

We state these propositions neither lightly nor as easy generalizations. We here stake out a lofty claim for the value of the written word. We do so because we believe that it is possessed of enormous variety and usefulness, worthy of cherishing and keeping free. We realize that the application of these propositions may mean the dissemination of ideas and manners of expression that are repugnant to many persons. We do not state these propositions in the comfortable belief that what people read is unimportant. We believe rather that what people read is deeply important; that ideas can be dangerous; but that the suppression of ideas is fatal to a democratic society. Freedom itself is a dangerous way of life, but it is ours.

A JOINT STATEMENT BY:
American Library Association
Association of American Publishers

SUBSEQUENTLY ENDORSED BY:
American Booksellers for Free Expression
The Association of American University Presses
The Children's Book Council
Freedom to Read Foundation
National Association of College Stores
National Coalition Against Censorship
National Council of Teachers of English
The Thomas Jefferson Center for the Protection of Free Expression

Libraries: An American Value

Adopted February 3, 1999, by the ALA Council

Libraries in America are cornerstones of the communities they serve. Free access to the books, ideas, resources, and information in America's libraries is imperative for education, employment, enjoyment, and self-government.

Libraries are a legacy to each generation, offering the heritage of the past and the promise of the future. To ensure that libraries flourish and have the freedom to promote and protect the public good in the 21st century, we believe certain principles must be guaranteed.

To that end, we affirm this contract with the people we serve:

- We defend the constitutional rights of all individuals, including children and teenagers, to use the library's resources and services;
- We value our nation's diversity and strive to reflect that diversity by providing a full spectrum of resources and services to the communities we serve;
- We affirm the responsibility and the right of all parents and guardians to guide their own children's use of the library and its resources and services;
- We connect people and ideas by helping each person select from and effectively use the library's resources;
- We protect each individual's privacy and confidentiality in the use of library resources and services;

- We protect the rights of individuals to express their opinions about library resources and services;
- We celebrate and preserve our democratic society by making available the widest possible range of viewpoints, opinions and ideas, so that all individuals have the opportunity to become lifelong learners—informed, literate, educated, and culturally enriched.

Change is constant, but these principles transcend change and endure in a dynamic technological, social, and political environment.

By embracing these principles, libraries in the United States can contribute to a future that values and protects freedom of speech in a world that celebrates both our similarities and our differences, respects individuals and their beliefs, and holds all persons truly equal and free.

CHAPTER 3
Creating Intellectual Freedom Policies for Your Library

POLICY TIPS

Libraries have a duty to meet the information needs of all community members. To do so, they must promote and protect intellectual freedom. The first step is to develop formal, written library policies and procedures. Once established and adopted by the governing body, policies should be reviewed regularly and updated as needed. The library should ensure that its governing body and all library workers (including volunteers), regardless of title, are aware of these policies and receive training in the principles of intellectual freedom and the implementation of policy.

Review Policies Regularly

The world doesn't stay static, and neither should your policies. Set a schedule to review them regularly. Identify who in your library is responsible for reviewing and updating each policy. Be sure to allow enough time for the full review cycle, which may be lengthy. The process often involves approval from the board, legal counsel, or a union. Think about which other stakeholders should be consulted. Some libraries even involve users in writing or updating policies. Regular updates can remove outdated language, address current issues, and improve clarity. However, avoid making changes to a policy while a formal challenge is underway.

Write in Plain Language

Policies should be clear and easy for anyone to read. Most users read policies to find answers or understand how to use the library. If a policy is written in complex legal terms or at a high reading level, the most important information can get lost. Plain language helps users understand policies on their own, which leads to fewer questions and less time that staff need to spend explaining. Library workers can learn more about writing in plain language at digital.gov/guides/plain-language.

Libraries can check policy readability using tools like readable (readable.com) or Hemingway (hemingwayapp.com/readability-checker). Aim for a sixth- to eighth-grade reading level on the Flesch-Kincaid scale. Libraries can also test policies with staff and users for clarity before finalizing them.

To ensure accessibility, policies should be translated into the most commonly used languages in the community.

Understand Public Forum

When creating policies, libraries need to understand public forum doctrine and what rights apply under the First Amendment. Please read "The Law Regarding Access to the Library: Public Forums and User Behavior Rules" in the next chapter for guidance.

Put Policies in Writing

Policies can't just exist in theory; they must be written down. Having well-written, board-approved policies and procedures helps the library:

- Provide stability and consistency in operations
- Reduce confusion and ambiguity
- Demonstrate professional, businesslike management
- Build trust in the library's decisions
- Communicate goals, values, and intent to the public
- Show accountability and invite public evaluation
- Respond more effectively to criticism
- Document standard practices, which can be important if legal questions arise
- Educate and empower staff to address policy questions

Post Policies Publicly

Make library policies easy to find. Post them in a clear, accessible spot on the library's website and physical locations when useful. Libraries may choose to post shortened versions of policies in public areas so they can be easily referenced and understood by users.

Consult Legal Counsel

Libraries should always consult legal counsel when creating policies. Legal counsel will have the most accurate information and specialized knowledge about local laws and how they impact the library.

The worksheets in this chapter are given as guidelines and are not meant as full lists of all the requirements or legal advice.

Essential Library Policies

The following six library policies are essential for supporting intellectual freedom. Libraries may have additional policies to guide their operations.

1. Collection Development and Resource Reconsideration
2. Internet Use (required by law if the library receives E-rate or LSTA funding)
3. Use of Meeting Rooms, Exhibit Spaces, and Bulletin Boards
4. Privacy and Confidentiality
5. Social Media (if the library chooses to use social media)
6. User Behavior and Library Use

OFFICIAL ALA POLICY STATEMENT

Guidelines for Library Policies

Formerly titled "Guidelines for the Development and Implementation of Policies, Regulations, and Procedures Affecting Access to Library Resources, Services, and Facilities." Adopted June 28, 1994, by the ALA Intellectual Freedom Committee; amended January 19, 2005; March 29, 2014; June 24, 2019; and February 10, 2025.

Publicly funded libraries follow the U.S. Constitution and federal, state, local, and tribal laws. These laws are put into action through regulations, policies, and procedures made by the library's leadership. These policies and procedures:

- define the library's mission;
- outline its functions, services, and operations; and
- clarify the rights and responsibilities of library users.

Publicly funded libraries must uphold the First Amendment's right to free expression. They provide free, equal, and equitable access to information. As government entities, libraries' policies and procedures allow them to act as limited public forums. This includes any public use of meeting rooms, exhibit spaces, or bulletin boards.

Libraries that are not publicly funded should also follow these guidelines when developing:

- policies;
- regulations; and
- procedures.

This is in line with the *Library Bill of Rights* that affirms, "all libraries are forums for information and ideas."

Library policies and procedures can sometimes restrict, deny, or create barriers to accessing the library as a public forum. Any rules that impact First Amendment rights must meet a higher standard of review than those of other public services and facilities.

Article V of the *Library Bill of Rights* states, "A person's right to use a library should not be denied or abridged because of origin, age, background, or views." Any policies that restrict access must be based on a compelling government interest. Libraries can set reasonable restrictions on when, where, or how people access resources, services, or facilities. These restrictions must be content-neutral and not based on personal characteristics. For example, libraries should not limit access based on:

- citizenship or immigration status;
- age;
- income or housing status; or
- disapproval of a user's beliefs or the information they seek.

Library workers should get training to understand the legal principles behind policies. This training should help staff respond to difficult situations in a timely, direct, and open way. Staff should learn trauma-informed practices to better understand and support library users facing barriers.

1. All library policies, regulations, and procedures should avoid denying, restricting, or creating barriers to access. All policies should:
    a. be created and carried out following the laws that apply to the library. This includes:
    b. the U.S. Constitution (especially the First Amendment);
    c. provisions ensuring due process and equal and equitable treatment under the law; and
    d. federal, state, local, and tribal laws.

2. refer to the specific laws that give the library the authority to make the policy;
3. be created and carried out following the *Library Bill of Rights* and its interpretations;
4. be based upon the library's mission and objectives;
5. avoid limiting access to library resources, services, or facilities unless it's needed to fulfill the library's mission and objectives;
6. make any restrictions as specific and limited as possible, applying them only when absolutely necessary to serve library objectives;
7. balance competing interests and make sure individual rights are protected—not favoring the majority;
8. avoid limiting access based upon arbitrary distinctions such as origin, age, background, or views;

9. not target specific users or groups based on an assumption that they might act in ways that will disrupt the library's objectives;
10. be clearly stated so that people of all reading abilities can understand them;
11. provide a way to appeal;
12. be reviewed regularly by the library's governing authority and legal counsel;
13. be communicated clearly and made available to all library users; and
14. be applied fairly and not in a way that benefits or disfavors any specific person or group.

CREATING POLICY FOR YOUR LIBRARY—COLLECTION DEVELOPMENT AND RESOURCE RECONSIDERATION

Consult "Censorship, Challenged Resources, and Internet Filtering" (part II, chapter 5) and "Collection Development and Management" (part II, chapter 7).

Every library should have a clear, written policy that guides the selection, deselection or weeding, and reconsideration of library resources. A strong selection policy is:

- reviewed and revised regularly;
- easy for everyone to access;
- available in the languages spoken in your community;
- understood by all library staff; and
- approved by the library's governing board or other decision-making body.

These policies tell users how and why the library selects and removes resources. They also outline how users can request items or ask for a resource to be reconsidered. Having a clear policy—and following it carefully—is essential when a challenge arises.

Start drafting your collection development and reconsideration policy by completing each of the following sections. Post the policy in a clear, accessible spot on the library's website and physical locations when useful.

Collection Development Policy Worksheet

Library Mission

Share your library's mission and vision statements. Explain how your selection of resources supports the library's mission.

Support for Intellectual Freedom

Intellectual freedom is a core value of librarianship. However, many users may not know what it means or why it's important to libraries. Use this section to explain intellectual freedom and how it protects users' First Amendment rights. Be sure to include references to professional documents and laws.

Objectives

Explain what your library aims to achieve with its collection. Describe who the library serves and why types of material are selected.

Responsibility for Selection

Many library workers are involved in selecting materials for the library. Use this section to explain which roles are responsible for different parts of the process. Be sure to clearly state that professional library staff make the final decisions. Do not include staff names—only the job title or designation.

Selection Criteria

Libraries use specific criteria to select items for their collections. Outline the criteria your library follows. Include criteria that are relevant to the library's mission and goals. Make note that all criteria are not required to be met for selection.

Work with your library's governing or policy-making body to decide how much detail to include in the policy. More specific guidelines can be added to a procedure manual instead of being included in the policy. Examples of criteria include:

- artistic or literary merit
- relevance to community interests
- current and historical significance
- suitability of format for library use
- availability in other libraries
- space and budget constraints
- various perspectives and minority points of view
- coverage of the topic in the current collection

- awards
- timeliness

Acquisitions Procedures

Explain the process for selecting and acquiring materials, from initial review to the final selection. Identify the resources consulted in making selection decisions. For example, the specific bestseller lists the library uses. Beware of *requiring* reviews.

You can give a general overview in the policy and be more specific in a procedure manual.

Special Collections

If your library has special collections, explain how selecting materials for these collections is different from the general collection. Include the scope and purpose of the collection. Describe any restrictions, such as limited access, borrowing rules, or environmental controls. Make sure to state that security measures are based on the value, rarity, or fragility of the items—not their content.

Gifts and Donations

Explain how your library decides whether to accept gifts or donations. List the criteria for accepting items and the steps users need to follow. Make it clear that donations must meet the library's selection criteria to be added to the collection.

User Requests

Explain how users can request that resources be added to the collection. Also, give details about how these requests are considered.

Discuss how the library will ensure a diverse and useful collection if using user-driven or order-on-demand collection processes.

Maintenance and Weeding

Step-by-step instructions for weeding and collection maintenance should go in a procedural manual, not a policy. In this section, explain why weeding and deselection are critical to keeping a collection healthy. Give an overview of the criteria for removing items. Clarify that weeding is not used to remove controversial materials based solely on their content.

Controversial Materials

Libraries often include topics in their collections that some people do not agree with. In this section, explain that these resources are chosen because they meet the library's selection criteria.

Resource Location

Explain how resources are arranged in the library. Let users know that prejudicial labels will not be used.

Prejudicial Labels

Prejudicial labels are used to try to influence opinions or behaviors and restrict access, which is a form of censorship. These types of labels might be based on a value judgment about:

- the content;
- language;
- themes; or
- the background or views of the creator.

These labels often mark materials as inappropriate or offensive for certain groups of users. They are used to warn, discourage, or block access. For more information, check out "Labeling and Rating Systems: An Interpretation of the *Library Bill of Rights*" (part II, chapter 7).

For More Guidance

Consult: "Selection & Reconsideration Policy Toolkit for Public, School, & Academic Libraries," ala.org/tools/challengesupport/selectionpolicytoolkit.

Reconsideration Process

Explain what users can do if they disagree with a library resource. Reference any local laws that may affect their ability to request a review, such as a Freedom to Read law.

State that challenged resources will be evaluated using the criteria in the collection development policy. Inform users that the resource will not be removed during the reconsideration process.

Indicate that the reconsideration process applies no matter what the source of the challenge is. A request for reconsideration from an elected official will be handled with the same process as a request from a library user.

This section should outline the process but will typically not include the form itself.

Some libraries use the phrase "statement of concern" instead of "request for reconsideration."

Request for Reconsideration or Statement of Concern

There are a few key components of the "request for reconsideration" process that are typically found in different documents.

1. *Collection Development Policy*: This public-facing document should explain what users can do if they have concerns about a library resource. Many libraries will choose to only outline the steps the user needs to take and how the library will respond. The specific details about what staff do after a request has been submitted may appear in a different document.
2. *Request for Reconsideration or Statement of Concern Form*: This document is the actual form users will submit to the library to request the reconsideration of a resource. Libraries should decide how to make the form available to users. Typically, libraries require speaking to a staff member about the concern, rather than making the form accessible to all.
3. *Procedure Manual*: This is an internal staff document that goes into detail about how the library and its staff will handle a request for reconsideration. If a committee is used, be informed about any open meeting and public records laws that apply to staff committees making policy decisions or recommendations.

Detailed examples of procedures for handling formal complaints can be found in the "Selection & Reconsideration Policy Toolkit for Public, School, & Academic Libraries," ala.org/tools/challengesupport/selectionpolicytoolkit/reconsideration.

Sample Form: Request for Reconsideration

Request for Reconsideration of Library Resources

The trustees of the Mainstream Public Library created a materials selection policy and a process for gathering input from community members about specific items. Fully completing this form is an essential step in that process. If you wish to request the reconsideration of a resource, please return the completed form to the library director. We only accept requests from those residing within the library's legal service area.

We take the review process seriously, so we dedicate significant time and effort to it. If you submitted a request for the reconsideration of another resource, please wait until that review process finishes before submitting an additional request. If reconsideration of the same resource was requested within the last three years, the outcome of the prior review will stand.

Date:	
Name:	
Address:	
City:	State/Zip:
Phone:	Email:
Representing: Yourself ☐ An Organization ☐	
Name of Organization:	
1. Resource Information	
Title:	
Author/Producer:	

Format:

___ Book	___ Movie	___ Digital Resource	___ Program
___ e-Book	___ Magazine	___ Game	___ Display
___ Audiobook	___ Sound Recording	___ Newspaper	___ Other

2. What brought this resource to your attention?

____

____

3. Did you examine the entire resource? If not, what sections did you review?

____

____

____

4. What do you think are the main themes of this resource?

---

5. What do you feel this resource does well?

---

6. What concerns you about this resource?

---

7. Are there other resources we should review that give more information or viewpoints about this topic?

---

8. What action are you requesting the review committee to consider taking?

Thank you for taking the time to share your feedback with us. We will let you know the results of our review, in writing, within 30 days.

CREATING POLICY FOR YOUR LIBRARY—INTERNET USE

Consult "Censorship, Challenged Resources, and Internet Filtering" (part II, chapter 5).

Public and school libraries that must comply with the Children's Internet Protection Act (CIPA) and the Neighborhood Children's Internet Protection Act (NCIPA) will have additional policy requirements for internet use. These requirements are not covered here. If your library is subject to these laws, consult legal counsel to ensure that your policies meet legal standards.

Any library that provides access to the internet should have an internet use policy. All libraries that receive E-rate or LSTA funding for internet access are required to have such policies.

Start drafting your internet use policy by completing each of the following sections. Post the policy in a clear, accessible spot on the library's website and physical locations when useful.

Internet Use Policy Worksheet

Purpose

Use this section to explain why your library provides internet access and how it supports your mission and vision. Highlight how providing internet access aligns with the library's values and principles, such as those in the federal and state constitutions, the U.S. Bill of Rights, the *Library Bill of Rights* and its interpretations, and the *Freedom to Read* statement.

Disclaimer

Add a statement explaining that the library is not responsible for the content found on the internet.

Illegal Activity

Clearly state that the library does not allow the use of its equipment or networks to access illegal content. Include a list of applicable laws in the policy or an appendix. Let users know what consequences they may face for breaking these rules.

User Responsibility

Explain what is expected of library users when they use library computers to access the internet. Include any restrictions on access and behavior guidelines.

Computer Use

Outline the library's procedures for using the internet. Cover details such as computer reservations and time limits. Explain that time limits are not based on a user's age or the content or activity, such as playing games.

Privacy and Confidentiality

Explain the library's commitment to protecting users' privacy and confidentiality. Include any limitations in protecting their privacy when users access the internet. Let users know if their computer session data is cleared after they sign out.

Minors

Inform caregivers about any guidelines for minors using the internet. Make it clear that caregivers, not library workers, are responsible for supervising their children's internet activity.

Filters

If your library uses filters, explain who is affected by them and how they can be turned off. Include instructions for users to request unblocking incorrectly filtered sites.

Monitored Use

School libraries may be required to monitor students' internet use. Disclose this to users so they know that their internet use is not private.

CREATING POLICY FOR YOUR LIBRARY—PRIVACY AND CONFIDENTIALITY

> Consult "Privacy and Confidentiality" (part II, chapter 11); "Visits and Requests from Law Enforcement" (part II, chapter 12); and "Library Privacy Guidelines," ala.org/advocacy/privacy/guidelines.

Privacy policies explain what data the library collects about users, their rights over that data, and how the library uses, shares, stores, and deletes the data. These policies also list which third parties can access personal information and provide links to their privacy policies. A clear privacy policy helps users understand how their data is handled by the library and its vendors and informs them about the laws that protect their information.

Records Management Plan

Libraries should also create a plan to manage records. This plan should include:

- a list of the types of records the library keeps;
- a schedule for how long records are kept; and
- the steps for deleting records when they are no longer needed.

When drafting this policy, consider open records laws, records management requirements, and your state's Freedom of Information Act.

Libraries should have clear procedures for staff to follow when handling records requests, including requests from law enforcement. These procedures should explain how to manage records that are part of a legal process or evidence of a crime.

Start drafting your privacy and confidentiality policy by completing each of the following sections. Post the policy in a clear, accessible spot on the library's website and physical locations when useful.

Privacy and Confidentiality Policy Worksheet

Purpose

This section explains why privacy is important to libraries and how your library is committed to protecting user privacy. Include details about any federal, state, and local laws that impact privacy. Mention any confidentiality statutes that may place special responsibilities on libraries and staff.

Your library should include commitments to:

- collect, monitor, store, and share only the minimum amount of personally identifiable information (PII) needed;
- notify users when their PII is collected;
- allow users to see what information has been collected about them;
- avoid creating unnecessary records or tracking library use beyond what is needed for operations;
- avoid using biometric technologies such as facial recognition; and
- protect PII from public view, such as:
  - avoiding self-service hold shelves that use full names;
  - not using postcard notices for renewals;
  - avoiding voicemail messages with hold details; and
  - positioning staff computers so private information is not visible to others.

Information Collected

Users have the right to know what information the library collects about them. This includes:

- PII such as names, addresses, and contact details;
- non-personally identifiable information, like borrowing history or room reservations; and
- data collected through analytics software.

Provide links to third-party vendors' privacy policies so users can understand how their data is handled by these companies.

Let users know how they can use the library's resources anonymously, such as accessing certain materials or services without providing personal information.

Record Retention

Inform users about the library's policies for keeping and deleting records. Let users know how long information is kept and that records not needed for library operations are destroyed.

These records may include:

- borrowing history;
- computer usage logs;
- account information;
- video surveillance footage;
- data collected by vendors; and
- system backups.

If possible, share a link to your retention policy for users to review.

Information Access

Discuss the fact that PII and library use data are confidential. Explain who is authorized to access the data. Inform users that their data is only accessed when needed to perform library operations.

Include policies about when one user can access another user's information. For example, explain when and how a caregiver can request access to their minor child's library records.

Students and Minors

If your library serves students or minors, explain how the library protects their privacy. Include any specific federal, state, or local laws.

Website and Public Computers

Users often share information with the library through technology. Use this section to explain how the library protects user privacy with online tools. If needed, ask your Information Technology Department for help with technical details.

HTTPS

HTTPS is a certificate that encrypts your library's network traffic to keep it secure. Let users know that the library's HTTPS/SSL certificates are valid and that they are revalidated annually.

Cookies

Explain what cookies are and which ones your website uses. If users can turn off certain cookies, provide instructions on how to do this.

Data and Network Security

Reassure users that the library is actively protecting their data from unauthorized access. You don't need to go into elaborate detail here. Avoid using phrases such as "we may protect your data" or "reasonable measures."

Public Computers and Connected Devices

If your library offers Wi-Fi device checkout, or public computers, explain the protections in place for users. Let them know:

- how long computer usage logs are kept (ideally not more than 24 hours);
- what happens to their data when they log out or return a device; and
- that their activity is not being monitored on internet-connected devices.

Third-Party Vendors

Library users might assume that everything accessed through the library's website is managed by the library. However, many services are provided by third-party vendors.

In this section:

- Summarize the types of information these vendors may collect, use, and share.
- Provide a link to a clear and regularly updated page with links to all third-party vendors' privacy policies.
- Explain the library's expectations for vendors, including any privacy requirements outlined in contracts or purchase agreements.

Surveillance

Many libraries use surveillance to ensure safety. Be upfront and honest with your users about the types of surveillance in place, such as:

- security cameras;
- body-worn cameras;
- facial recognition software; or
- smart devices.

Include details about how long surveillance data is kept and who is authorized to access it.

Requests for Information

Explain the steps the library follows when someone requests access to a user's records. Include information about staff training to handle these requests, especially when the request comes from law enforcement or other authorities.

For More Guidance

- ALA Privacy Field Guides: ala.org/advocacy/privacy/fieldguides.
- State Privacy Laws Regarding Library Records: ala.org/advocacy/privacy/statelaws.

CREATING POLICY FOR YOUR LIBRARY—SOCIAL MEDIA

Consult "The Law Regarding Social Media" (part II, chapter 9).

Libraries are not required to use social media or host public conversations online. A library may choose to use social media only for one-way communication, such as announcements or sharing content created by the library. It does not need to invite or respond to questions or comments.

If a publicly funded library allows conversation on the social media it uses, it may create a "designated public forum." In that case, the library must uphold users' First Amendment rights to free expression. It cannot restrict speech based on content or viewpoint.

To prevent the library's social media from being used for content unrelated to its mission, such as commercial posts or off-topic comments, the library should adopt a social media policy. This policy should clearly state the purpose of using the platform and define acceptable online behavior that aligns with the library's mission.

Start drafting your social media policy by completing each of the following sections. Post the policy in a clear, accessible spot on the library's website and physical locations when useful.

Social Media Policy Worksheet

Purpose

Use this section to explain why your library uses social media and how it supports your mission and vision. Highlight how using social media aligns with the library's values and principles, such as those in the federal and state constitutions, the U.S. Bill of Rights, the *Library Bill of Rights* and its interpretations, and the *Freedom to Read* statement.

Audience

Identify the intended audience of the library's social media messages, such as:

- people living in the library's official service area;
- university faculty, students, staff, administrators, and alumni; or
- students attending K–12 schools and their parents.

Disclaimer

Let users know that comments on social media don't always reflect the library's views or opinions.

Information Accuracy

Encourage users to decide for themselves if the information they see on social media is accurate or trustworthy.

Behavior Guidelines

Explain what kinds of behavior are and aren't allowed. For example, users may not post anything illegal or not protected by the First Amendment, such as:

- copyright violations;
- obscene content;
- child sexual abuse materials (CSAM);
- false or harmful statements about others (defamation or libel); and
- real threats toward the library, staff, or anyone else.

Clearly say what will happen if someone breaks the rules in the library's social media policy.

Privacy

Let users know that their comments and posts are public. State that the library does not collect personal information through social media. Remind users that social media sites have their own privacy policies and refer users to those policies.

Complaints and Concerns

Give users a way to share complaints or concerns about content on the library's social media.

Explain how the library reviews these concerns and the steps it follows to reconsider content. Make clear that posts will only be removed through the approved process—not by a single staff member or administrator.

Consult Your Library's Legal Counsel

A public library's social media policy must carefully balance legal considerations and communications goals. Public libraries that value a vigorous and engaged social media presence must ensure they have enough resources and routinely reevaluate their policies. Legal concerns include First Amendment, copyright, trademark, risk of defamation, and applicable record-keeping laws. The lawyer selected to advise on such policies should have significant experience in each of these areas.

CREATING POLICY FOR YOUR LIBRARY—USE OF MEETING ROOMS, EXHIBIT SPACES, AND BULLETIN BOARDS

Consult "Meeting Rooms, Exhibit Spaces, and Programming" (part II, chapter 9).

Publicly funded libraries are not required to allow the community to use library meeting rooms, auditoriums, exhibit spaces, or bulletin boards. If they do, libraries must follow First Amendment protections for free expression and access. Libraries should have clear, easily accessible policies available to users.

Some libraries will choose to have one policy for meeting rooms and another for displays, exhibits, and bulletin boards. Think about how your library uses these spaces and what meets your needs.

Start drafting your policy for meeting rooms, exhibit spaces, and bulletin boards by completing each of the following sections. Post the policy in a clear, accessible spot on the library's website and physical locations when useful. For example, it can be helpful to have applicable parts of the policy posted in the meeting room or on the bulletin board.

Use of Meeting Rooms, Exhibit Spaces, and Bulletin Boards Policy Worksheet

Purpose

Use this section to explain why your library provides access to its spaces. Connect how providing access supports your library's mission and vision, including principles from federal and state constitutions, the U.S. Bill of Rights, the *Library Bill of Rights* and its interpretations, and the *Freedom to Read* statement.

Disclaimer

Explain that library spaces are available as a public service and that the library does not endorse the beliefs, views, or speech of those using its spaces. State that the library will not remove or censor displays or programs because someone disagrees with the content, identity, beliefs, or affiliations of the sponsor.

Also explain that library use takes priority over community reservations as space is limited.

Space Description

List the general spaces available and who can use them. Include the specific details about each space in a separate document or section of the website. This will avoid having to go through a full policy update anytime spaces change.

Eligibility and Use Guidelines

Use inclusive language to describe eligibility and rules. Include details about:

- when, where, and how the spaces can be used (time, place, manner rules);
- any fees or limitations on how often a space can be used;
- any restrictions on display materials (such as size requirements);
- when items will be removed from a display; and
- whether meetings must be open to the public.

Rules must not be based on the content of meetings or displayed materials. Policies should not exclude religious groups or other users based on their beliefs or speech. Court rulings state that libraries cannot discriminate against religious or controversial groups or speakers when providing access to spaces.

Marketing

Let users know the guidelines for marketing their programs or exhibits. Libraries may require users to add a notice to marketing materials that explicitly states that the library is not sponsoring or affiliated with the event or display.

Behavior Guidelines

Inform users that the library's behavior policy applies to all users of meeting rooms, even outside regular hours. If there are additional behavior rules, such as those about food, noise, or private security, list them here.

Abandoned Items

State how unclaimed exhibit items will be handled and include a deadline for retrieval.

Appeal Process

Give a process for users to appeal decisions about using library spaces.

CREATING POLICY FOR YOUR LIBRARY—USER BEHAVIOR AND LIBRARY USE

OFFICIAL ALA POLICY STATEMENT

Guidelines for the Development of Policies and Procedures Regarding User Behavior and Library Usage

These guidelines were adopted January 24, 1993, by the ALA Intellectual Freedom Committee; amended November 17, 2000; January 19, 2005; March 29, 2014; March 24, 2019; July 29, 2019; August 16, 2020; and August 5, 2025.

No user should disrupt another person's ability to use and enjoy the library.[1] Library staff should also be able to do their jobs without disruption. To support this, libraries need clear, written policies and procedures to address user behavior. These policies should be approved by the library's governing body and grounded in:

- the American Library Association's (ALA) *Code of Ethics;*
- the *Library Bill of Rights;* and
- federal, tribal, state, and local law, including the First and Fourteenth Amendments.

There is a significant government interest in ensuring that libraries are places where all users can exercise their constitutionally protected right to receive information.[2] This interest gives publicly supported libraries the authority to maintain safe and healthy environments where users and staff are free from harassment and threats. Libraries also have a legal responsibility to take prompt and appropriate corrective action when their employees experience harassment.[3]

To support this, libraries may place reasonable restrictions on the time, place, or manner of access to:

- protect everyone's right to use the library;
- ensure the safety of users and staff; and
- prevent damage to library resources and facilities.

The *Library Bill of Rights* "affirms that all libraries are forums for information and ideas." Libraries should follow these guidelines when developing policies and procedures.

Policy Guideline

Publicly supported libraries can use the following guidelines to develop policies and procedures about using library facilities:

- Make sure all policies and procedures reflect the principles in the *Library Bill of Rights*.
- Use existing laws and law enforcement tools as the main way to address:
  - public safety issues;
  - criminal behavior;
  - anything already covered by federal, tribal, state, or local laws.
- If the library creates its own policies, cite the law or ordinances that gives the library the authority to do so.
- Policies and procedures should be reasonable and narrowly focused. They can be used to stop someone from interfering with others' use of the library or to stop activities that do not align with the library's mission and goals.
- Ask library legal counsel to review policies often. Legal counsel should provide guidance on updating policies to comply with all applicable laws.
- Respond to behavior issues in a timely, direct, and transparent way. Use common sense, reason, and empathy to resolve issues without escalation.
- Develop ongoing staff training based on the user behavior policy. Training should include:
  - de-escalation methods;
  - how to report harassment of staff to the employer;
  - serving people with disabilities;
  - working with members of marginalized and underserved groups;
  - supporting those experiencing poverty and homelessness; and
  - understanding the diversity in the community.
- Training should also cover the unique challenges of working in tribal, urban, suburban, and rural libraries.
- Libraries should balance different needs and avoid favoring the majority at the expense of a person's right to access or use library resources and services. One person's choice or belief should not override those of the majority of library users.

Policies and regulations that place restrictions on library access should:

- Apply only to activities that seriously interfere with:
  - the public's right to access the library;
  - the safety of users and staff; and
  - the protection of library resources and facilities.
- Be narrowly written so they do not restrict more than is needed to meet their goals.
- Be based solely on actual behavior and not on personal characteristics like:
  - race;
  - ethnicity;
  - national origin;
  - sexual orientation;
  - gender or gender identity;

  - religious affiliation;
  - age;
  - disability; or
  - disease.
- Be enforced consistently and fairly, not in a way that benefits or harms any person or group without reason. Clearly describe what behavior is not allowed and the consequences for engaging in that behavior; and
- Explain how the policy is enforced, including due process and fair warning.

Policies and regulations that place restrictions on library access should not:

- Target specific users or groups based on assumptions or expectations that they might disrupt library services.
- Leave people without a reasonable way to access information in the library.
- Be used to limit library users' access to constitutionally protected speech, even if the content may be considered controversial or objectionable by some.
- Restrict access to people simply because they anger or annoy others. Policies based on appearance, mildly annoying behavior, or on negative personal reactions from others do not meet the necessary standard. Instead, policies should use a reasonable, objective standard based on actual behavior.

Many user behaviors come from a wide range of individual and societal conditions. Libraries should work with local social service agencies, advocacy groups, mental health professionals, law enforcement officials, and other community partners to create strategies that support the needs of a diverse population.

The policy should be clearly and consistently shared with users in all languages commonly used in the library's communities.

Definitions

Due process: Neither the federal nor state and local governments may deprive life, liberty, or property without appropriate legal procedures and safeguards. For example, a person has the right to appeal an adverse decision by a court or a government agency. This principle is embedded in the Fifth and Fourteenth Amendments.

Protected speech: Speech that the government cannot censor or regulate under the First Amendment, as interpreted by the U.S. Supreme Court. By law, speech is considered protected unless a court determines it falls into a category that is not protected. The Supreme Court has identified several types of speech that are not protected by the First Amendment.

Publicly supported libraries: Libraries established by a government entity or libraries that receive most of their financial support from government funding.

Significant or compelling government interest: A term used by courts when assessing if a government regulation or action unfairly limits a fundamental right, like free speech. To pass this test, the government must show more than just an important reason for the rule. The reason for the rule must be compelling—so important that it outweighs even the most valued freedoms it negatively affects.

Strict scrutiny: Test applied to determine whether a restriction on speech is unconstitutional under the First Amendment. To justify a restriction on speech, the government must show that:

1. it has a compelling interest in enforcing the restriction;
2. the restriction is narrowly tailored to achieve that compelling interest; and
3. there is no less restrictive alternative to achieving that interest.

Unprotected speech: Speech or expressive activity that is not protected by the First Amendment. The main categories of unprotected speech identified by the Supreme Court include:

- obscenity;
- child sexual abuse material (CSAM);
- defamation; and
- expression intended and likely to incite imminent lawless action, such as fighting words or true threats.

NOTES

1. The word "enjoyment" is used in many court decisions about regulating library users' behavior and appearance. For example, in *Kreimer v. Morristown* the court states that libraries may create rules to prevent people from "unreasonably interfering with other patrons' use and enjoyment of the Library." In legal terms, "quiet enjoyment" refers to the right to use a space or property without disturbance.
2. *Kreimer v. Bureau of Police for Morristown,* 958 F.2d 1242 (3d Cir. 1992).
3. Title VII of the Civil Rights Act of 1964, the Age Discrimination in Employment Act of 1967, and the Americans with Disabilities Act of 1990.

User Behavior and Library Use Policy Worksheet

Consult "The Law Regarding Access to the Library: Public Forums and User Behavior Rules" (part II, chapter 4).

No user should disrupt another person's ability to use and enjoy the library. Library staff should also be able to do their jobs without disruption from users. Libraries need clear policies and procedures to address behavior. These policies should rely on the ALA *Code of Ethics*, the *Library Bill of Rights*, and federal, tribal, state, and local laws, including the First and Fourteenth Amendments.

Everyone has the constitutional right to access information, and publicly funded libraries have a duty to protect that right. Libraries must maintain a safe and healthy space where users and staff are free from harassment and threats to their safety and well-being.

Libraries can set reasonable rules about where, when, and how people use the library. These rules help:

- keep users and staff safe; and
- protect library resources and facilities from damage.

Start drafting your user behavior and library use policy by completing each of the following sections. Post the policy in a clear, accessible spot on the library's website and physical locations when useful.

Purpose

This section explains that all users have the right to access information in a space that is respectful, safe, and free from disruptions. Describe how this policy supports the library's mission.

Highlight that the policy is guided by:

- the ALA *Code of Ethics*;
- the *Library Bill of Rights*; and
- federal, tribal, state, and local laws, including the First and Fourteenth Amendments.

Guidelines

Provide a list of activities that are not allowed because they disrupt someone's use of the library or prevent staff from doing their work. Include only activities that significantly affect users' access, safety, or the protection of library resources.

Prohibited activities should:

- Be the least restrictive possible
- Be based only on actual behavior, not arbitrary distinctions like:
  - race;
  - ethnicity;
  - national origins;
  - sexual orientation;
  - gender or gender identity;
  - religion;
  - age;
  - disability; or
  - disease.

Write the guidelines clearly and concisely so they are easy for all users to understand.

Enforcement

Explain what happens if a user violates this policy. If possible, provide details about how enforcement is handled based on the specific type of behavior. Include a link to the enforcement guidelines if they are available for public viewing.

Let users know how they can appeal a suspension or ban on accessing library services.

Laws

Include any local laws or ordinances that apply—for example, a penal code that allows arrest for trespassing.

When to Call Law Enforcement

Calling law enforcement in response to a library user's behavior is a serious decision that should not be made lightly. While libraries must not permit illegal activity, involving law enforcement can have severe consequences for individuals—particularly for Black and Brown community members, who are disproportionately affected by police violence. According to Mapping Police Violence, Black people are 2.8 times more likely to be killed by police than white people in the United States.[1] Libraries should take this reality into account when deciding whether to contact law enforcement.

Law enforcement should be reserved for serious situations involving immediate danger or illegal activity, not as a default response to behavioral issues or to enforce library rules. Library workers should never use the threat of calling law enforcement to control user behavior.

Library workers should call law enforcement if a person:

- threatens physical harm against another person (user or staff);
- strikes or physically harms another person;
- refuses to leave library property after being asked to leave (a library representative must be prepared to sign a criminal complaint or testify in court);
- views child sexual abuse material; or
- sexually assaults another person.

How can the library provide evidence to law enforcement while protecting user confidentiality?

If library workers believe a crime has been committed, they should make reasonable efforts to preserve any direct evidence, such as video surveillance footage. They should give the evidence to the library director or legal counsel, who will decide whether to involve law enforcement. Library workers must always follow state and local laws, including library confidentiality laws.

If the evidence includes personally identifiable information about library users, the library should:

- preserve the evidence;
- inform law enforcement that it exists; and
- keep it confidential until a court order allows law enforcement to access it.

What if allegations of a crime are reported to library workers?

If no library worker witnessed the incident or has firsthand knowledge of a crime, the library should give the person making the complaint the information they need to contact law enforcement directly. Law enforcement can determine the facts and may interview the witness(es).

What if someone is viewing pornography or text and images that people find offensive?

"Pornography" is not a legal term. It is often used to refer to materials and images that are sexually explicit or considered by some to be objectionable. Often these materials are protected by the First Amendment, and it is *not* illegal to possess or view them. The decision about what is pornographic is largely subjective and reflects changing community standards and the individual's views.

In contrast, it is appropriate to call law enforcement if a user is viewing images or video depicting the sexual abuse of children.

What about other activities that some people find offensive or inappropriate?

The following activities are not criminal:

- violating library policy, such as cell phone use or talking in quiet areas;
- making abusive comments that do not include threats of physical harm;
- wearing clothing or other symbols of gang affiliation or hate groups; or
- being unhoused or having an offensive body odor or poor bodily hygiene.

In these cases, the library should follow its user behavior and other relevant policies.

Note: Behaviors that violate conduct policies may be driven by mental health conditions, reactions to sensory stimuli, or illicit or prescription drug effects. Leaning on resources other than police is often the most appropriate response. Community resources can:

- support the individual's needs;
- increase the likelihood for future compliance with the policy; and
- decrease the danger associated with police presence.

Libraries should create partnerships with local behavioral health organizations, implement mental health first-aid training for staff, and have crisis phone numbers easily accessible.

For more about when you should not call law enforcement, read Jarrett Dapier and Emily Knox's article, "When Not to Call the Cops: A Plea to Protect Black Patrons," *American Libraries*, July 8, 2020, americanlibrariesmagazine.org/2020/07/08/rethinking-when-to-call-the-cops/.

NOTE

1. Mapping Police Violence, mappingpoliceviolence.org.

Intellectual Freedom: The Law in Flux

OFFICE FOR INTELLECTUAL FREEDOM STAFF

As we draft the eleventh edition of the *Intellectual Freedom Manual,* the freedom to read is under threat. Small, organized groups of activists are challenging well-settled legal principles. They want to force their reading preferences on entire communities and limit what materials library users can access and read. In some cases, they even try to close or defund the library.

Their efforts to censor books and other library materials have spread to state legislatures and the courts. This section examines recent court decisions, legislative efforts, and administrative actions that threaten the ability of libraries to serve their communities and defend each library user's right to read.

Coordinated Public Censorship Efforts

Demands to censor and restrict library materials are at record levels. Libraries of all kinds in communities across the nation are facing attempts to remove and limit access to books and other materials. Library workers and administrators are being harassed and intimidated. Some library boards and politicians are also taking steps to deny library users' freedom to read.

These censorship efforts are part of a larger well-funded, organized campaign to curb access to information and ideas. The campaign is driven by ideology, not facts. In 2024, 72 percent of demands to censor books in school and public libraries came from pressure groups, elected officials, board members, and administrators—not parents or individual library users. These organized efforts have led to skyrocketing levels of censorship. From 2001 to 2020, these organized groups and like-minded officials challenged only an average of 46 titles per year. In 2024, they tried to censor 4,190 titles. Most of the challenged materials focused on the lives, experiences, and concerns of LGBTQIA+ people, Black people, Indigenous people, and people of color.

Beyond these overt censorship activities, library workers are facing harassment and attacks. This has created a climate of fear. Many library workers are now afraid to shelve, display, and purchase materials that may become controversial. This includes materials with LGBTQIA+ themes and books about race and racism in the United States.

As Deborah Caldwell-Stone, who was the director of the Office for Intellectual Freedom, describes in the 2024 "State of America's Libraries" report: "We are witnessing an effort to eliminate entire genres and categories of books from library shelves in pursuit of a larger goal of placing politics and religion over the well-being and education of young people and everyone's right to access and find information in our libraries. It is impacting our youth and our communities."

Adverse Library Legislation

The censorship campaigns have pressured state lawmakers to introduce anti-library bills. Legislatures in multiple states are reinforcing the efforts of pro-censorship pressure groups. They are sponsoring bills intended to restrict readers' access to disfavored books in libraries and schools.

Some of this legislation proposes censoring books with "sexual content," "sensitive materials," and other vague, undefined categories.[1] Other laws could lead to criminal charges or private right-of-action lawsuits against library workers for providing books that one person believes are inappropriate for minors.[2] Some lawmakers want to limit or remove library workers' role in collection development. Others want to take away the local control of library resources.[3] In some states, new laws now require libraries to create physical barriers to certain books, locking them away in "adult only" rooms or staff areas.[4]

Other states are responding to these efforts to legalize censorship by passing laws that protect the right to read and library workers. Legislators in California, Illinois, Maryland, Minnesota, New Jersey, Washington, and Rhode Island have passed laws that protect intellectual freedom in libraries.

Defunding, Reorganizing, and Board Takeovers

In addition to censorship laws and actions, some people are trying to defund libraries and fill their boards with pro-censorship special interest group members. These efforts to cut funding and degrade the integrity of library leadership are a threat to intellectual freedom. Political moves to strip power from communities make it harder for libraries, staff, and boards to provide materials, resources, and programs. These legislative and political efforts are part of the larger campaign to advance censorship and limit access to education. Even when framed as budget or policy changes, these efforts are driven by ideology instead of by community needs.

Library Litigation

Censorship-focused laws and organized efforts have led to lawsuits. Community members are suing states, local governments, and library boards for removing books from shelves, claiming it violates their First Amendment rights. These cases are moving slowly through state and federal courts across the country. Each case creates a chance for judges to overrule and eliminate long-settled legal precedents protecting the freedom to read as a central tenet of the First Amendment.

In more than a dozen states, attorneys general are part of the censorship campaign. For decades, courts have held that libraries are spaces where everyone has the right to access information and ideas, and that the First Amendment protects that right. Now these lawyers are trying to get judges to overturn that legal precedent. They want courts to say that library materials are the expression of elected officials. If that happens, the government could remove materials just because it disagrees with the opinions and ideas contained in them.

Federal courts in Arkansas and Iowa have rejected claims that libraries belong to politicians and pressure groups rather than the communities they serve. However, one court, the U.S. Court of Appeals for the Fifth Circuit, issued an opinion in 2025, *Little v. Llano County*, that contradicts those court opinions.[5]

Families brought the Llano County case after county commissioners, and the public library board removed books based on their personal opinions about the ideas in them. The families argued that taking the books off the shelves violated their First Amendment rights. The district court agreed with the families. But when the county appealed, a majority of judges in the federal Fifth Circuit Court of Appeals ruled against them. In an opinion written by Judge Kyle Duncan, those judges held that children have fewer First Amendment rights than adults. The judges also held that no one has a right to receive information in the public library. This ruling contradicts current law and the very purpose of public libraries. Some of the judges even agreed that library collections are government speech and not subject to the First Amendment.

In December 2025, the Supreme court declined to hear *Little v. Llano*, creating a patchwork of freedom to read rights that vary across the country. Courts are now deciding if they will adopt the Fifth Circuit's denial of library users' rights, or if they will uphold the long-standing precedent, as in the Arkansas and Iowa cases. Until the Supreme Court resolves this split by hearing a salient case and issuing an opinion, the future of the freedom to read remains uncertain.

Wherever First Amendment protections of library access erode, library workers and administrators must stand behind their professional ethics to uphold the freedom to read.

NOTES

1. Texas SB 13 (2025); Utah HB 29 (2024); Iowa SF 496 (2023).
2. Idaho HB 710 (2024); Texas SB 412 (2025).
3. Texas SB 13 (2025).
4. Arkansas SB 1646 (2025).
5. The Fifth Circuit Court of Appeals has jurisdiction in Louisiana, Mississippi, and Texas.

Part II
Intellectual Freedom Topics and Best Practices

CHAPTER 4
Access to Library Resources and Services

BIG IDEA BREAKDOWN

Key Concepts

- Library resources and services should be available to everyone in the community.
- Libraries should work to provide free access to resources and services without barriers. This includes unfiltered internet access. Everyone in the community should have access regardless of:
  - origin;
  - background;
  - disability;
  - age;
  - reading level;
  - economic or housing status;
  - views;
  - sex;
  - gender identity or expression; or
  - sexual orientation.
- Restricting materials because they contain controversial, unusual, or sensitive subjects is censorship.
- Libraries should avoid creating economic barriers, such as requiring a phone number or physical address to use services.
- Equity, diversity, inclusion, and belonging are central to promoting and practicing intellectual freedom.
- Library workers should provide inclusive collections and services that reflect the diversity of the world.
- Incarcerated people have the right to access library services and materials while they are detained.

- Libraries should provide equal access to collections, services, and facilities for all users. If full access is not possible, libraries should quickly provide reasonable accommodations so people with disabilities have similar experiences.

What Does the Law Say?

The First Amendment gives all people the right to free expression. Based on this right:

- Public libraries, schools, and colleges or universities that are owned and funded by the government are considered state actors. Their actions must follow the First Amendment.
- Private libraries, schools, and colleges or universities that are not funded or controlled by the government are considered private actors. They are not required to follow the First Amendment. However, they may become subject to government rules if they accept public funding or follow government accreditation standards. These institutions can still protect free expression and academic freedom through their own policies or contracts.
- Private institutions may choose to close their libraries to the public, but they do not have to. Libraries that are government depositories under Title 44 of the U.S. Code must allow the public to access their government information collections.

Creating Policy for Your Library

- Adopt the *Library Bill of Rights* (part I, chapter 2) as policy for your library. It includes statements that support access to library resources for a diverse group of people.
- Make sure your policies clearly outline the procedures and rules for accessing library resources (part I, chapter 3). Policies about using the library and its services should be:
  - written;
  - objective;
  - consistently and fairly enforced regardless of a person's identity or beliefs; and
  - reasonable and directly related to library use.
- If a user is denied access or banned from the library or a resource, the policy should include an appeal process.

For Academic Libraries

- Special collections materials are often kept in closed stacks because they are unique, expensive, and fragile. If the goal is to protect them so they are available for future library users, this practice supports the intellectual freedom principle of ensuring access.

For Public Libraries

- Libraries may place certain materials in a children's or young adult section. This is not considered restricting access, as long as all library users are still able to access all parts of the collection.

For School Libraries

- Reading level systems that assign a specific age, grade, or developmental level to materials should not be used to restrict students from reading above or below their assigned level. Labels showing a reading level should not be placed on the outside of a book, as they can stigmatize students' reading at lower levels and may lead them to self-censor their reading.
- Overly restrictive internet filtering impacts students' access to information, including constitutionally protected speech.

To Learn More

Consult "Access to Library Resources and Services," ala.org/advocacy/intfreedom/access.

Reflection Questions

- How is access to information and services an intellectual freedom issue?
- What strategies can you use to reach out to underserved populations in your community?
- What kinds of restrictions on library use are permissible? Why?
- Does your library have any policies that seem to unfairly harm people who are unhoused or are struggling financially? What alternative options could your library provide to ensure access?
- Your library director has put up signs saying that the library is a safe space open to all and that offensive language or actions won't be tolerated. How do you feel about this from an intellectual freedom perspective? How do you feel about this from a diversity and inclusion perspective?

What Is Meant by "Origin," "Age," "Background," and "Views"?

In the *Library Bill of Rights* and all its interpretations:

- Origin means all the traits someone is born into and can't change.
- Age means all the traits that come with a person's stage of life and maturity.
- Background means all the traits that are a result of a person's life experiences.
- Views means all the opinions and beliefs held and expressed by a person.

OFFICIAL ALA POLICY STATEMENTS

Access to Digital Resources and Services: An Interpretation of the *Library Bill of Rights*

Formerly titled "Access to Digital Information, Services, and Networks: An Interpretation of the *Library Bill of Rights*." Adopted January 24, 1996, by the ALA Council; amended January 19, 2005; July 15, 2009; June 25, 2019; and May 29, 2025.

The library's key mission is to provide everyone with access to information. They do this no matter the content or format. Today, this mission also includes providing access to digital resources and services.

Libraries are critical in connecting people to digital resources and services, such as computers and the internet. Libraries must follow the *Library Bill of Rights* when offering these resources. They should prioritize intellectual freedom and equity, ensuring that technology expands access rather than restricting it.

Libraries should stay up to date on digital creation, distribution, retrieval, and archiving issues. When reviewing these issues, they should consider:

- users' First Amendment rights;
- users' rights to privacy;
- the *Core Values of Librarianship;*
- the *Library Bill of Rights;*
- the American Library Association's (ALA) *Code of Ethics;* and
- the library's collection policies.

These reviews should guide policy updates to ensure access to digital information. Many people don't have access to, or the skills needed to use or create digital resources. Libraries must provide spaces where people can access, use, or create digital information without barriers. These barriers may include:

- physical;
- mental;

- economic;
- educational; or
- political challenges.

Providing access doesn't mean the library agrees with the content. Libraries should resist the censorship of digital resources and services. This includes attempts by individuals, governments, and private entities to censor or limit access.

Libraries should carefully plan how to provide access to digital resources, services, tools, equipment, and networks. These decisions should follow the principles of intellectual freedom and equity, while reflecting the library's:

- mission;
- goals;
- objectives;
- cooperative agreements; and
- community needs.

Users' Rights

Libraries should review all policies, procedures, and regulations to ensure they don't violate users' rights. All digital access policies should follow the guidelines set by the ALA.[1]

Users have a right to express, receive, create, or participate in constitutionally protected speech. Their access to digital resources and services cannot be blocked for exercising this right. If access is limited for other reasons, users must receive due process. This includes formal notice and an option to appeal. These rights extend to minors as well as adults.[2]

Libraries should use technology to expand digital access, not restrict it. Digital information that users find, use, or create is constitutionally protected unless a court rules otherwise. Users also have the right to be free of unreasonable limitations set by:

- libraries;
- library workers;
- system administrators;
- vendors; and
- network service providers.

Library contracts, agreements, and licenses must respect users' rights. Libraries should provide training and support to help users find, evaluate, use, and create digital information.

Libraries should protect users' rights to privacy and confidentiality, as stated in Article VII of the *Library Bill of Rights*.[3] This right applies to all users, regardless of their abilities, origin, age, background, or views.

To uphold these rights, libraries should maintain secure systems and networks. When offering digital resources, libraries should ensure third-party vendors protect users' privacy. Many online services collect, store, use, and share user data without their knowledge. Libraries should educate users about these risks and advocate for stronger privacy protections from vendors.

Equity of Access

The digital world offers many opportunities for people to participate in our information society. However, serious barriers, often called the "digital divide," prevent access for many. These barriers include a lack of:

- infrastructure for internet connectivity;
- tools (hardware or software);
- skills;
- knowledge; or
- means of accessing digital resources.[4]

Libraries should address the digital divide and work to reduce it when providing access to digital resources in their communities.

All digital resources and services from the library should be equitably accessible to everyone. The ALA doesn't support publicly funded libraries charging fees for access.[5]

Libraries should create digital access policies that follow ALA's guidelines. When new digital resources are added, libraries must provide equitable training opportunities to users and staff. This training should include privacy and security issues to help users navigate these resources safely.

Information Resources and Access

Libraries should provide access to all types of information that meet the community's needs and interests. They do this regardless of a user's age or the content of the material.

To preserve cultural information and prevent its loss, libraries may need to expand their collection policies. These policies should ensure digital information is selected and preserved in the appropriate formats. Libraries also have a duty to provide access to government information in digital formats.

Connecting users to global information, services, and networks is different from adding materials to the library's collection. Some digital information may not meet the library's collection policy. As such, each user must decide what is right for their needs.

Libraries should not deny or limit access to digital resources simply because they are considered controversial. Access should not be limited based on staff members' personal beliefs or fear of conflict. Resources should not be restricted just because they are seen as lacking value.

Parents and legal guardians should guide their own children in using digital resources if they have concerns.

Publicly funded libraries must legally provide access to constitutionally protected information. However, laws or governing bodies require some libraries to use internet filters or technology to block access to this information. This practice goes against the *Library Bill of Rights*.[6] Libraries that use these tools must set them at the least restrictive level. This ensures they do not block protected information needlessly.

Adults have the right to access all constitutionally protected information. They can ask for filters or tools to be disabled promptly and confidentially. Minors also have the right to access this information. At a minimum, they can ask for access to wrongly blocked information. Those requests should also be handled quickly and confidentially. To protect user privacy, records of these requests should not contain personally identifiable information. Libraries have a duty to inform users about their rights and provide clear ways for users to exercise those rights.[7]

Digital resources and services greatly expand the amount of information available to users. Libraries should treat these resources the same as non-digital ones and follow the principles of the *Library Bill of Rights*. This ensures equitable access, no matter the content or platform.

Questions to Explore in Choosing an Online Service

For information about choosing and using an online service, including questions about how to better understand how vendors should properly collect, store, use, share, and retain personal data, please see the ALA's "Privacy Guidelines,"[8] which includes more specific information in the "Library Privacy Guidelines for Vendors" document.[9]

NOTES

1. "Guidelines for Library Policies," approved June 28, 1994, by the ALA Intellectual Freedom Committee; amended January 19, 2005; March 29, 2014, under the previous name "Guidelines for the Development and Implementation of Policies, Regulations, and Procedures Affecting Access to Library Resources, Services and Facilities"; amended June 24, 2019, and February 10, 2025.
2. *Tinker v. Des Moines Indep. Cmty. Sch. Dist.*, 393 U.S. 503 (1969); *Bd. of Educ., Island Trees Union Free Sch. Dist. No. 26 v. Pico*, 457 U.S. 853 (1982); *Am. Amusement Mach. Ass'n v. Teri Kendrick*, 244 F.3d 954 (7th Cir. 2001); *cert. denied*, 534 U.S. 994 (2001).
3. "Privacy: An Interpretation of the *Library Bill of Rights*," adopted June 19, 2002, by the ALA Council; amended July 1, 2014; June 24, 2019; and June 29, 2025.
4. Martin Hilbert, "The End Justifies the Definition: The Manifold Outlooks on the Digital Divide and Their Practical Usefulness for Policy-Making," *Telecommunications Policy* 35, no. 8 (2011): 715–36, https://doi.org/10.1016/j.telpol.2011.06.012.

5. "Economic Barriers to Information Access: An Interpretation of the *Library Bill of Rights*," adopted June 30, 1993, by the ALA Council; amended June 25, 2019; and June 29, 2025.
6. "Internet Filtering: An Interpretation of the *Library Bill of Rights*," adopted June 30, 2015, by the ALA Council; amended June 29, 2025.
7. "If some libraries do not have the capacity to unblock specific Web sites or to disable the filter or if it is shown that an adult user's election to view constitutionally protected internet material is burdened in some other substantial way, that would be the subject for an as-applied challenge, not the facial challenge made in this case." *United States, et al. v. American Library Association*, 539 U.S. 194 (2003) (Justice Kennedy, concurring).
8. "Library Privacy Guidelines: Overview and Listing," American Library Association, https://www.ala.org/advocacy/privacy/guidelines.
9. "Library Privacy Guidelines for Vendors," approved June 29, 2015, by the ALA Intellectual Freedom Committee under previous title "Library Privacy Guidelines for E-book Lending and Digital Content Vendors"; revised January 26, 2020.

Economic Barriers to Library Access: An Interpretation of the *Library Bill of Rights*

Adopted June 30, 1993, by the ALA Council; amended June 25, 2019; and June 29, 2025.

The core mission of most libraries, and particularly publicly funded libraries, is to provide free, equal, and equitable access to all types of information. While libraries may have different roles, goals, and objectives, this mission is shared by all. Economic challenges can affect a library's ability to fulfill this mission and can also create barriers for individual users.

Libraries and their governing bodies sometimes face economic pressure and competition for funding. Even so, they must remain committed to the library's core mission. To support this mission, the American Library Association (ALA) offers guidance in the *Library Bill of Rights* and related policies. In particular, the *Library Bill of Rights* states: "A person's right to use a library should not be denied or abridged because of origin, age, background, or views."

The ALA opposes economic barriers for access to services and resources in all publicly funded libraries. All library resources should be accessible to all users, regardless of format or delivery method. This ensures equitable access for everyone. Libraries should not impose any financial barriers that may disadvantage users. Libraries of all types should eliminate barriers that limit access to library resources and services.

Libraries should thoughtfully design services to deliver information and resources equitably to all users. They should regularly review these services to ensure that the library's core mission stays intact.

The "Resolution on Monetary Library Fines as a Form of Social Inequity" states that fines create a barrier to accessing library services.[1] Libraries should review policies and procedures related to fines, fees, or other user charges.

Libraries should work to remove any policies that create barriers to access or academic success. They should also consider waiving or reducing fees for individuals based on their ability to pay. This may include fees for:

- lost or damaged items;
- borrowing fees for non-residents; or
- program participation.

Economic barriers go beyond a user's ability to pay fines or fees. Many policies and procedures unfairly harm people who:

- are struggling financially;
- are experiencing homelessness; or
- come from marginalized communities.

Examples of such policies include those about:

- personal belongings;
- hygiene requirements;
- verifying a permanent address; and
- accessing an email account, phone number, or computer.

These policies can restrict or deny access for some community members by singling out certain users and reinforcing inequalities.

Libraries and their governing bodies should find other ways to reduce differences between users based on economic status. They should resist charging user fees to address financial pressures, as these can harm public trust and the library's integrity. Policies should not favor those who are economically fortunate at the expense of those who are not.

The ALA opposes any laws or regulations that impose content restrictions on library resources as a condition of funding. It also opposes efforts to limit user access to resources or services tied to funding for publicly supported libraries.

Libraries and their governing bodies should review all terms and conditions attached to funding or gifts, whether from public or private sources. They should reject any conditions that limit equal or equitable access to content. They should also work to build community agreement that libraries require funding free from conditions that limit equal or equitable access to content. Such an agreement supports the library's mission of providing free and open exchange of information and ideas.

NOTE

1. "Resolution on Monetary Library Fines as a Form of Social Inequity," adopted January 28, 2019, by the ALA Council.

Equity, Diversity, Inclusion, and Belonging: An Interpretation of the *Library Bill of Rights*

Adopted June 27, 2017 by the ALA Council (under previous name "Equity, Diversity, Inclusion"); amended May 29, 2025.

Equity, diversity, inclusion, and belonging are central to promoting and practicing intellectual freedom. Libraries play a vital role in:

- democracy;
- self-government;
- personal development;
- social progress; and
- everyone's right to life, liberty, and the pursuit of happiness.

To support these goals, libraries and library workers should embrace equity, diversity, inclusion, and belonging in all that they do.

Equity means considering differences to ensure a fair process and outcome. It recognizes that some groups have faced barriers to education and employment. Many of these barriers still exist today. As a result, these groups are often underrepresented or marginalized. Equity focuses on increasing diversity, inclusion, and belonging by improving the conditions of disadvantaged groups.

Diversity means the sum of the ways people are the same and different. Embracing diversity means recognizing and valuing the unique qualities in each person.

Inclusion is an environment where everyone:

- is treated fairly and with respect;
- is valued for their unique skills, experiences, abilities, and perspectives; and
- has equitable access to resources and other opportunities.

Belonging is when every person feels truly welcomed and included. To create this environment, library workers, administrators, and governing bodies should reflect the origins, age, background, and views of their community. Library spaces, programs, and collections should meet the needs of every user to ensure everyone feels they belong.

The principles of equity, diversity, inclusion, and belonging are guided by the *Library Bill of Rights:*[1]

I. Books and other library resources should be provided for the interest, information, and enlightenment of all people of the community the library serves. Materials should not be excluded because of the origin, age, background, or views of those contributing to their creation.
   - Origin means all the traits someone is born into and can't change.
   - Age means all the traits that come with a person's stage of life and maturity.

- Background means all the traits that are a result of a person's life experiences.
- Views means all the opinions and beliefs held and expressed by a person.

Libraries must provide equitable and inclusive access. To do this, they must work closely and talk with diverse communities to understand their needs and goals. This helps libraries offer collections and services that meet those needs.

A diverse collection includes content by and about a wide array of people and cultures. This ensures it authentically reflects a variety of ideas, information, stories, and experiences. Library collections should reflect the languages spoken and read by the community. Materials should come in various formats to serve the needs of all community members.

Mainstream publishers and other producers have historically underrepresented diverse authors and viewpoints. Finding, reviewing, and acquiring those materials may take extra effort. Libraries should seek out alternative, small-press, independent, and self-published content in a variety of formats.

Libraries may benefit from partnerships and cooperative efforts to help find and acquire diverse materials. Interlibrary loans can support this effort but should not replace building local diverse local collections.

The entire community the library serves should be able to access all materials. Books and resources should meet the needs of a broad range of abilities, skills, tools, and preferences. They should also be compatible with adaptive or assistive technologies.

Library materials should be easy for the community to find. Cataloging, labeling, and displays help make this possible. Libraries must avoid systems that limit or restrict access to resources.

II. Libraries should provide materials and information presenting all points of view on current and historical issues. Materials should not be proscribed or removed because of partisan or doctrinal disapproval.

Intellectual freedom is the key to equitable library services. It means providing free access to a wide range of ideas so people can explore questions, causes, and movements. Libraries should do more than avoid excluding materials representing unorthodox or unpopular ideas. They should actively include a diverse range of genres, ideas, and expressions. Underrepresented and marginalized people the library serves should see themselves in the resources and programs the library offers.[2] A full commitment to equity, diversity, belonging, and inclusion requires that library collections and programming represent many kinds of ideas, stories, and experiences—even those that some find controversial.

III. Libraries should challenge censorship in the fulfillment of their responsibility to provide information and enlightenment.

Libraries are forums for information and ideas. By challenging censorship, they create an inclusive environment where people can explore ideas, information, stories, and experiences from a wide range of people and cultures. Materials and programming don't need to appeal to everyone. Libraries have a responsibility to provide access to all points of view, not just the most popular opinions.

Library workers have a professional and ethical duty to defend a user's right to read, view, or listen to content protected by the First Amendment. They must do so fairly and justly, regardless of the user or creator's viewpoint or personal history.[3] To prepare for challenges, libraries should adopt clear policies and procedures. While community objections and complaints should be considered respectfully, controversy alone should not dictate policy.

Governing bodies, administrators, and library workers must discourage self-censorship. Fears and biases can suppress diverse voices in collections, programming, and services.[4] Libraries should counter censorship by practicing inclusion and censorship awareness programming.

IV. Libraries should cooperate with all persons and groups concerned with resisting abridgment of free expression and free access to ideas.

American society has always included people of diverse origin, age, background, and views. The constitutional principles of free expression and free access to ideas support and affirm this diversity. Limiting these freedoms threatens the core American values of equity, diversity, inclusion, and belonging.

Libraries should build and maintain strong ties to groups that support the rights of socially excluded, marginalized, and underrepresented people. Libraries should stand with anyone working to protect free expression and free access to ideas.

V. A person's right to use a library should not be denied or abridged because of origin, age, background, or views.

The principle of inclusion is clear and unambiguous in the *Library Bill of Rights* and its interpretations and supporting documents.

To uphold this principle, libraries should regularly review their policies to increase access to collections and services. Policies, services, and programming should evolve to meet the community's changing needs. Libraries should remove or revise policies that restrict access. Examples of exclusionary policies include:

- identification requirements;
- overdue charges and fees; or
- deposits for service.[5]

Libraries must base access restrictions solely on behavior, not unfair differences between people or groups. Libraries may not base restrictions on:

- race;
- ethnicity;
- national origin;
- sexual orientation;
- gender or gender identity;
- religious affiliation;
- age;
- disability;[6] or
- disease.[7]

VI. Libraries which make exhibit spaces and meeting rooms available to the public they serve should make such facilities available on an equitable basis, regardless of the beliefs or affiliations of individuals or groups requesting their use.

Publicly available library spaces serve as forums for people and groups of all origins, ages, backgrounds, and views. These spaces should have clear policies that define when and how they can be used. Policies should be inclusive and not limit access based on the content, beliefs, affiliations, or views of people using the space.

Libraries should actively encourage and support participation from marginalized and underrepresented community members in public forums. Policies should be available in languages and formats that are accessible to the community. The use of public forums and library spaces should not block access to library facilities or resources.

Libraries should welcome diverse content in exhibits and diverse ideas, people, and groups in their meeting rooms. This includes content and groups that some community members may find objectionable or offensive.

For more guidance on use of meeting rooms in libraries, see ALA's "Meeting Rooms: An Interpretation of the *Library Bill of Rights*."[8]

VII. All people, regardless of origin, age, background, or views, possess a right to privacy and confidentiality in their library use. Libraries should advocate for, educate about, and protect people's privacy, safeguarding all library use data, including personally identifiable information.

The right to privacy and confidentiality in libraries is essential. These rights allow people to access information without fear of consequences. Without privacy, people may avoid reading or viewing certain materials. This limits their ability to explore ideas and connect with the world. Surveillance and monitoring harms marginalized groups the most. For these reasons, privacy and confidentiality are essential to equity, diversity, inclusion, and belonging.

Libraries should have policies and practices that minimize surveillance and the tracking of someone's library use. These policies should be easy to find and available in formats and languages that everyone can access. Children and youth have the same rights to privacy as adults.

People should always have a choice to consent—or not to consent—to being tracked and monitored. Any data collection or surveillance should only happen when it's required to provide services.

Library workers must protect privacy in everything they do, including:

- selecting and using library content;
- selecting software tools;
- designing library spaces;
- interacting with users; and
- responding to law enforcement.

For more guidance on the rights of library users and responsibilities of libraries, see ALA's "Privacy: An Interpretation of the *Library Bill of Rights*"[9] and "Library Privacy Guidelines."[10]

Conclusion

Library workers, governing bodies, administrators should uphold the *Library Bill of Rights* to serve the entire community. They can do this by embracing equity, diversity, inclusion, and belonging.

NOTES

1. "Library Bill of Rights," adopted June 19, 1939, by the ALA Council; amended October 14, 1944; June 18, 1948; February 2, 1961; June 27, 1967; January 23, 1980; January 29, 2019.
2. "Library-Initiated Programs as a Resource: An Interpretation of the *Library Bill of Rights*," adopted January 27, 1982, by the ALA Council; amended June 26, 1990; July 12, 2000; June 26, 2018, under previous name "Library-Initiated Programs as a Resource"; June 24, 2019, under previous name "Library-Initiated Programs and Displays as a Resource"; and June 29, 2025.
3. "Diverse and Inclusive Collections: An Interpretation of the *Library Bill of Rights*," adopted July 14, 1982, by the ALA Council; amended January 10, 1990; July 2, 2008; and July 1, 2014, under the previous name "Diversity in Collection Development"; amended June 25, 2019; and May 29, 2025.
4. "Challenged Resources: An Interpretation of the *Library Bill of Rights*," adopted June 25, 1971, by the ALA Council; amended July 1, 1981; January 10, 1990; January 28, 2009; July 1, 2014; January 29, 2019; and May 29, 2025.
5. "Guidelines for the Development of Policies and Procedures Regarding User Behavior and Library Usage," adopted by the Intellectual Freedom Committee, January 24, 1993; revised November 17, 2000; January 19, 2005; March 29, 2014; March 24, 2019; July 29, 2019; August 16, 2020; and August 5, 2025.
6. "Services to People with Disabilities: An Interpretation of the *Library Bill of Rights*," adopted January 28, 2009, by the ALA Council, under the previous name "Services to Persons with Disabilities"; amended June 26, 2018; and June 29, 2025.
7. "Economic Barriers to Information Access: An Interpretation of the *Library Bill of Rights*," adopted June 30, 1993, by the ALA Council; amended June 25, 2019; and June 29, 2025.

8. "Meeting Rooms: An Interpretation of the *Library Bill of Rights*," adopted July 2, 1991, by the ALA Council; amended June 26, 2018; amended version rescinded August 16, 2018; amended January 29, 2019; and June 29, 2025.
9. "Privacy: An Interpretation of the *Library Bill of Rights*," adopted June 19, 2002, by the ALA Council; amended July 1, 2014; and June 24, 2019; and June 29, 2025.
10. "Library Privacy Guidelines," https://www.ala.org/advocacy/privacy/guidelines.

Intellectual Freedom Principles for Academic Libraries: An Interpretation of the *Library Bill of Rights*

Approved by ACRL Board of Directors: June 29, 1999 and adopted July 12, 2000 by the ALA Council; amended on July 1, 2014; and June 29, 2025.

Academic libraries must prioritize intellectual freedom when developing collections, services, and instruction. This supports efforts to ensure that information and resources are provided fairly and without bias or restriction, supporting education and research.

This interpretation explains how intellectual freedom applies to academic libraries. These principles should be included in all relevant library policies.

1. **Follow the Library Bill of Rights.** The principles in the *Library Bill of Rights* provide a crucial foundation for building collections, services, and policies for the entire academic community.
2. **Protect library users' privacy.** Libraries should have policies to minimize collection and retention of borrowing records and other personal use information, and to keep that information confidential.
3. **Build diverse, unbiased collections.** Library collections should support the institution's instruction and research programs. Personal values should not influence what is selected. Collections must include diverse perspectives, even on controversial topics.
4. **Preserve and replace materials fairly.** Libraries should maintain a balanced collection. Materials may be removed from the collection for a variety of reasons, including withdrawal, routine wear and tear, theft, or damage. Particular care may be needed with controversial materials, which may be targeted by individuals or groups based on ideology. Library workers should take a thoughtful and intentional approach to maintaining the collection, considering all forms of material loss or removal.
5. **Ensure licensing agreements uphold access.** Licensing agreements should align with the *Library Bill of Rights* and maximize access.
6. **Provide open internet access.** Academic libraries should provide easy access to an open, unfiltered internet. Content filtering and restrictions go against the library's mission to offer a wide range of information for research and learning. These limits violate intellectual freedom.

7. **Support free expression.** Library policies and exhibits should support freedom of information and creative expression.
8. **Make library spaces available to all.** Library spaces should be available to all academic users, regardless of their research topic or discussion subject. Any restrictions should be based on space availability, not content, and should follow library policy. Restrictions on access may be required by local, state, or federal law. Spaces include:
   - meeting rooms;
   - research carrels;
   - exhibit spaces; and
   - other facilities.
9. **Minimize service fees.** Library services should be free whenever possible. If a fee is required, a free or low-cost alternative should be provided.
10. **Guarantee equal access to information.** Library services should ensure equal access to information for all in the academic community. No one should face discrimination based on:
    - race;
    - age;
    - values;
    - gender or gender identity;
    - sexual orientation;
    - cultural or ethnic background;
    - physical, sensory, cognitive, or learning disability;
    - economic status;
    - religious beliefs; or
    - views.
11. **Establish a fair collection development policy and reconsideration process.** Libraries should have a clear, fair process for handling all requests to remove or add resources, exhibits, or services. This process should prioritize the research and academic needs of users inside and outside of the institution.
12. **Seek institutional endorsement.** Institutional governing bodies, such as the faculty senate, should endorse these statements.

Library Access and Representation for All Sexes, Gender Identities and Expressions, and Sexual Orientations: An Interpretation of the *Library Bill of Rights*

Adopted June 30, 1993, by the ALA Council; amended July 12, 2000; June 30, 2004; July 2, 2008; January 28, 2020 (under previous name "Access to Library Resources and Services Regardless of Sex, Gender Identity, Gender Expression, or Sexual Orientation"); and June 29, 2025.

American libraries operate within the framework of laws established by the U.S. Constitution and the First Amendment. The *Library Bill of Rights* outlines the principles that guide libraries in offering services, materials, resources, and programs. These principles allow libraries to offer a full range of information and ideas.

The American Library Association (ALA) maintains that libraries and library workers have a duty to resist efforts that exclude materials concerning someone's:

- sex;
- gender identity;
- gender expression; or
- sexual orientation.

The ALA affirms that materials are protected by the *Library Bill of Rights* when they:

- focus on lesbian, gay, bisexual, transgender, queer/questioning, intersex, and asexual/aromantic (LGBTQIA+) topics;
- are created by LGBTQIA+ people; or
- include content about LGBTQIA+ life.

Library workers should provide inclusive collections and services that reflect the diversity of the world. Refusing to include or removing resources because of the sex, gender identity, gender expression, or sexual orientation of its creator—or because the content covers LGBTQIA+ life—is censorship.[1]

Libraries should offer services, materials, and programs that reflect diverse views on sex, gender identity, gender expression, and sexual orientation.[2] Removing or restricting resources about LGBTQIA+ life without following library policy violates the *Library Bill of Rights.*

Library resources and services must be available to all members of the community. Libraries cannot restrict access based on someone's sex, gender identity, gender expression, or sexual orientation. Concerns, questions, or complaints should follow the same policies and procedures used to reconsider other library resources.

Attempts to restrict or remove access to library services and resources must be resisted to protect First Amendment rights. Library workers have a duty to ensure that all users have free and equal access to all library services and materials. The ALA urges library workers to actively support the First Amendment rights of all library users, regardless of sex, gender identity, gender expression, or sexual orientation.

NOTES

1. "Evaluating Library Collections: An Interpretation of the *Library Bill of Rights*," adopted February 2, 1973, by the ALA Council; amended July 1, 1981; June 2, 2008; and June 25, 2019.
2. "Challenged Resources: An Interpretation of the *Library Bill of Rights*," adopted June 25, 1971, by the ALA Council; amended July 1, 1981; January 10, 1990; January 28, 2009; July 1, 2014; January 29, 2019; and May 29, 2025. "Diverse and Inclusive Collections: An Interpretation of the *Library Bill of Rights*," adopted July 14, 1982, by the ALA Council; amended January 10, 1990; July 2, 2008; and July 1, 2014, under the previous name "Diversity in Collection Development"; amended June 25, 2019; and May 29, 2025. "Meeting Rooms: An Interpretation of the *Library Bill of Rights*," adopted July 2, 1991, by the ALA Council; amended June 26, 2018; amended version rescinded August 16, 2018; amended January 29, 2019; and June 29, 2025.

PERSONAL STORY

Finding Belonging Through Drag: Why Drag Story Hour Matters

SANTANA TAPIA

They say to be the change you want to see in the world. As I reflect on my journey growing up in the United States as a chubby, immigrant kid who felt disconnected from her identity, I marvel at how I found belonging through an art form that is now under attack—drag.

My family was made up of farm workers, constantly migrating with the harvest seasons across California. I never had the chance to put down roots, let alone discover who I was. By the time we finally settled in San Francisco, I felt utterly lost. That's when I met Miss Sequoia, a statuesque drag queen who radiated joy and confidence. For the first time, I saw someone who celebrated difference rather than hiding from it. Miss Sequoia inspired me to try drag, and through drag, I found a sense of belonging I had been searching for my entire life.

Drag gave me permission to reconnect with my Mexican roots, to embrace my creativity, and to reclaim parts of myself I thought I had lost forever. It was an art form that helped me piece together my identity, reminding me that being "different" was not only okay—it was powerful. Still, I can't help but wonder how much sooner I might have begun this journey if I had a space like Drag Story Hour as a child.

There is a unique magic to meeting a drag performer. Drag artists create a world of possibility, a space where everyone—especially the most marginalized—feels seen, welcomed, and celebrated. That's why I became involved in Drag Story Hour: to ensure that kids, and even adults carrying wounded inner children, experience that magic and safety. These events make reading fun, nurture curiosity, and teach kids that diversity is something to be celebrated, not feared.

In the face of growing protests and anti-drag legislation, hosting Drag Story Hour has become an act of resilience. I've seen the fear and hatred in protesters' faces as they scream outside libraries, trying to shut down events that are rooted in love and joy. But I've also seen the transformative power of drag. I've watched children light up as they listen to stories about courage and friendship, and I've heard parents thank us for showing their kids that it's okay to be themselves.

The attacks on Drag Story Hour are not just about drag—they're about silencing difference, suppressing creativity, and erasing the spaces where marginalized people feel safe. But we can't let that happen. These events are more than storytimes; they are celebrations of intellectual freedom and inclusivity. They remind us that every child deserves a world where they can imagine and create without fear.

For every protest we face, we find strength in the lives we touch. Drag has taught me resilience, and Drag Story Hour continues to inspire me to share that with others. The fight to protect these spaces is about more than just books or performances—it's about ensuring that no child grows up feeling as lost as I once did. It's about preserving the magic of belonging.

OFFICIAL ALA POLICY STATEMENT

Prisoners' Right to Read: An Interpretation of the *Library Bill of Rights*

Adopted June 29, 2010, by the ALA Council; amended July 1, 2014; January 29, 2019; and January 26, 2025.

The American Library Association strongly believes in protecting intellectual freedom for all, regardless of age or location. This includes people held in:

- Jails
- Prisons
- Detention centers
- Juvenile facilities
- Immigration centers
- Prison work camps
- Segregated units within any facility
- Any other type of facility—whether public or private.

As Supreme Court Justice Thurgood Marshall once wrote:

> When the prison gates slam behind an inmate, he does not lose his human quality; his mind does not become closed to ideas; his intellect does not cease to feed on a free and open interchange of opinions; his yearning for self-respect does not end; nor is his quest for self-realization concluded. If anything, the needs for identity and self-respect are more compelling in the dehumanizing prison environment.[1]

In a democracy, everyone needs open access to various kinds of information:

- social;
- political;
- legal;
- economic;
- cultural;
- scientific; and
- religious.

Having access to the same information as those outside of a carceral facility is essential to a successful transition to freedom. Learning to thrive in a free society requires access to a wide range of knowledge. Suppression of ideas does not prepare incarcerated people of any age for life in a free society. Even those who will never leave prison require access to books and information in any format, so that they may have a window into the world.

Just because material contains unpopular views or is considered offensive doesn't mean it should be censored.[2] Censorship is when authorities decide to block certain ideas or viewpoints. Unlike censorship, selection is a process of inclusion. It's about seeking out a diverse range of ideas in any format. The carceral library collection, like all library collections, should reflect the needs of its community.

Carceral libraries and their staff may be required to prohibit materials that promote illegal acts or harm. These restrictions are because of the following:

- Federal, state, or local laws
- Administrative rules
- Court decisions

Staff should only restrict items posing a real and imminent risk to safety and security. These limiting factors may reduce available materials. However, following the *Library Bill of Rights* and its interpretations can help minimize the impact.

Use these principles to serve people who are incarcerated or detained. They apply to everyone, regardless of their citizenship status or if they've been convicted of a crime.

- **Collection Management:** Libraries should follow a written policy for how to maintain their collections. Library workers and carceral administrators should agree on the policy. The policy should align with the *Library Bill of Rights* and its interpretations.
- **Challenges Procedures:** If someone challenges a library item, the library should have written procedures to follow. This includes a policy that explains what makes an item unacceptable.[3]
- **Materials Selection:** Library workers should select materials based on the people they serve. This means choosing items that reflect their backgrounds, information needs, interests, and diverse cultural values.
- **Acquisition Independence:** Library workers should be able to acquire materials that meet written selection criteria. Carceral agency review should not be required during acquisition. Material selection should not be limited to a pre-approved list of materials or vendors.
- **Language Diversity:** Library workers should provide materials to meet the information needs of people who read in languages other than English.
- **Findability:** Library workers should have enough support to make it easy for people to find library resources.
- **Age:** Incarcerated children and youth should have access to a wide range of fiction and nonfiction. Age is not a sufficient reason for censorship.[4]
- **Disability Access:** Equitable access to information should be provided for people with disabilities.[5]
- **Non-traditional Bindings:** Libraries should avoid banning materials with non-traditional bindings. The exception would be if they pose real and imminent risk to safety and security.
- **Sexual Content:** Material with sexual content should not be banned unless it violates state or federal law.
- **Digital literacy:** Digital literacy skills are crucial in society today. Libraries should offer training to help incarcerated people learn how to become digitally literate.[6]
- **Digital access:** Incarcerated people should have access to digital services and materials at no cost. Incarcerated people should have controlled access to digital legal resources. These legal resources should include legal databases. Access to the internet should only be limited as required by law or sentencing restrictions.
- **External Material Access:** Incarcerated or detained people should be able to acquire materials from outside of the carceral facility.

When free people, through judicial procedure, segregate some of their own, they incur the duty to provide humane treatment and essential rights. Among these are the rights to read and to access information. The right to choose what to read is crucial, and the suppression of ideas is fatal to a democratic society. The denial of intellectual freedom—the right to read, to write, and to think—reduces the humanity of those segregated from society.

NOTES

1. *Procunier v. Martinez,* 416 U.S. 428 (1974).
2. 28 C.F.R. 540.71(b): "The Warden may not reject a publication solely because its content is religious, philosophical, political, social or sexual, or because its content is unpopular or repugnant."
3. "Challenged Resources: An Interpretation of the *Library Bill of Rights,*" adopted June 25, 1971, by the ALA Council; amended July 1, 1981; January 10, 1990; January 28, 2009; July 1, 2014; January 29, 2019; and May 29, 2025.
4. "Access to Library Resources and Services for Minors: An Interpretation of the *Library Bill of Rights,*" adopted June 30, 1972, by the ALA Council; amended July 1, 1981; July 3, 1991; June 30, 2004; July 2, 2008, under previous name "Free Access to Libraries for Minors"; July 1, 2014; June 25, 2019; and May 29, 2025.
5. "Services to People with Disabilities: An Interpretation of the *Library Bill of Rights,*" adopted January 28, 2009, by the ALA Council, under the previous name "Services to Persons with Disabilities"; amended June 26, 2018; and June 29, 2025.
6. A person who has the ability to use information and communication technologies to find, evaluate, create, and communicate information, requiring both cognitive and technical skills.

PERSONAL STORY

Intellectual Freedom Incarcerated

ELDON RAY JAMES

When I arrived at the Big Spring Federal Prison Camp in 1997, I had never heard the term "intellectual freedom." I always worked from the assumption that I could read, write, or think as I wished. Within a few months I learned the hard lesson that this was not true. By the time I left in 2002 I still did not know the term "intellectual freedom," but I had felt the impact of not having it.

However, within a few months of beginning study at the University of Texas School of Information, I not only knew what intellectual freedom was but also that it had, in subtle and forceful ways, been stripped from me in prison.

While incarcerated, I began writing letters from prison that were published in *The Mountain Mail*. In the first one, I wrote about the journey from Salida to Big Spring. I wrote about some of the people I met along the way, including a correctional officer. I then received a copy of the letter as printed. The prison had read it in my mail and called me to task. The message: We will not stop you from writing, but do not describe correctional officers or the prison itself. Not wanting to test the limits, all future letters focused on my state of mind or opinions about national or world issues.

The next problem came from the prison's policy of allowing only ten books, including a Bible, in the possession of each incarcerated person. After ten weeks I exceeded the limit. I received a warning. Since other folks in my unit had no books, I managed to give out the excess books. Since the camp did not have a library, except for the law library, there were no alternatives.

When I began college correspondence courses, the limit on books changed to an unspecified number. Unfortunately, not all correctional officers were informed of this. A shakedown search often resulted in the officer confiscating the excess books as contraband. Sometimes I was able to get them back and more often, not.

When I moved into a job at UNICOR (Federal Prison Industries), there was a lot of space in my cubicle. I asked the correctional officer, who was my boss, if I could store some books and other school materials there. After checking with her supervisor, she agreed.

Once again, not all the correctional officers got the word. In a search for drug contraband at my workplace, the officers took some schoolwork and the books that my boss said I could store. Eventually, in response to numerous requests, the prison returned the bag I used to carry, but none of its contents. They told me they did not know what happened but that it was probably destroyed.

I confess that the continual pressure over what I could write, read, and even think caused me to withdraw. I followed the rules as exactly as I could, knowing they could change instantly. I still read and thought, but I kept that reading and those thoughts to myself. I stopped putting ideas down on paper. My formerly colorful letters turned banal.

I concentrated on schoolwork and managed to earn enough credits for an Associate of Science degree only to discover that I could not receive the degree because I could not get credit for a computer class. I pleaded to be allowed to go to the college to test out on the class. No. Could I take the test at the prison? No.

On my last day at the camp the person in charge came to me to ask if I would still like to get the computer class credit. Yes! I took a test on a computer and keyboard that I was unfamiliar with, and with programs I did not know. Two years later I found out that I had passed the test and was awarded the degree.

I will admit that in my time in prison I led a privileged life. I consider myself reasonably intelligent. Given all of that, I had a difficult time dealing with the prison rules. I keenly felt the losses of intellectual freedom. But the real pain I feel now is that most of my fellow incarcerated peers then (and now) do not have my advantages. Is it any wonder that recidivism is so high because the tools that might make a difference are out of reach or behind opaque walls?

Now I use my unfettered intellectual freedom to break down the barriers for my brothers and sisters inside.

OFFICIAL ALA POLICY STATEMENTS

Restricted Access to Library Materials: An Interpretation of the *Library Bill of Rights*

Adopted February 2, 1973, by the ALA Council; amended July 1, 1981; July 3, 1991; July 12, 2000; June 30, 2004; January 28, 2009; July 1, 2014; and May 29, 2025.

Libraries are places for the free exchange of information. Restricting access to library materials based on content violates American Library Association's *Library Bill of Rights*.[1]

Some libraries have fragile or special collections that need careful handling to prevent damage. While these items may have restricted access due to their condition, access should not be limited based on content.

Some libraries use physical or digital barriers to control access to materials. This might include the following practices:

- Labeling materials
- Placing materials in locked cases
- Organizing materials into a "high demand" collection
- Creating "adults only" or "restricted" sections

These measures may be used because of legal requirements, institutional rules, or to prevent theft or damage. However, such actions can unintentionally support censorship. Restricting materials because they contain controversial, unusual, or sensitive subjects is censorship. Listing a title as restricted in the catalog or in the library creates a barrier. This may cause users to feel embarrassed or hesitate to ask for access.[2]

Libraries may organize collections by reading level, ability, grade, or age. This practice can restrict access and make users uncomfortable selecting resources from sections that don't match their assigned category.

Some libraries use programs that assign reading levels to library materials or users. Such programs should not be used to limit choice. These programs may not reflect a user's full reading skills, needs, or interests because they may categorize users by age or grade. Users should be free to choose materials outside of their assigned level. Library staff should be free to choose any materials in alignment with their Collection Development Policy, even if that item does not have an assigned reading level.

Federal and state laws may require libraries receiving certain funds to use internet filters. These filters can block access to a wide range of constitutionally protected information. Libraries should have policies and procedures to manage internet filters. This helps to ensure users can access information.[3]

Donated items also need special consideration. Libraries should avoid donor agreements that permanently restrict access to these collections. Libraries must ensure equal access to all research materials they hold.

Library policies that restrict access to resources must be written and managed carefully to ensure they adhere to the principles of intellectual freedom. This caution is evident in many ALA policies:

- "Evaluating Library Collections"[4]
- "Access to Library Resources and Services for Minors"[5]
- "Preservation Policy"[6]
- ACRL "Code of Ethics for Special Collections Librarians"[7]

Libraries provide access to diverse viewpoints on current and historical issues. Proposals to restrict access should be scrutinized to ensure that they don't suppress viewpoints or create barriers. Libraries must have policies and procedures that serve the diverse needs of their users and protect the First Amendment right to access information.

NOTES

1. "Library Bill of Rights," adopted June 19, 1939, by the ALA Council; amended October 14, 1944; June 18, 1948; February 2, 1961; June 27, 1967; January 23, 1980; January 29, 2019.
2. "Labeling Systems: An Interpretation of the *Library Bill of Rights*," adopted July 13, 1951, by the ALA Council; amended June 25, 1971; July 1, 1981; June 26, 1990; January 19, 2005; July 15, 2009; and July 1, 2014. Divided into two interpretations, "Labeling Systems: An Interpretation of the *Library Bill of Rights*," and "Ratings Systems: An Interpretation of the *Library Bill of Rights*," both adopted June 30, 2015; "Rating Systems" amended June 25, 2019. "Labeling Systems" and "Ratings Systems" merged into a single document, "Labeling and Rating Systems: An Interpretation of the *Library Bill of Rights*," adopted May 29, 2025.
3. "Access to Digital Resources and Services: An Interpretation of the *Library Bill of Rights*," adopted January 24, 1996, by the ALA Council; amended January 19, 2005; July 15, 2009, under the previous name "Access to Digital Information, Services, and Networks"; June 25, 2019; and May 29, 2025.
4. "Evaluating Library Collections: An Interpretation of the *Library Bill of Rights*," adopted February 2, 1973, by the ALA Council; amended July 1, 1981; June 2, 2008; and June 25, 2019.
5. "Access to Library Resources and Services for Minors: An Interpretation of the *Library Bill of Rights*," adopted June 30, 1972, by the ALA Council; amended July 1, 1981; July 3, 1991; June 30, 2004; July 2, 2008, under previous name "Free Access to Libraries for Minors"; July 1, 2014; June 25, 2019; and May 29, 2025.
6. "ALA Preservation Policy 2008," adopted by ALA Council at 2008 Annual Conference.
7. "Code of Ethics for Special Collections Librarians," approved by ACRL in October 2003.

Services to People with Disabilities: An Interpretation of the *Library Bill of Rights*

Adopted January 28, 2009, by the ALA Council under the previous name "Services to Persons with Disabilities"; amended June 26, 2018; and June 29, 2025.

The American Library Association (ALA) recognizes that people with disabilities are a significant and vibrant part of society. Libraries should be fully inclusive and work to remove barriers to access. By providing accessible resources and services, libraries can help all users take part more fully in their communities and promote the full inclusion of people with disabilities.

The Americans with Disabilities Act (ADA) defines a person with a disability as:

- someone with a physical or mental impairment that substantially limits one or more major life activities;
- someone with a history or record of such impairment; or
- someone who is perceived by others as having such an impairment.[1]

There is no exhaustive list of disabilities. The term "person with a disability" includes people with a diversity of abilities, identities, and appearances. This intersectional group shares common experiences of discrimination and barriers to access.

Libraries must follow all applicable laws, including the ADA requirements and state or local disability accessibility guidelines. Libraries should check with legal counsel to understand their legal responsibilities.

Libraries should:

- learn about the technical and legal standards for digital accessibility;
- offer training for staff and volunteers on how to serve users with disabilities and work with colleagues who have disabilities;
- provide equal access to collections, services, and facilities for all users. If full access is not possible, libraries should quickly provide reasonable accommodations so people with disabilities have a similar experience;
- have policies and procedures which are inclusive of people of all abilities; and
- have policies to support hiring people with disabilities and including them on governing boards.

Libraries remove barriers to information when they offer content in accessible formats. Library workers should research and use new and existing accessible technologies to support users. Libraries should provide equal access to physical and online spaces and make sure all users know these tools and services are available.

Library workers:

- should never assume a person's limits based on disability.
- should not let their personal and professional biases shape services or resources.
- should connect with people with disabilities and advocacy and support groups to build partnerships. These partnerships should help guide program planning, collection development, and changes to library spaces.
- should include as many diverse community members as possible in all stages of planning and implementation.

Library Resources and Collections (print and online)

Libraries must act legally, ethically, and inclusively to meet the information needs of all users. This should include materials by and about people with disabilities. This group has historically not been treated equitably. Libraries should not limit access to materials based on assumptions about what users need, are interested in, or can understand. The collection should include perspectives by persons with disabilities and representation across:

- age;
- race;
- gender;
- class; and
- orientation.

To be inclusive, libraries must provide accurate, up-to-date, and representative materials. They should also preserve historic materials that show the progress toward inclusion and equality in American society.

Library collections should also be accessible to everyone. All resources should be available in accessible formats to people of all ages and abilities. This includes the library website and online resources. Library administrators should work closely with vendors to ensure accessibility of resources. They should make sure vendors set reasonable deadlines to fix accessibility issues. Libraries should not license, subscribe, or buy a resource or product until these issues are addressed.[2]

Physical Spaces, Exhibits, Meeting Rooms and Programs

Physical access should never stop anyone from using the library. Buildings should be accessible, or reasonable accommodations should be provided.

Information about the library facility should be available on the library's website in an accessible format.

If libraries offer exhibit spaces and meeting rooms, these spaces should be as physically accessible as other public spaces. Examples of accessible features include:

- automatic doors;
- handrails;
- elevators;
- ramps;
- clear travel paths; and
- accessible tables, desks, restrooms and parking.

To ensure accessibility for all, libraries should provide reasonable accommodations, including:

- sign-language interpreters;
- open captions during presentations; and
- visual description during programming.

These accommodations should be available upon request. Information about all available accommodations and how to request them should be easily accessible to all users in-person and on the library website.

Privacy, Confidentiality, and Censorship

A person's rights to privacy and confidentiality and quality of service should not be affected based on their disability.

Censorship often silences the voices of those who are already marginalized. Libraries give everyone a chance to be heard, including those whose voices are quieter or heard less often. As stated in "Equity, Diversity, Inclusion, and Belonging: An Interpretation of the *Library Bill of Rights*," "Libraries should counter censorship by practicing inclusion."[3]

NOTES

1. U.S. Department of Justice, "Guide to Disability Rights Laws," last modified July 2009, ada.gov/cguide.htm.
2. "Fact Sheet: New Rule on the Accessibility of Web Content and Mobile Apps Provided by State and Local Governments," last modified April 2024, ada.gov/resources/2024-03-08-web-rule/.
3. "Equity, Diversity, Inclusion, and Belonging: An Interpretation of the *Library Bill of Rights*," adopted June 27, 2017 by the ALA Council, under previous name "Equity, Diversity, Inclusion"; amended May 29, 2025.

PERSONAL STORY

Access Begins at the Door: A Librarian's Perspective on Disability and Inclusion

REBECCA WEBER

For me, information access and barriers to libraries begin at the door. I have cerebral palsy and walk with crutches. Preplanning is essential when I am going someplace new. I consider whether accessible parking is available and how best to access the building. Most of this is second nature because I do it all the time. I am used to looking at pictures of buildings on the internet to see how accessible they are and using websites to see if I can find something about their accessibility. Seeing that a library has accessibility features or a web page about its services makes me feel welcome and included before I enter the space.

At my local public library, the staff usually offer assistance when I walk in. I tell them thank you, but I want to browse before I ask for help. I will ask for assistance later if I want too many books or if they are too high on the shelf. If I am in a hurry, I take advantage of curbside pickup or have a book reserved to pick up at the desk. All of these services make it easier for me as a person with a disability.

As a librarian, familiarity with how libraries work gives me an advantage when navigating a library space. However, one issue that often comes up in disability advocacy discussions is discrimination in the workplace. Those of us with disabilities worry that when we disclose our disability, our capabilities will be judged by what people think of our physical appearance or neurodivergence. For example, when I was leaving a previous library position, a colleague came into my office and said, "When we first interviewed you, I thought, 'Here we go; she won't be able to do this.' But you proved smarter than I thought you were." I sat in shock, unsure how to answer in the face of blatant discrimination when my colleague thought she was complimenting me.

Accommodations for people with disabilities allow for gainful employment and are not just extra perks. They enable people with disabilities to have the same chance in the workplace as non-disabled people, and providing them isn't just the right thing to do—it is the law.[1]

In the last couple of years, I have worked with many librarians and library workers with disabilities through the American Library Association (ALA) and the Reference and User Services Association's Accessibility Assembly. I have had Deaf and Hard of Hearing (HOH) librarians and staff request something as simple as closed captions for the movies shown at ALA or having interpreters for all sessions because they cannot fully participate otherwise. People who are blind need websites and presentations with alt text to use their screen readers. Individuals who use wheelchairs have relayed that others judge their intelligence because of their mode of mobility. I have worked with librarians with autism or learning disabilities whose lived experience helps them design programming for neurodivergent users. Everyone's needs for support or access differ, but their contributions are rich. Their perspectives allow me to consider the many aspects of disability and intellectual freedom when working with ALA or at my university.

NOTE

1. U.S. Department of Labor, Office of Disability Employment Policy, "Accommodations," dol.gov/agencies/odep/program-areas/employers/accommodations.

A DEEPER LOOK

The Law Regarding Access to the Library: Public Forums and User Behavior Rules

This section was written by a legal expert in the field. The author's name has been withheld by mutual agreement.

Public Forum Doctrine

There are three types of government property:

- traditional;
- designated or limited; and
- nonpublic.

Traditional Public Forums

A traditional public forum is a location such as a street, park, or sidewalk. Historically, these spaces are set aside for public use, free expression, and open discussion. They have traditionally been accessible to the public for activities like gathering, sharing ideas, and "discussing public questions."[1]

In a traditional public forum, any content-based restrictions are reviewed under a strict scrutiny standard to determine if they are constitutional. Under strict scrutiny, the government must show that the restriction:

- serves a compelling government interest;
- is narrowly tailored to achieve that interest; and
- uses the least restrictive way to reach the goal.

If the government cannot meet these requirements, the restriction is unconstitutional.[2]

Designated or Limited Public Forums

A designated or limited public forum is "property that the State has opened for expressive activity by part or all of the public."[3] This type of forum does not come into existence automatically or by accident. Simply allowing some limited public use of a space or not actively restricting it does not make it a designated public forum. Instead, the government must make a clear and deliberate decision to open a nontraditional space for public expression or discussion.[4]

To decide whether a place is a designated or limited public forum (and not a traditional public forum), courts examine the government's "policy and practice." They determine whether the government "intended to designate a place not traditionally open to assembly and debate as a public forum."[5]

Governments may impose valid time, place, and manner restrictions in limited public forums. These restrictions must be content-neutral, narrowly tailored to serve a significant government interest, and must leave communication channels open.[6] Examples of such restrictions in the library setting include:

- hours of operation;
- handling disruptions in the library;
- copying costs;
- time limits on using materials or services;
- meeting room capacity;
- meeting room sign-up procedures; and
- limits on the number of days exhibit spaces may be used.

These restrictions must have a clear purpose, be content-neutral, and be applied consistently.

There are limited circumstances in which content-based restrictions can be applied in a designated public forum. If a court finds that a government entity has created a designated or limited public forum, it will evaluate any content-based restrictions to see if the restriction:

- serves a compelling government interest;
- is narrowly tailored to achieve that interest;
- and uses the least restrictive way to reach the goal.[7]

If the government cannot meet that test, the restriction will be held to be unconstitutional.

Nonpublic Forums

A nonpublic forum is government property reserved for an intended purpose, even if it is used for communication. For example, a public library might use a meeting room for its own purposes without making it available for public use. The room could be used for staff meetings, library programming, or meetings of the Friends of the Library. Even though the library uses the room for communication, it remains a nonpublic forum.

The Supreme Court has held that the government can control who uses a nonpublic forum and base that access "on subject matter and speaker identity." However, these rules must be "reasonable in light of the nature of the purpose served by the forum" and viewpoint-neutral.[8]

Courts generally look at the entity's policies, how the forum is used, and "its compatibility with expressive activity."[9] To determine the type of forum the government has created, courts look at factors such as:

- whether there is a written policy;
- whether the policy is applied consistently;
- whether the policy is based on subjective or overly general criteria;
- which criteria are used to determine access; and
- consistency with the principal function of the forum.[10]

Restrictions based on viewpoint are never allowed in any forum, including in a nonpublic forum.[11]

Court precedents show that a library's policies and practices determine the type of forum it creates. How these principles are applied may vary based on the services the library provides.

Courts have generally held that public libraries are *designated* or *limited* public forums for the receipt of information. Any restrictions on library access must be evaluated using First Amendment principles. This critical issue was first considered in *Kreimer v. Bureau of Police for the Town of Morristown.*[12] A man experiencing homelessness, Richard Kreimer, was banned from the Morristown Public Library in New Jersey for disrupting users and because others found his personal hygiene offensive. He sued the library in federal court. The Third Circuit Court of Appeals held unequivocally that the First Amendment protects the right to receive information and "includes the right to some level of access to a public library."[13]

The court found that the Morristown Library had "intentionally opened the Library to the public" for "specified purposes: reading, studying, using the Library materials." The court held that libraries can put reasonable rules in place to govern library use and that libraries can regulate user behavior even when there is no "actual disruption." The court also held that libraries may regulate non-expressive activity (including loitering, following people, and playing audio equipment so others can hear it) to ensure safety or efficient access to resources. The Third Circuit remanded the case back to the lower court so that it court could determine whether the library's rules were applied in a manner that did not violate Richard Kreimer's constitutional rights, but the case settled before the lower court made that determination.

Importantly, the *Kreimer* case was settled before the lower court could apply these general principles to the particular facts of the case. As a result, the court never determined whether the Morristown rules had been applied to Richard Kreimer in a constitutional manner.[14]

The principles established by the *Kreimer* case have been applied and expanded by many courts. Critically, however, a restriction on user access to a library upheld as constitutional in one library may not necessarily be upheld in another. In each case, courts evaluate whether the particular library has a compelling need for the restriction in light of its particular mission.

The cases show the types of issues related to restrictions on access that are not constitutional. For example, in *Brinkmeier v. City of Freeport*, a library user was banned from entering the library on the grounds that he had harassed a library employee in a location removed from the library premises.[15] Relying on *Kreimer*, the district court held that library users have a First Amendment right to access the public library but that the right has some limits.

The court held that Freeport's policy against harassment was unreasonable for the following reasons:

1. it was unwritten and broadly stated;
2. terms such as "harassing" and "intimidation" were undefined;
3. the ban was not tied to use of the library by other users or staff;
4. it did not have geographical limits, since it seemed to apply to conduct that happened outside the library; and
5. there was no formal or informal procedure for challenging denial of access to the library.[16]

Of course, the library employee could seek other remedies, such as applying for a court-issued stay-away order to prevent the person from approaching her anywhere, including her place of employment at the library.

In *Armstrong v. District of Columbia Public Library*, a user was banned from the library because his appearance was considered "objectionable." The court held that the ban was unconstitutional.[17] The district court held that the standard was unconstitutionally vague and overly broad.[18] The court also held that the appearance rule violated the user's due process rights. The court explained that "not only does the vague appearance regulation increase the risk of discriminatory decisions regarding library access, its arbitrary nature and application prevents the type of uniform decision-making required to provide fair notice of what hygiene conditions will be prohibited."[19]

In contrast, courts have upheld user bans when the rules are objective and clearly defined. For example, in *Neinast v. Board of Trustees*, the court held that banning a barefoot user from the library was constitutional.[20] The district court explained that the library was a limited public forum but that the shoe requirement was constitutional because it is "a valid, content-neutral regulation that promotes communication of the written word in a safe and sanitary condition." To demonstrate the need for the ban, the library provided evidence in the form of incident reports to show that its "floor sometimes contains feces, semen, blood, and broken glass, all of which pose a significant danger to barefoot individuals."[21] The Sixth Circuit appellate court affirmed the decision, adding that the rule also protected the library from the potential of lawsuits and litigation costs if a barefoot user was injured.[22]

Library policies on user behavior must be:

1. written;
2. objective;
3. consistently enforced;
4. reasonable and directly related to library use; and
5. accompanied by an appeal process, even if informal.

NOTES

1. *Perry Educ. Ass'n v. Perry Local Educators' Ass'n,* 460 U.S. 37, 45 (1983) (quoting *Hague v. CIO,* 307 U.S. 496, 515 [1939]).
2. *Perry,* 460 U.S. at 45; Widmar v. Vincent, 454 U.S. 263, 269–70 (1981).
3. *Int'l Soc. for Krishna Consciousness, Inc. v. Lee,* 505 U.S. 672, 678 (1992).
4. *Cornelius,* 473 U.S. at 802; see also *Ark. Educ. Television Com'n v. Forbes,* 523 U.S. 666, 677 (1998) (holding that designated public forums are created by "purposeful government action").
5. *Cornelius,* 473 U.S. at 802.
6. *Perry,* 460 U.S. at 45.
7. *Ark. Educ.,* 523 U.S. at 677.
8. *Cornelius,* 473 U.S. at 806.
9. *Id.* at 802.
10. *Hopper v. City of Pasco,* 241 F.3d 1067 (9th Cir.), *cert. denied,* 534 U.S. 951 (2001) (holding that the city violated the First Amendment when it denied artists access to a city hall display area); *see also Planned Parenthood/Chicago Area v. Chicago Transit Authority,* 767 F.2d 1225 (7th Cir. 1985) (concluding that the city violated the First Amendment when it denied a nonprofit group access to advertising space on transit authority vehicles). An example of how this might apply in the library context: If a library designated a meeting room for use only by library staff in a written policy, but then allowed some public groups to use the meeting room without allowing for such use in its policy, it would be inconsistent with the principal function of the forum as a nonpublic forum for library use only. In that case, if another group had asked the library to use the meeting room and the library replied that it could not because the meeting room is a nonpublic forum, the court might determine that the denial was unconstitutional because the room was actually open to some groups for their own use.
11. *Cornelius v. NAACP Legal Def. & Educ. Fund, Inc.,* 473 U.S. 788, 806 (1985).
12. 958 F.2d 1242 (3d Cir. 1992); but see *Little v. Llano County,* No. 23-50224 (5th Circuit, May 23, 2025) (holding that users do not have a right to receive information in a public library).
13. *Id.* at 1255.

14. In examining constitutional challenges, a court must determine if a restriction is facially unconstitutional or unconstitutional as applied. A statute will be deemed facially unconstitutional if it could never be applied in a constitutional manner. If a statute is facially constitutional, then a court examines whether it has been applied in an unconstitutional manner to the complaining party.
15. (Case No. 93C 20039), 1993 U.S. Dist. Lexis 9255 (N.D. Ill. July 2, 1993).
16. *Id.*; see also *Wayfield v. Town of Tisbury*, 925 F. Supp. 880, 884–85 (D. Mass. 1996) (holding that a library card was a type of license giving its holder access to the library, deprivation of which infringed upon a liberty or property right requiring the library to provide due process before imposing restrictions on the right to enter the library).
17. 154 F. Supp. 2d 67, 75 (D.D.C. 2001).
18. *Id.* at 79.
19. *Id.* at 81.
20. 190 F. Supp. 2d 1040 (S.D. Ohio 2002), *aff'd*, 346 F.3d 585 (6th Cir. 2003), *cert. denied*, 541 U.S. 990 (2004).
21. *Id.* at 1044.
22. 346 F.3d 585 (6th Cir. 2003), *cert. denied*, 541 U.S. 990 (2004); see also *People v. Taylor*, 630 N.Y.S.2d 625, 164 Misc. 2d 868 (N.Y. Sup. Ct. 1995) (upholding the conviction for trespass of a user who violated a ban against playing cards and board games in the library after being unsuccessful in his attempt to have the library lift its ban and despite being requested by the director of the library and three police officers to abide by the library rules).

Intellectual Freedom: The Law in Flux

The right to receive information in libraries has faced recent legal challenges. For more information, refer to "Intellectual Freedom: The Law in Flux" (part I, chapter 3).

CHAPTER 5
Censorship, Challenged Resources, and Internet Filtering

BIG IDEA BREAKDOWN

Key Concepts

- People have the right to express their opinions about library resources and services.
- Libraries should follow their collection development policies when selecting resources and have formal procedures for reconsidering challenged resources.
- Reconsideration policies should also address challenges to resources and services such as:
  - subscription databases;
  - programs;
  - displays; and
  - exhibits.
- Resources should not be removed from the collection because of:
  - partisan or doctrinal disapproval;
  - the origin, background, or views of the creator; or
  - because some may consider the item offensive.
- Challenged resources should remain in the collection during the reconsideration process. Resources that meet the library's selection criteria should not be removed.
- Using internet filters to block constitutionally protected speech, including social media and gaming content, compromises First Amendment freedoms and goes against core library values. Internet safety is best supported by educational programs that teach people of all ages how to find and evaluate information.

What Does the Law Say?

- The U.S. Constitution protects free expression and the related right to receive the protected expression of others. The Supreme Court has held that the Bill of Rights requires a process to critically examine any challenged expression before it can be suppressed.
- Libraries are only required to follow the Children's Internet Protection Act (CIPA) and use internet filters if they accept funding for internet access through the E-rate discount program or LSTA grants. Libraries are not required to seek or accept this funding.
- "Pornography" is not a legal term. It is often used to describe sexually explicit materials or materials some people find objectionable, but these materials are often protected by the First Amendment.
  - In contrast, "obscenity" and "child pornography" are legal terms. These materials are designated by a court of law and are not protected by the First Amendment. While "child pornography" is still the term used in federal law, "child sexual abuse material" (CSAM) is preferred because it more accurately reflects the abuse involved.[1]
  - "Harmful to minors" is another legal term. It refers to sexually themed materials that are legal for adults but restricted for minors. (Refer to appendix 1, "Glossary of Terms," for more detail.)
- Hate speech is protected by the First Amendment. This protection is based on the belief that freedom of speech requires the government to allow strong debate on public issues—even if the speech is offensive, hurtful, or hateful. Under current law, hate speech can only be criminalized if it directly incites imminent criminal activity or contains a specific threat of violence aimed at a person or group.

Creating Policy for Your Library

- Adopt the *Library Bill of Rights* and the *Code of Ethics of the American Library Association* as policies for your library (part I, chapter 2). They have statements about resisting censorship and not removing resources based on partisan or doctrinal disapproval.
- Have a collection development policy that covers all types of resources, including online resources. Follow this policy when selecting, removing, or responding to challenges to materials (part I, chapter 3).
- Make sure your collection development policy includes a clear procedure for reconsidering challenged resources, no matter the type or format (part I, chapter 3).

For Academic Libraries

- Academic libraries are sometimes pressured to remove resources labeled as "unscholarly," "pseudoscience," or offensive to certain groups (for example, Holocaust denial literature). These materials are often part of the collection to support research, study the controversy, or preserve the historical record.
- Refer to "Intellectual Freedom Principles for Academic Libraries" (part II, chapter 4).

For Public Libraries

- Challenges often begin at the front desk or in the stacks. That's why all library workers should understand their library's reconsideration policy and know how to respond to user concerns. It's also important to educate the library's governing body about the process and why public libraries include materials that some may find controversial.

For School Libraries

- The courts have distinguished between a school board's control over materials used in the curriculum (used by all students) and materials in the school library collection, which is a "marketplace of ideas." If a resource is selected using the school's collection development policy, it should not be removed without due process.
- School libraries should not filter the internet beyond what CIPA and state law require. Doing so may restrict students' access to constitutionally protected resources. School districts should have a process to unblock sites that do not include images that are obscene, CSAM, or defined by a court as "harmful to minors."
- Public school libraries should not favor or promote materials that advance a certain point of view on a potentially controversial topic. This is considered "viewpoint discrimination." Libraries should provide access to resources that give a range of views of these topics.

To Learn More

- Visit these ALA websites for links to information about censorship, challenges, internet filtering, banned books, and hate speech:
  - "Banned and Challenged Books," ala.org/advocacy/bbooks
  - "Filters and Filtering," ala.org/advocacy/intfreedom/filtering
  - "First Amendment and Censorship," ala.org/advocacy/intfreedom/censorship

- "Selection & Reconsideration Policy Toolkit for Public, School, & Academic Libraries," ala.org/tools/challengesupport/selectionpolicy toolkit
- "Hate Speech and Hate Crime," ala.org/advocacy/intfreedom/hate

Reflection Questions

- What are the steps in your library's reconsideration process? How frequently is the process reviewed with staff?
- The author of a popular and controversial nonfiction book admits to falsifying some of their data. You have multiple copies in your collection. What do you do?
- At a meeting, a colleague says that the library should change its collection development policy to exclude items that contain hate speech. About half of the group agrees. What would you say?

Please Report Challenges to the American Library Association

To report a challenge to your library's materials, use the reporting form at ala .org/tools/challengesupport/report. All information is kept confidential. ALA reports information about challenges only in aggregate or after the challenge has been reported in the press.

Need Help Handling a Challenge?

- Contact the intellectual freedom committee of your state or regional library association.
- Call the ALA Office for Intellectual Freedom at (800) 545-2433, ext. 4221, or email oif@ala.org.

NOTE

1. U.S. Department of Justice, "Child Sexual Abuse Material," Subject Matter Expert Working Group, June 2023, justice.gov/d9/2023-06/child_sexual _abuse_material_2.pdf.

OFFICIAL ALA POLICY STATEMENT

Challenged Resources: An Interpretation of the *Library Bill of Rights*

Adopted June 25, 1971, by the ALA Council; amended July 1, 1981; January 10, 1990; January 28, 2009; July 1, 2014; January 29, 2019; and May 29, 2025.

Libraries: An American Value states, "We protect the rights of individuals to express their opinions about library resources and services."[1] The American Library Association (ALA) maintains that every library should have a written policy and procedure for review of challenged resources. These should cover:

- library materials;
- library provided resources;
- library initiated programs; and
- library services.

A person's right to freedom of expression is protected by the U.S. Constitution. This right also applies to students and minors.[2] Freedom of expression includes the right to share and access content, even if some people may find it objectionable. It also includes the right to object to content and have those concerns considered and addressed by governing entities, like library boards. The Supreme Court has held that the Constitution requires a careful process to review all challenged expression before it can be suppressed.[3]

Libraries should have procedures to review concerns and challenges raised by groups or individuals. These procedures should be open, transparent, and comply with all applicable open-meeting and public-records laws. They should not be used to suppress constitutionally protected expression. Library policies should:

- protect the rights of library users;
- follow applicable laws; and
- align with the guidance of the *Library Bill of Rights*, and *Freedom to Read* and *Freedom to View* statements.

A review procedure is used to decide if a resource aligns with the library's mission and policies. Resources that meet these standards should not be removed. During the review process, resources must stay available to users. Access should not be restricted, even for a short time.

To protect free expression, libraries must carefully evaluate any effort to control or restrict resources. These efforts can take many forms, such as:

- Updating a collection development policy based on a new law or legal advice, even if the law may later be ruled unconstitutional.

I., Ch. 5 Censorship, Challenges, & Internet Filtering

- A library cataloger placing a juvenile book in the adult collection out of fear of complaints about the content.
- A school board member implying that a library worker's job depends on them removing a specific item.
- A mayor claiming the authority to decide what the library collects, ignoring the library's collection development policy.
- A state legislature passes a bill tying funding to removal of specific library materials.

Some of these actions may have legal ramifications for the library or for library staff. Legal counsel should be consulted to determine the legality or illegality of the action and how to proceed.

Libraries and library workers should be proactive in resisting efforts to restrict access that do not follow the legally required process, library policies, and ethical guidelines.

NOTES

1. "Libraries: An American Value," adopted February 3, 1999, by the ALA Council.
2. "Access to Library Resources and Services for Minors: An Interpretation of the *Library Bill of Rights,"* adopted June 30, 1972, by the ALA Council; amended July 1, 1981; July 3, 1991; June 30, 2004; July 2, 2008, under previous name "Free Access to Libraries for Minors"; July 1, 2014; June 25, 2019; and May 29, 2025.
3. *Bantam Books, Inc. v. Sullivan,* 372 U.S. 58 (1963).

PERSONAL STORY

Information Deserts: The Scarcity of Knowledge in Prisons

STACY LYN BURNETT

In the United States, incarceration is alarmingly common—tens of millions of people have experienced it. Yet getting information into prisons is far more difficult than being sentenced to a term of incarceration. Navigating the barriers to knowledge means confronting complex and often predatory technologies, along with restrictive policies that limit access. Prisons are information deserts, where even the smallest source of knowledge can feel like an oasis. Inside, finding information is not a simple search. It is a relentless scavenger hunt.

When I was incarcerated, my housing unit was the farthest from the library. Every Tuesday I would wait by the door for movement to be called, determined to be the first one out. I needed to get to the library before others to ensure that, in the twenty minutes I had, I could read last Sunday's *New York Times*. Would it be on the rack? Had someone else already taken it? Would I have to wait for a list? Could I ask the person reading it to share the book reviews and bestseller list? This was how I found titles to request from the interlibrary loan system.

That Tuesday's ritual was a solo power walk with my head down so no one would slow me down. This urgency for a two-day old *New York Times* is a mundane experience for anyone in the free world. But what I found in those pages would determine the books I could request and the knowledge that would sustain me in the months ahead. This is how I discovered *Cutting for Stone* by Abraham Verghese and Stieg Larsson's *Millennium* series. I once received *The Poisonwood Bible* through Books Through Bars, but because the word "poison" appeared in the title, the package room officer refused to give it to me. A week later I found it on the library shelf, and I took a journey with the Price family through the Congo—out of defiance as much as curiosity.

When I transferred to a new facility, I had the opportunity to enroll in college. As a student in the Bard Prison Initiative, the world opened up through classroom resources. For the first time, I used JSTOR. The database had been modified for offline access, and I took full advantage. Some of my classmates were overwhelmed by the sheer number of search results. After years of having every aspect of our lives controlled, many of us had adapted to the illusion of autonomy while losing the ability to seek out knowledge independently. Professors encouraged my curiosity and filled every request I submitted—more than 35,000 pages in a single year.

Today, I work for JSTOR, making its resources available to more than a million incarcerated people worldwide. But access is only the first step. Getting JSTOR into correctional facilities, whether online or offline, is a challenge in itself. Another is helping departments of corrections manage content at scale and ensuring educators know that JSTOR is available for their students.

Curiosity is not confined to a syllabus. The most profound intellectual growth I experienced in prison was sparked by an Oscar Wilde obsession that had nothing to do with coursework. Yet many correctional systems restrict educational content to materials tied directly to classes, extending institutional control into the classroom without any true security justification.

Librarians inside correctional institutions have been some of the strongest allies in expanding access to knowledge. When they, rather than security teams, oversee content, a prison's information desert can transform into a thriving landscape of learning and opportunity.

OFFICIAL ALA POLICY STATEMENTS

Censorship by Altering Library Resources: An Interpretation of the *Library Bill of Rights*

Adopted February 2, 1973, by the ALA Council; amended July 1, 1981; January 10, 1990; July 2, 2008; July 1, 2014 (under previous name "Expurgation of Library Resources"); and June 29, 2025.

Altering library resources by deleting, editing, or removing content for the purpose of censorship violates the *Library Bill of Rights.*

Who might alter library resources for the purpose of censorship?

Resources might be altered by:

- employees;
- administrators;
- governing authorities;
- parent institutions (if any);
- third-party vendors; or
- library users.

What are some examples of altering library resources for the purpose of censorship?

- obscuring words, passages, or images in physical or digital resources;
- removing or gluing together pages;
- altering displays based on user complaints;
- adding commentary in the margins; or
- publishing a version of a material with changed language, without the approval of the creator.

Why is altering resources for the purpose of censorship harmful?

- **It denies access to the full work.** Censorship removes or edits parts of a work, denying access to the full range of ideas it expresses.
- **It violates intellectual freedom.** Suppressing information—especially under the belief that it is harmful to minors—goes against the *Library Bill of Rights.*
- **It may violate copyright law.** Altering a work without permission from the rights holder can breach U.S. copyright law.

Preserving Original Works

Library workers do not have to remove or edit earlier versions of a work just because a rights holder decides to change future versions. In some cases, original versions of a work should be retained in order to preserve historical copies and prevent censorship. This should not interfere with a library's regular collection maintenance and efforts to keep collections accurate and up to date, according to the library's purpose.

Library workers should oppose altering resources in licensed collections. Any alteration of library resources limits access to ideas and information. This disregards users' right to experience works in their original form.

Internet Filtering: An Interpretation of the *Library Bill of Rights*

Adopted June 30, 2015, by the ALA Council; amended June 29, 2025.

Many schools and libraries use online content filters for different reasons. The most common reason is to comply with the Children's Internet Protection Act (CIPA), which allows them to receive federal funding or discounts through:

- the Library Services and Technology Act (LSTA);
- Title III of the Elementary and Secondary Education Act; or
- the Universal Service discount program (E-rate).

Some libraries and schools also follow state filtering rules to qualify for state funding. Many believe that having filtered access is better than having no access at all. The American Library Association (ALA) does not recommend the use of internet filters. When they are used, libraries should adopt practices and policies to reduce their negative impacts.

CIPA requires public libraries and schools that receive E-rate discounts to use content filters. These filters must block two categories of images that are not protected by the First Amendment: obscene images and child sexual abuse material. The Supreme Court has ruled that these types of content do not have constitutional protection.

CIPA also requires libraries and schools to block a third category—images that courts deem "harmful for minors." These images are legal for adults but not for minors. CIPA does not require blocking any other constitutionally protected speech or images.

Research shows that filters often block too much or too little content. They frequently prevent access to a wide range of legally protected speech for multiple reasons. Filtering technology often struggles to interpret and categorize complex human communication, whether in text or images, or video. Filters can be ineffective in handling new types of content because they lag behind the always changing and growing internet.[1] Also, filter settings may be set by administrators in ways that go beyond the legal requirements and restrict access to legally protected speech.[2]

Using filters shifts the control of important library and school resources to outside companies. These third parties can influence basic library functions without accountability.[3] Also, library workers and educators often find that filters are unreliable and tech-savvy users can easily bypass them. Some filters allow local library workers to modify settings. Other filters require approval from higher-level administrators.

Most content filters are designed for larger markets beyond libraries and schools. They often block broad categories of legally protected speech, such as:

- objectionable language;
- violence;
- unpopular or controversial opinions; and
- entire online services like email and social media.

Many filters operate on an "opt-out" model, meaning they are turned on by default. These filters often default to the strictest settings, which can only be changed by an administrator.

The Supreme Court upheld CIPA requirements in public libraries based on the idea that adults could request filters be turned off.[4] However, in practice, this often doesn't happen. Some libraries are unwilling or unable to unblock content when requested. This is especially true if system administration is outside of the library's control or when staff are unsure of what content is protected for adults. This can lead to long delays in unblocking mistakenly filtered content.

This same issue happens in schools. Delays in unblocking content function as a form of censorship. This is because most users don't have the time to wait hours or days for access. This problem is made worse by the filtering industry's secrecy about how content is categorized and blocked, often protected as trade secrets.

Filters also raise privacy concerns. Users must identify themselves and their interests when asking for specific websites to be unblocked. This can discourage both adults and minors from accessing information on personal or controversial topics. No one should have to give up their privacy to access information that should be freely available.

In schools, the CIPA rules are often misinterpreted. This leads to:

- overly strict filtering that blocks legally protected content;
- preventing educators from using the internet for teaching; and
- stopping students from accessing content for assignments and personal interests.

Students may also be blocked from using interactive websites and social media for learning. This limits opportunities to create and share original content like documents, videos, and music.

These issues arise when library workers and educators are not involved in setting filtering policies and procedures. Minors, educators, and library workers should not be blocked from legally protected content just because some may find it objectionable. Anyone should be able to request that non-CIPA-required content be unblocked.

CIPA-mandated content filtering has several major impacts on schools and libraries:

1. It widens the digital divide between those who can afford personal internet access and those who must rely on filtered, publicly-funded access.
2. Minority viewpoints, religions, or controversial topics are often labeled as objectionable or offensive and blocked.
3. Filters can reinforce bias and discrimination by restricting access to certain content.

When filters block too much content, people without other internet access are left with only what the unreliable filters allow.

The negative effects of internet content filters are well documented. Because of this, the ALA cannot recommend using filters.[5] However, the ALA recognizes that many libraries and schools rely on federal or state funding for internet access and may be required to use them.

Libraries and schools that use filters should have policies to reduce their negative impact. They should make it easy for users to request blocked content to be unblocked. These requests should be carried out with minimal delay and with respect for user privacy.

For further guidance, see "Guidelines to Minimize the Negative Effects of Internet Content Filters on Intellectual Freedom."[6]

NOTES

1. Dhanaraj Thakur and Emma Llansó, "Do You See What I See? Capabilities and Limits of Automated Multimedia Content Analysis," Center for Democracy & Technology, May 2021.
2. Elizabeth Laird, Madeleine Dwyer, and Hugh Grant-Chapman, "Off Task: EdTech Threats to Student Privacy and Equity in the Age of AI," Center for Democracy and Technology, September 2023, https://cdt.org/wp-content/uploads/2023/09/091923-CDT-Off-Task-web.pdf.
3. Kristen Batch, "Fencing Out Knowledge: Impacts of the Children's Internet Protection Act 10 Years Later," OITP and OIE Policy Brief No. 5, American Library Association, June 2014, https://www.ala.org/sites/default/files/advocacy/content/intfreedom/censorshipfirstamendmentissues/FINALCIPA_Report.pdf.
4. *United States v. Am. Library Association, Inc.*, 539 U.S 194 (2003).
5. "Resolution on the Use of Filtering Software in Libraries," adopted 1997 by the ALA Council; and "Resolution on Opposition to Federally Mandated Internet Filtering," adopted 2001 by the ALA Council.
6. "Guidelines to Minimize the Negative Effects of Internet Content Filters on Intellectual Freedom," https://www.ala.org/advocacy/intfreedom/filtering/filtering_guidelines.

A DEEPER LOOK

Responding to Challenges and Concerns About Library Resources

BECKY CALZADA AND ERIC STROSHANE

Introduction

Libraries strengthen communities by supporting literacy and providing access to information and culture.[1] Library workers fulfill this mission by collecting resources spanning the horizon of human thought and experience.

Attempts to limit the freedom to read are attempts to limit whose stories can be told and who gets to tell them. Restrictions on access to books are restrictions on the ideas available for consideration and discussion.

The *Code of Ethics of the American Library Association* (ALA) directs library workers to "uphold the principles of intellectual freedom and resist all efforts to censor library resources."[2]

Libraries need approved collection development and resource reconsideration policies. The policies should provide criteria for selecting resources, and procedures for handling challenges to materials. These policies help library workers defend the freedom to read. (Consult chapter 3, "Creating Intellectual Freedom Policies for Your Library.")

Libraries serve community members who have differing needs, interests, and viewpoints. The materials valued by some community members may be considered objectionable by others. A library user may complain when they disapprove of a resource.

Library workers should handle all complaints in the same way. Policy must be followed no matter who raises concerns about the resource. This is true even if the complainant is a staff member, an administrator, or an elected official.

This section provides guidance on handling complaints, censorship requests, and efforts to go around policy.

Verbal Concerns and Complaints

Every library needs a process for handling verbal complaints about resources. When someone expresses concerns, politely refer them to the person responsible for responding. When handling complaints:

- Do not agree with the person or promise to act.
- Remain calm and respectful.
- Remember that everyone has the right to question library resources.
- Listen attentively, ask clarifying questions, and seek to understand their concerns.

- Determine if they have read the entire work.
- Ask if there is something they would like the library to do.
- Offer the complainant help in finding something better suited to their interests.
- When the concerns are about a resource for children or young adults, affirm that parents have the right to guide their own children's reading and library use, and they must allow other parents that same right.
- If the complainant requests censorship of the resource, explain that other library users may not share their perspective. Describe how library resources are selected. Share that a library's mission is to provide resources for all members of the community and must collect resources from many points of view to fulfill that mission. Explain that every library user has the First Amendment right to experience the resources they choose and to form their own opinions about them.
- If the complainant is satisfied, thank them for their interest.
- If the complainant is not satisfied:
  1. Explain the formal reconsideration process and its timeline. Consult "Formal Requests for Reconsideration or Statements of Concern" in this chapter.
  2. State your policy on the resource's availability during the reconsideration process.[3]
  3. Provide a copy of the library's collection development policy and a resource reconsideration form.[4]
  4. Stress that the form must be fully completed for the library to act.
  5. Explain that the reconsideration process begins when a completed form is received and that the form becomes part of the public record.
  6. After the conversation, make notes, date them, and retain them for background in case a reconsideration request form is filed. These notes may become public records.[5]
  7. Notify your director or principal of the concerns expressed, how concerns were handled, and any actions the complainant said they would take next. This information helps administrators:
     a. Respond knowledgeably if the complainant contacts them.
     b. Prepare for the reconsideration process, if started. Coordinate with the board or other governing body if someone raises concerns directly to them.

If the complainant becomes belligerent:

- Enforce your library's user behavior policy.
- Report harassment to your human resources department.
- Report threats to the police.

Be aware that some people attempt to subvert the process by taking their concerns directly to the board or another governing body. Consult "Responding to Attempts to Undermine the Process" in this chapter.

Formal Requests for Reconsideration or Statements of Concern

A formal request for reconsideration is a written document listing concerns about a resource and the reasons to reconsider its place in the library. Each library needs a policy on receiving and handling formal challenges to resources. If your library has a governing board, the policy should be approved by your board.

ALA's Office for Intellectual Freedom (OIF) is available to assist you if you receive a reconsideration request. If you require support, do not hesitate to contact OIF by submitting a confidential report at: www.ala.org/challengereporting.

> Some libraries are now calling this form "Statement of Concern" instead. This title is clearer for users and avoids library jargon. The process for staff stays the same, no matter what the form is called. But using "Statement of Concern" can help set clearer expectations for users.

> Avoid personal opinions in all official communications, as paper and electronic documents can be obtained with an open records request. If you have questions, check with your library's legal counsel.

If the library receives a completed reconsideration form, the party designated in the library's policy to evaluate challenges should:

1. Promptly acknowledge receipt of the request and share the steps and timeline for the process with the complainant.
2. Identify:
    a. if the request is from an individual or from a representative of a group;
    b. if the complainant reviewed the entire resource;
    c. if action was requested; and
    d. the reasons provided by the complainant.
3. Prepare a document for the library director or school administrator that includes:

   a. the resource's title;
   b. a summary of the plot or content;
   c. the selection criteria the resource meets;
   d. a list of positive reviews;
   e. awards received;
   f. how frequently the item was checked out;
   g. how many libraries in the area own it; and
   h. a summary of the reconsideration process.

4. Meet with your administration to discuss the challenge. If an administrator attempts to remove a library resource without following policy, explain the legal and ethical issues:
   a. Going around policy to censor a resource puts a school district or library in jeopardy of a lawsuit. (Consult "Creating Intellectual Freedom Policies for Your Library," part I, chapter 3.)
   b. Decisions about which resources are available should be deliberate and objective, not emotional or reactive.
   c. Disregarding policy sends the message that bypassing policy is legal and that censoring library resources is easy and appropriate—a precedent that can be quickly repeated.

5. Follow your reconsideration procedure as written. The review process must be transparent, objective, and should include the following steps:
   a. reviewing the challenged work in its entirety;
   b. determining if the resource meets the selection criteria in the library's collection development policy;
   c. deciding if the resource will be kept or if another action will be taken; and
   d. sharing the decision with the complainant in a written response (do not use an impersonal form letter).

6. If the library's policy includes an appeals process, also:
   a. explain how to appeal the decision;
   b. state the deadline for appeal;
   c. inform the complainant if their appeal requires public disclosure of the reconsideration request and related documents, such as in a meeting agenda;
   d. inform public-facing staff about the reconsideration process; and
   e. keep records as required by your library's document retention policy.

7. Once a final decision about the resource is made, communicate the decision to library workers, keep a dated record, and report the result to OIF at: ala.org/challengereporting. OIF uses this information for statistics but keeps the details of the challenge confidential.

8. Reflect on the experience:
    a. Was community access to a resource retained?
    b. Did you learn something you can apply to the next challenge?
    c. Did you gain allies?
    d. Do you need to improve relationships with community leaders or with the local media?
    e. Can the experience support library advocacy in the community?
9. If the process can be improved, create a list of recommendations. Meet with the administration to discuss if the timing is right to revise the policy.

Additional information on the reconsideration process in libraries is available in the ALA document "Selection & Reconsideration Policy Toolkit for Public, School, & Academic Libraries" at ala.org/tools/challengesupport/selection policytoolkit.

Responding to Attempts to Undermine the Process

Some people attempt to undermine a library's approved process for handling complaints. Those doing so usually take excerpts from books out of context to create outrage and discredit library workers. Such efforts erode trust in public schools and libraries. An effective response to this requires preparation.

If you learn someone plans to approach a governing body directly, brief its members about the situation. Provide the board's members with copies of the policies and other information needed, including book résumés and talking points.

Alert your network of allies about the situation. Building coalitions and developing allies through advocacy helps defend libraries and library workers. Allegiances must be formed before you need them. (Refer to part III, "Advocacy and Assistance.")

Book Résumés

Book résumés are free resources that help teachers, library workers, parents, and community advocates support access when others demand that books should be censored. Each résumé contains a synopsis of the book, reviews, awards, accolades, and links to resources and relevant media. The résumé may also include information about how the title has been successfully retained in schools and public libraries where it has been challenged.

The "Book Résumés" resource, containing hundreds of such résumés, is maintained and updated by Unite Against Book Bans at bookresumes.uniteagainst bookbans.org.

The following steps can help the board president defuse undermining efforts and retain control of meetings so the board can conduct business. Always consult legal counsel before implementing changes, so as to ensure compliance with local laws and ordinances.

1. Set rules on how public comment takes place:
   a. Hold public comments until the end of the meeting.
   b. Require advance sign-in to make public comments at the meeting.
   c. Allow only community and residents of the library's service area to speak at the meeting.
   d. Set a reasonable time limit for each speaker.
   e. Set a reasonable overall time limit for the public comment period.
   f. Restrict comments to matters on the agenda, policies, past actions, and concerns.
   g. Prohibit discussing library workers by name, to protect them from harassment during and after the meeting.
   h. Disallow outbursts, verbal demonstrations, and interacting with other speakers.
   i. Remind attendees of the rules governing public comment.
2. When complaints about library materials come up, the board president should share information on the library's process for handling complaints.
3. The board president should thank each speaker for their comments, but not express opinions, indicate agreement, or promise action.
4. If allowed, the board president can correct the record when false statements are made. Such statements typically involve:
   a. which materials are in the collection;
   b. where materials are held;
   c. misrepresentations of law or policy; and
   d. mischaracterizations of library workers' professionalism.

Some people abuse the reconsideration process by challenging multiple titles that they have found in lists online. These attempts drain the resources needed to carry out the library's mission and responsibilities. To prevent this, strengthen your reconsideration policy by:

- defining who in your community can challenge library resources;
- allowing only one item to be challenged per request form;
- requiring that reconsideration forms be fully completed;
- setting a reasonable limit on the number of items an individual can challenge at a time (e.g., one per month, three per year, etc.);
- specifying the deadline for appeal before the decision becomes final (if your policy includes an appeals process); and
- indicating how long the decision will stand before a resource can be challenged again.

Follow ALA's "Guidelines for Reconsideration Committees" to help keep the process within constitutional guardrails: ala.org/tools/challengesupport/reconsiderationcommittees.

The following practices can further blunt the effectiveness of reconsideration abuse:

- Document the time and resources consumed by abuses of the reconsideration process. This supports policy changes and demonstrates the harm caused by those seeking censorship.
- Refer to the "Book Résumés" site to show challenged titles' literary value and educational merit: bookresumes.uniteagainstbookbans.org.
- Report all challenged titles and intellectual freedom issues to OIF and your state library or school library association's intellectual freedom committee.

When library workers, administrators, and other stakeholders are on the same page, it blunts the effectiveness of pressure tactics. Annually review the library's selection and reconsideration policies with library workers, administrators, and other decision-makers. Orient new board members, administrators, and officials on intellectual freedom and the library's policies, mission, and role. Public library trustees should review and sign an ethics statement, such as the one from United for Libraries that can be found at ala.org/sites/default/files/united/content/trustees/orgtools/Ethics%20Statement.pdf.

An administrator may circumvent the library's policy out of fear of controversy, in response to social media outrage, or in the face of political pressure. This can include prohibiting the purchase of certain materials and removing resources or canceling events without formal review. If it is safe to do so, remind the administrator that:

- Following the policy maintains objectivity and transparency, prevents discrimination, is a legal and fiduciary responsibility, and protects the library from lawsuits.
- Soft censorship and shadow bans encourage abuse of the system and generate liability.
- Lawsuits are time-consuming and expensive, especially when constitutional rights are violated.

Finally, there can be legislative threats to the right to read. When a law or ordinance is in effect, it must be followed. This is true even when the law or ordinance is facing or likely to face a legal challenge.

Follow all administrative guidance regarding compliance with such laws. Maintain detailed records of materials removed for compliance. These records could become important court documents. If possible, retain the materials withdrawn in a secure location. If the law is overturned or enjoined, you will be able to return materials to the shelves.

Libraries are on the front line in the culture wars. Proponents of culture wars are intentionally cruel, intimidating, and demeaning; they inflict physical, emotional, and psychological trauma. Nurture yourself by:

- practicing mindfulness and self-care;
- getting help from employee assistance programs;
- making time for creative outlets;
- safeguarding your personal social media accounts;
- disconnecting during days off;
- spending time with family, friends, and pets; and
- getting outdoors and away from where you live and work.

For additional guidance, consult "Hateful Conduct in Libraries: Supporting Library Workers and Patrons" at ala.org/advocacy/hatefulconduct.

It is natural to feel torn between your ethical principles and authoritative pressures to censor. Library workers do profound good that radiates throughout their communities. Because of this, library workers are needed and cherished, especially during the darkest times. If you work in a library, do the best you can, with the books you have, for as long as you can. Every reader served will appreciate, learn from, and remember your help and courage. Those who defend the power of stories to uplift and unite will never stand alone.

NOTES

1. Throughout this chapter, the term "libraries" is used to refer to all publicly funded school, public, special, and academic libraries, except in cases where a specific library type is referred to. While it is best practice for private libraries to adhere to the principles outlined here, they are generally not obligated to do so under the First and Fourteenth Amendments.
2. *Code of Ethics of the American Library Association*, adopted at the 1939 Midwinter Meeting by the ALA Council; amended June 30, 1981; June 28, 1995; January 22, 2008; and June 29, 2001.
3. Best practice is for the resource to remain available without restriction throughout the process. If this isn't possible, minimize the amount of time it is not available. See "Challenged Resources: An Interpretation of the *Library Bill of Rights*."
4. If the library does not have a collection development policy, affirm the principles of intellectual freedom found in the *Library Bill of Rights*. See "Creating Policy for Your Library—Collection Development and Resource Reconsideration"; "Challenged Resources: An Interpretation of the *Library Bill of Rights*"; and "Access to Library Resources and Services for Minors: An Interpretation of the *Library Bill of Rights*."
5. Complainants' names may need to be redacted to comply with state statute when reconsideration request forms are publicly disclosed. In *Brookhart v. Reaman* 2022CV30017, the Colorado Court of Appeals found that "the identifying information in the requesters' reconsideration forms is protected under the second category of section 24-90-119(1). Under the plain language of the statute, the identifying information of a person who 'requested or obtained [a] specific ... service' from the library may not be disclosed. The

> requesters 'requested ... [a] specific ... service' from the library district when they submitted their reconsideration forms and 'obtained' a benefit from such service by initiating the process of determining whether the book should be removed from the library's collection or placed in a restricted status." While this could be persuasive precedent, it has no direct application outside of Colorado.

The Law Regarding Internet Filtering

DEBORAH CALDWELL-STONE

CIPA

The Children's Internet Protection Act (CIPA)—and its requirement to use filtering software—applies *only* to schools and libraries that accept federal E-rate discounts or LSTA grants for their internet access. There is no requirement that a school or library accept these federal funds.

The term "child pornography" is used in this chapter because it is the term currently used in U.S. federal law. However, the term "child sexual abuse material" (CSAM) is widely recognized as more accurate, as it describes the abuse and exploitation involved and centers the harm done to the child. Many organizations, including the U.S. Department of Justice, have called for a shift to using CSAM instead of the outdated legal term. Refer to the Department of Justice's 2023 memorandum: https://www.justice.gov/d9/2023-06/child_sexual_abuse_material_2.pdf.

The Internet and the First Amendment

As the internet became a common way to communicate, lawmakers debated whether it should be regulated by the government because of the growing availability of materials some people considered pornographic or controversial. In response to these concerns, federal and state lawmakers passed laws making it a crime to publish or view online materials they deemed "indecent." The lawmakers passed these laws even though the First Amendment protects the right to publish and view these materials. Library workers, readers, publishers, and civil liberties groups challenged these laws in the courts. They argued that these laws violated the First Amendment by making it a crime to read or view protected speech.

In 1997, the Supreme Court resolved this debate. It ruled that the First Amendment applies without restriction to all material published or provided through the internet.[1] It also ruled that people using the internet enjoy the same right to publish and receive information as those who use print media.[2] The court's decision overturned all existing laws restricting access to controversial or explicit internet content.

The Children's Internet Protection Act

After the Supreme Court's decision, Congress passed the Children's Internet Protection Act (CIPA) in response to public concerns about youth access to controversial and explicit online content in libraries.[3] CIPA requires libraries and schools to use internet filters and have an internet use policy in order to receive federal funds for internet access. These funds come from the Universal Service E-rate program and the Library Services and Technology Act (LSTA).[4] Schools and libraries accepting these funds must certify that they have an internet use policy. This policy must include using filtering software to block online images that are obscene under federal law.

The American Library Association (ALA) and the Freedom to Read Foundation joined with public library users to challenge CIPA in the courts. The trial court held that CIPA's content-blocking requirement could harm library users' First Amendment rights.[5] But the Supreme Court disagreed. It ruled that the First Amendment does not prohibit Congress from requiring a library to use internet filters to receive federal funding. However, adults aged seventeen and older can ask for the filter to be disabled without explaining their request.[6]

What CIPA Requires

Because Congress can set requirements on the funds it provides to public schools and libraries, it can pass laws like CIPA that control how those funds are used.[7] However, schools and libraries are not required to accept federal funds. CIPA only applies to those schools and libraries that choose to accept E-rate discounts or LSTA grants for internet access.

To comply with CIPA, schools and libraries must adopt a written internet use policy that addresses minors' online safety and requires content filters on all computers. Schools must also have a policy to educate students about:

- social media use;
- cyberbullying; and
- appropriate online behavior.

Filters must be installed on all school- or library-owned computers and other devices that can access the internet. This includes computers and devices used by staff. Filters must be set to prevent adults and minors from accessing online visual images that are obscene or qualify as child pornography under federal law.

Filters must also prevent minors from accessing visual images that federal law classifies as "harmful to minors," or obscene for minors. Adults have a First Amendment right to view these images. However, to be deemed harmful for minors, the images must lack any serious value for minors in the following areas:

- literary;
- artistic;
- political; or
- scientific purposes.

Library staff can disable the filters or unblock websites for adult users. They may also unblock websites for users of all ages that are wrongfully blocked by the filters.[8] It is important to note that CIPA does not require schools or libraries to block text-based publications or messages.

The use of filters must comply with the First Amendment. CIPA does not allow blocking access to controversial topics or viewpoints. It also does not allow blocking information for discriminatory reasons. Filters cannot be set to block platforms or social media sites like Facebook and YouTube.[9] Additionally, CIPA does not allow software that tracks or monitors a person's internet use.[10]

Liability for Blocking Constitutionally Protected Content

School boards and libraries have been sued for blocking access to materials protected by the First Amendment. They have also faced lawsuits for failing to disable internet filters when requested to do so by adults.[11] In one case, a court ruled that the school board violated students' First Amendment rights by blocking their access to websites affirming civil rights for the gay, lesbian, bisexual, and transgender communities.[12] As a result, the board was ordered to pay $125,000 in legal fees to the American Civil Liberties Union. To avoid such lawsuits, libraries should not use filters to block access to controversial topics or viewpoints. They should consult legal counsel to ensure that their internet use and filtering policies comply with the law.

Liability for Unfiltered Access

A federal law, 47 U.S.C. § 230, protects libraries and other internet service providers from lawsuits. This law prevents people who claim that they were harmed by accessing controversial or explicit material published by a third party from suing internet service providers and libraries that only provide access to the internet. In one case, a parent sued a public library for not using a filter after her son used library computers to download images the parent found inappropriate.[13] The California Court of Appeals ruled against the parent, citing the protections provided in 47 U.S.C. § 230. The court also ruled that public libraries do not have a special duty to protect minors from inappropriate online materials since they do not have a special custodial relationship with minor users.

State Laws and Internet Filtering

Many states have their own versions of CIPA. These "mini-CIPA" laws require schools and libraries to use filters on their computers to receive state funding.

Some state lawmakers are passing laws that require filters on online databases and e-book platforms. Other new state laws would mandate filtering on all internet-capable devices.

Additionally, nearly half of state legislatures in the United States have passed laws requiring age verification for all internet users. Age verification laws harm both adult and minors' rights to free expression, anonymity, and privacy online. These laws are currently being challenged in the courts. Several courts, including in Ohio, Utah, Mississippi, and Indiana, have stopped enforcement of these laws because the courts found that the laws, as written, violate internet users' First Amendment rights. However, in the case of *Free Speech Coalition v. Paxton*, the Supreme Court upheld a Texas age verification law that requires commercial websites publishing sexually explicit content that is obscene to minors to verify that visitors are eighteen or older.

While the Texas age-verification law does not impose new legal duties on libraries or digital service providers providing access outside of Texas, the Supreme Court's approval of the age verification scheme suggests that similar laws impairing users' access to online information and privacy may be adopted in other states.

For this reason, it is important to stay informed about proposed legislation and to consult legal counsel about new laws that regulate how libraries provide internet access. State library associations and the ALA track and report on new legislation that may restrict or regulate access to online library materials, and they advocate against legislation that harms library users' intellectual freedom. The Freedom to Read Foundation tracks and reports on court cases challenging restrictions on internet access and also challenges laws impairing intellectual freedom in the courts.

What Should I Do If I'm Required to Install an Internet Filter?

Libraries and schools can take these steps to minimize the negative impact of filtering:

1. Take care when choosing and installing filtering software. Choose software that:
    a. clearly explains how it decides what content to block;
    b. lets the library block only narrow and specific types of content; and
    c. allows staff to permanently unblock content that was blocked by mistake.

    Make sure the library can opt out of any content or viewpoint-based blocking that goes against the First Amendment. Make sure that the filter correctly blocks illegal content.

    Before using the software, test the list of blocked websites and adjust the filter to avoid blocking too much. Staff should regularly check how the filter works. They should also be able to turn off the filter or unblock websites on public computers when needed.
2. Create a written internet use policy. CIPA requires this policy to address online safety for minors and the use of filters. The rules must be fair, reasonable, and not based on personal beliefs or viewpoints. The policy should clearly explain internet users' rights and responsibilities. It should also list the consequences for breaking the rules and explain how to appeal decisions. The library should have a process for adults and minors to ask for blocked content to be reviewed and unblocked quickly if it was blocked by mistake. Adults must also be allowed to ask that filters be turned off promptly.
3. Use alternatives to filtering, such as:
    a. arranging computer stations to give users more privacy;
    b. creating spaces just for families and children; and
    c. using privacy screens on monitors.

    Libraries should also offer educational programs that teach people of all ages how to search the internet safely, protect their personal information, and avoid unwanted content.
4. Do a cost-benefit analysis to track the costs of filtering. These costs may include:
    a. filtering software;
    b. network support and maintenance; and
    c. staff time for training and administration.

    In some cases, the cost of filtering may be higher than the value of the federal funding your institution receives.

Note: A version of this section originally appeared in the tenth edition of the *Intellectual Freedom Manual* and was written by Deborah Caldwell-Stone and Sarah Houghton.

NOTES

1. *Reno v. American Civil Liberties Union*, 521 U.S. 844, 897 (1997).
2. *Id.*
3. The Children's Internet Protection Act, P.L. 106-554 (2000), codified at 47 U.S.C. § 254(h)(5) and 20 U.S.C. § 9134(f).
4. 47 U.S.C. § 254(h)(5) (E-rate) and 20 U.S.C. § 9134(f) (LSTA).
5. *American Library Association v. United States*, 201 F. Supp. 2d 401 (E.D. Pa. 2002).
6. *United States v. Am. Library Association*, 539 U.S. 194 (2003).
7. *Id.* at 203.
8. 20 U.S.C. § 9134(f)(3) and 47 U.S.C. § 254(h)(6)(D).
9. FCC Report and Order 11-125, August 21, 2011 (Report and Regulations Implementing CIPA).
10. Pub. L. 106–554, §1(a)(4) [div. B, title XVII, §1702(b), Dec. 21, 2000.
11. *Bradburn, et al. v. North Central Regional Library District* (E.D. Wash. 2012); *PFLAG v. Camdenton R-III School District*, 853 F. Supp. 2d 88 (W.D. Mo 2012); and *Hunter v. Salem Public Library* (E.D. Mo. 2013).
12. *PFLAG v. Camdenton R-III School District*, Case 2:11-cv-04212, Consent Judgment (April 4, 2012), aclu.org/cases/pflag-v-camdenton-r-iii-school-district?document=pflag-v-camdenton-r-iii-school-district-consent-judgment.
13. *Kathleen R. v. City of Livermore*, 87 Cal. App. 4th 684 (2001).

Intellectual Freedom: The Law in Flux

The law regarding access to and the removal of library resources has been changing. For more information, refer to "Intellectual Freedom: The Law in Flux" in part I, chapter 3.

CHAPTER 6
Children and Youth

BIG IDEA BREAKDOWN

Key Concepts

- Each library user has unique needs and interests. Library workers cannot decide what resources will meet those needs based on just one factor, such as:
  - age;
  - apparent maturity;
  - education level;
  - literacy skills; or
  - legal status.

  No one's right to use the library should be denied or limited because of these factors.
- A lack of access to information can harm young people. Teaching them how to evaluate information and make informed choices helps support healthy, safe development into adulthood.
- Library workers and governing bodies cannot take on the role of parents (in loco parentis). Only parents and guardians have the right and responsibility to decide what their children—and only their children—can access in the library.

What Does the Law Say?

- Children and young adults have First Amendment rights. This includes the right to receive information and the right to privacy.
- The right of parents or guardians to access their minor children's public library and public school library records varies from state to state. Consult the law in your state. Parents' and guardians' access to their minor children's school library records is also governed by the Family Educational Rights and Privacy Act (FERPA).

Creating Policy for Your Library

- Adopt the *Library Bill of Rights* (part I, chapter 2) as policy for your library. It contains statements about people's right to use a library regardless of age.

For Academic Libraries

- Courts do not require college or university libraries to supervise the intellectual activities of minors, whether they are students or visitors. However, academic libraries should have internet use policies. These should ban illegal computer use and make clear that parents—not library workers—are responsible for monitoring their children's online activity.
- Academic libraries may collect and keep controversial titles in children's and young adult literature. These materials serve as historical artifacts and examples of past cultural norms, supporting research and the study of children's literature over time.

For Public Libraries

- Libraries may place certain materials in a children's or young adult section. This is not considered restricting access, as long as all library users are still able to access all parts of the collection.

For School Libraries

- School libraries may be the only place where minors can access information. Restrictions on access, including internet filtering, should be kept to a minimum.
- Teaching information literacy skills is a vital part of a school library's role.

To Learn More

- "Schools and Minors' Rights," ala.org/advocacy/intfreedom/minors.
- Visit the websites of these organizations:
  - American Association of School Librarians (ala.org/aasl)
  - Association for Library Service to Children (ala.org/alsc)
  - Cooperative Children's Book Center (ccbc.education.wisc.edu)
  - Public Library Association (ala.org/pla)

Reflection Questions

- A parent asks to see what their child has checked out. The books include a title about alcoholic parents. What do you do?

- When checking out movies, a parent removes one from their twelve-year-old child's stack and says they're not ready to watch it yet. The child comes back later and wants to check out that movie. What do you do?
- You're helping a high school student with a research project on sexually transmitted diseases. Many of the sites they're trying to access are blocked by the library's internet filter. What are your options?
- Your school automatically sends library checkout history to the parents of all students. You realize this includes high school seniors who have turned eighteen. What do you do?

For More Information About Minors and the Library

Refer to the following chapters of this manual:

- "Access to Library Resources and Services" (part II, chapter 4)
- "Censorship, Challenged Resources, and Internet Filtering" (part II, chapter 5)
- "Collection Development and Management" (part II, chapter 7)
- "Privacy and Confidentiality" (part II, chapter 11)

OFFICIAL ALA POLICY STATEMENTS

Access to Library Resources and Services for Minors: An Interpretation of the *Library Bill of Rights*

Adopted June 30, 1972, by the ALA Council; amended July 1, 1981; July 3, 1991; June 30, 2004; July 2, 2008 (under previous name "Free Access to Libraries for Minors"); July 1, 2014; June 25, 2019; and May 29, 2025.

All people, of all ages, should have equal and equitable access to all library resources and services. The American Library Association (ALA) opposes any efforts to restrict access based on age. Policies and procedures that prevent minors from accessing the same resources and services as adults violate the ALA's *Library Bill of Rights*.[1] Libraries and their governing bodies should not use age as a reason to avoid potential objections. Not acquiring materials because minors might access them reduces the credibility of the library and limits access for everyone.

Article V of the *Library Bill of Rights* states, "A person's right to use a library should not be denied or abridged because of origin, age, background, or views." The right to use a library means that people should have free access to all services, materials, and facilities and unrestricted use of everything the library offers. Any restriction based solely on the following criteria violates Article V:

- age;
- apparent maturity;
- educational level;
- literacy skills; or
- legal status.

Further violations of Article V include setting limits on:

- how old someone must be to get a library card;
- demonstrated skills or abilities required to get a library card (like signing their name);
- requiring parental/guardian permission to get a card for anyone old enough to be in the library without parental/guardian supervision;
- how many or what kinds of items minors can check out compared to adults; or
- creating trial periods for library use based on age.

Violations to Article V also include restricting access for minors who don't have a parent or guardian available to sign a library card application or permission slip, who can't provide legal ID to verify their name or address, or who can't visit a library in person.

Libraries can make reasonable exceptions to protect the safety of minors or financial liability to the library. Reasonable exceptions may include limiting access to multipurpose rooms, expensive/rare materials, or high cost circulating items or technology.

Libraries: An American Value states the following: "We affirm the responsibility and the right of all parents and guardians to guide their own children's use of the library and its resources and services."[2] Libraries and their governing bodies can't take on the role of parents or act "in loco parentis." Examples include:

- setting up computer systems that hide or block certain materials without parental permission;
- limiting which parts of the library or what kinds of books and services minors can use;
- not letting minors check out certain items or making comments about whether materials are appropriate based on assumed age or maturity; and
- using ratings to stop young people from getting certain materials.

There are many resources available for parents/guardians to find information on how a book, resource, or other material aligns with their family's values. Libraries are not responsible for determining the appropriateness of any book, material, or resource for an individual beyond the already existing collection designations. Only parents or guardians should restrict their own children's access to library materials and services.

The freedom to read is guaranteed by the U.S. Constitution.[3] This includes minors. Minors have the right to receive information from the library in all forms, such as:

- print;
- sound;
- images;
- data;
- social media;
- online applications;
- games;
- technologies;
- programming; and
- other formats.[4]

The right to privacy is fundamental to the freedom to read.[5] Article VII of the ALA *Library Bill of Rights* states, "All people, regardless of origin, age, background, or views, possess a right to privacy and confidentiality in their library use." Minors also have the right to use the library without being watched or monitored.[6]

Libraries and their governing bodies have a legal and professional obligation to provide free and equitable access to a diverse range of library resources and services that is inclusive, regardless of content, approach, or format to everyone in their community equally, including minors. School and public libraries, in particular, must provide resources and services to meet the diverse interests and informational needs of everyone in their community. This means:

- offering services, materials, and spaces that work for all community members, no matter their age;
- curating developmentally appropriate collections;
- understanding that people need different things at different stages of their lives; and
- not making decisions about what's appropriate for each person individually.

Libraries cannot censor constitutionally protected speech to protect minors from ideas or images lawmakers deem unsuitable.[7] Denying access to information to anyone, including minors, can be harmful. Libraries and their governing bodies must uphold this principle to protect the rights to intellectual freedom and the freedom to read for people of all ages.

NOTES

1. Check local laws for definitions.
2. "Libraries: An American Value," adopted on February 3, 1999, by ALA Council.
3. "The Freedom to Read Statement," adopted June 25, 1953, by the ALA Council and the AAP Freedom to Read Committee; amended January 28, 1972; January 16, 1991; July 12, 2000; June 30, 2004; reaffirmed by ALA, AAP on June 26, 2023.
4. *Brown v. Entertainment Merchant's Association, et al.* 564 U.S. 08-1448 (2011).
5. "Privacy: ALA Core Values of Librarianship," adopted January 2024 by the ALA Council.
6. "Privacy: An Interpretation of the *Library Bill of Rights*," adopted June 19, 2002, by the ALA Council; amended July 1, 2014; June 24, 2019; and June 29, 2025.
7. *Erznoznik v. City of Jacksonville*, 422 U.S. 205 (1975): "Speech that is neither obscene as to youths nor subject to some other legitimate proscription cannot be suppressed solely to protect the young from ideas or images that a legislative body thinks unsuitable for them. In most circumstances, the values protected by the First Amendment are no less applicable when government seeks to control the flow of information to minors." See also *Tinker v. Des Moines School Dist.*, 393 U.S.503 (1969); *West Virginia Bd. of Ed. v. Barnette*, 319 U.S. 624 (1943); *AAMA v. Kendrick*, 244 F.3d 572 (7th Cir. 2001).

Access to Resources and Services in the School Library: An Interpretation of the *Library Bill of Rights*

Adopted July 2, 1986, by the ALA Council; amended January 10, 1990; July 12, 2000; January 19, 2005; July 2, 2008; July 1, 2014; and June 29, 2025.

School libraries are dynamic learning environments. They bridge the gap between access and opportunity for all learners. The American Library Association's *Library Bill of Rights* applies to all school libraries. This means every student should have equitable access to the library's facilities, resources, and programs. School libraries play a crucial role in supporting learners' freedom to explore and learn about different ideas. School libraries should be staffed by full-time certified librarians. School librarians play a crucial role in the ongoing process of selecting, acquiring, evaluating, and deselecting library materials. They do this to ensure the collection meets the diverse needs of learners and supports their intellectual freedom rights. School librarians consider curriculum requirements, learner interests, and community needs.

School libraries ensure that students of all abilities can fully participate in their education. They do this by integrating adaptive technologies and digital resources into the curriculum and classrooms in collaboration with teachers. This inclusive approach makes sure everyone can join in discussions, a vital part of a democracy. It also ensures that every student has equitable access to information.

School librarians ensure access for all learners by including resources in different languages, not just English. When choosing materials, school librarians should consider the languages of learners in their community. These resources assist learners who are learning English and allows all learners to see and learn about different languages.

School librarians choose materials that meet the needs and maturity levels of the learners. These resources:

- support the school's goals and curriculum;
- offer a variety of viewpoints on both current and historical issues, including those considered controversial;
- foster intellectual growth and personal development; and
- meet learners' recreational reading needs.

By providing these resources, school librarians support lifelong learning for all students.

School librarians select materials that support the curriculum and independent reading. They do this without letting personal beliefs or biases get in the way. The goal is to provide access to resources and services without restrictions imposed by personal beliefs or group opinions. Common barriers that prevent students from accessing resources in school libraries include:

- age- or grade-level restrictions
- limitations on interlibrary loans

School library policies should remove any barriers and support free and open access to information. School librarians recognize that every parent reserves the right to guide what their learner reads and to select instructional resources that support their family's unique set of views and opinions but this right to exercise control extends only to their own learner.

The role of school librarians extends beyond the library walls. They provide transformational leadership that prepares students to excel in a complex, interconnected world. School boards are responsible for supporting these roles. They do this by creating policies that:

- ensure students can access a wide range of ideas;
- foster a well-rounded educational experience; and
- prepare students for lifelong success.

Policies should include how to handle concerns about library resources in a fair and timely manner and should include a certified school librarian in the review process for challenged materials. The review process should be guided by professional standards and educational relevance, not by partisan or doctrinal viewpoints. School librarians should implement these policies to make sure all students have equitable access to the library's resources and services.

PERSONAL STORY

Standing Strong: School Librarians Lead

CATHI FUHRMAN

In the last three years, local school boards in Pennsylvania have tried to ban, censor, restrict access to, and deny selection of material for K–12 students. To support school librarians, I proposed the creation of the Intellectual Freedom Task Group to the Pennsylvania School Librarians Association (PSLA) in 2022. As a school librarian since 1994, I knew that my colleagues' experience hinged on the basis of having a selection policy. They were not prepared for what was happening in our communities.

Like other areas of the country, we began seeing parents and community members quoting from books out of context at school board meetings. Later, school boards were proposing to revise selection policies with vague, discriminatory language. This was happening in more school districts than we could keep track of.

To address these growing concerns, our Task Group formed a Rapid Response Team. This enabled school librarians in Pennsylvania to send confidential alerts about mounting intellectual freedom issues. We established protocols and procedures to support and advise school librarians. This support grew to include community members and students. While revising selection policies remains a major part of our work, we are now battling internal administrative regulations that shift acquisition and selection decisions to administrators, school board members, and community members. Certified school librarians are being forced to allow untrained and biased people to approve, select, and curate the library materials for K–12 students.

Fortunately, I have not had to deal with censorship in my role as a high school librarian. I can channel my energy into standing up for intellectual freedom for K–12 students across Pennsylvania. I have the capacity to pick up the sword and shield for librarians who are not able to publicly fight for their students' rights.

Supporting school librarians, libraries, and community members is rewarding professionally and personally, but it is also stressful and overwhelming. We watch long school board meetings, pore over proposed policy revisions to offer suggestions, develop talking points and position statements, and talk with school librarians who need support.

The hardest work is helping school librarians and community members stay mentally healthy as we work through situations together. It is difficult for me to make sense of the attacks on our profession, our values, and our motives as school librarians—especially when those attacks come from a place of misinformation, rhetoric, fear, bias, and attempts to control public education.

Struggling to stay strong for others in this atmosphere takes its toll, but our team strives to hold each other up so we can continue the fight.

Our successes in Pennsylvania have greatly hinged on the coalition partners we've established at state and local levels. Becoming a partner in Pennsylvanians for Welcoming and Inclusive Schools continues to be the game changer for our intellectual freedom work. Groups like the Education Law Center, the ACLU, Red, Wine, & Blue, PA Education Voters, and the Human Rights Campaign provide a team of Freedom Fighters to work with the PSLA to protect our students' First Amendment rights. School librarians cannot do this work alone. We have begun to turn the tide here in Pennsylvania, but we must still stand together for intellectual freedom where the battle has not yet been won.

OFFICIAL ALA POLICY STATEMENT

Minors and Online Activity: An Interpretation of the *Library Bill of Rights*

Adopted July 15, 2009, by the ALA Council; amended July 1, 2014 under the previous name "Minors and Internet Activity: An Interpretation of the Library Bill of Rights"; June 24, 2019; and June 29, 2025.

The internet gives people the ability to access, create, and share information. Minors have First Amendment rights to seek, create, and interact with online information in schools and libraries. In particular, they have the right to free expression and the right to privacy.

Minors should have access to social media and other online tools for both learning and recreation. The internet can help develop their social, interpersonal, and academic skills. Examples include:

- creating and sharing documents online;
- uploading pictures, videos, and other visual content;
- playing interactive games;
- organizing and categorizing information; and
- participating in online communities.

Library workers should curate and provide access to age-appropriate online resources and teach minors how to stay safe online. They should help young people develop the skills needed to be responsible digital citizens.

Parents and guardians play a critical role in preparing their children to be online. They should communicate their values and guide their children's internet use. Libraries and their governing bodies should make it clear that only a parent or guardian can decide what their child—and only their child—can access online.

Libraries and schools often use filters to restrict access to online content. These filters can go beyond what state laws and the Children's Internet Protection Act require, limiting access to information and social media. Such restrictions deny minors their right to free expression online.

Protecting minors' online privacy rights is essential. Concerns about sharing personal information or cyberbullying often lead to restrictive policies. These policies can limit minors' right to free expression and online privacy.

Blocking minors from social media and online communities can prevent them from learning important digital skills. Library workers should teach them how to engage online in ways that match their maturity level. This should be done without restricting access for others.

Library workers should also support strong privacy policies that prevent the collection and use of minors' online activity for marketing or profit.

The First Amendment protects all speech created by minors and shared online. Blocking social media in schools and libraries violates the *Library Bill of Rights* and minors' right to free expression.

Improper use of online tools should be handled as an individual behavior issue, not as a reason to restrict or ban access. Online safety concerns should not justify limiting access for minors. Library workers, educators, and administrators must stay informed about these risks while continuing to support minors' intellectual freedom.

Libraries defend intellectual freedom and the First Amendment, and they should advocate for greater access when it is limited or restricted. Libraries have a responsibility to provide unrestricted access to online resources to the greatest extent allowed under local, state, and federal laws and to support minors' right to free expression and online privacy.

A DEEPER LOOK

The Private Lives of Public Readers: Teens, Books, and Belonging

NICK HIGGINS AND ROBIN LESTER-KENTON

Teens have long been at the center of efforts to ban books in the United States. They are in a time of profound change—trying on different identities and reading about a variety of life experiences, realities, and fantasies. As they explore, they begin to discover who they are and who they want to become. To do this, they need the freedom to access a wide range of stories. This access is key to self-actualization.

While a natural part of development, this exploration of identity is often disruptive and confusing. That makes it an especially hard time to be caught in today's current culture war over book bans. Parents and families may feel concerned as their children begin to take their first steps toward independence. This shift can also feel unsettling to people in power who fear losing control.

The regulation of young people's private inner lives—what they are allowed to think, feel, and access—is central to the book ban movement. It's rooted in a familiar moral panic about the imagined loss of childhood innocence. This fear is used to push policies that take away rights and impose strict rules on how children should be raised—all in the name of protection and safety. Community campaigns based on fear often tap into parents' worries about their children's futures. As a result, teens have less freedom to explore and understand who they are.

The tension between children's rights and society's expectations has long played out in public policy, education, and popular culture. Parents may feel scared as their child's private inner life begins to grow. That fear is understandable—parents remember their own journey of self-discovery. But this fear doesn't take away a child's right to this private experience.

As library workers, we have a unique opportunity and responsibility to provide teens with physical and digital spaces where they can explore, learn, and grow without judgment or limits. In this era of life online, young people are often overwhelmed by a constant stream of information that isn't always accurate. The isolation caused by the COVID-19 pandemic has made this worse. By opening our doors to teens, we help:

- nurture their private inner lives;
- support them as they learn to navigate the world; and
- connect them to the public lives of others.

We have the power to create spaces that unify and build trust across lived experience, gender, race, sexuality, and more. Our mission of free and open access to information must extend to *all* community members.

Books are banned and challenged for many reasons. Most often, it's because they cover topics like:

- violence;
- sexual content;
- LGBTQIA+ life;
- mental illness; and
- race.

Supporters of book bans argue that these topics are "harmful to minors." They claim the books may make people uncomfortable or lead to "deviant" behavior—meaning anything that isn't traditional, white, straight, and Christian.

But these claims ignore what we know to be true: reading books with different points of view helps young people build empathy, think critically, and better understand the world and themselves.

In 2022, the Brooklyn Public Library (BPL) took a bold step to support teens' right to read by launching *Books Unbanned*. This national program gives digital library cards to young people from ages 13 to 21. These cards give full access to the BPL's digital collections. The program doesn't require an ID or parental permission—though many parents have helped their children apply.

The program doesn't just focus on books that are often on banned books lists. Instead, it gives teens access to a wide range of books and ideas. That access can help build stronger connections and relationships within their communities.

In speaking with *Books Unbanned* cardholders, we found that young readers believe exposure to diverse views is essential to their growth. Reading books that address race, identity, trauma, and LGBTQIA+ issues helps them better understand the world. Titles like *The Hate U Give* by Angie Thomas, *Gender Queer* by Maia Kobabe, and *Beloved* by Toni Morrison challenge their assumptions and help them develop empathy for others. These books aren't just stories—they are critical tools for shaping compassionate, informed individuals.

They also tell us that banning books sends a message about whose voices and stories matter. When books are removed from libraries or classrooms, it can feel like certain groups' experiences are not important enough to be shared. For many teens, reading about people who are different from them builds solidarity and understanding. Removing these books undermines the values of inclusivity and diversity that schools and libraries aim to promote.

When books are banned, teens can feel othered and isolated. This adds to the feelings of invisibility and marginalization they may already have. Reading books that reflect someone's experience can literally help save a teen's life—or help them save someone else's.

Empowering teenagers to seek diverse books is an act of bravery. Open access may come with threats to funding and safety, but this work ensures that libraries remain truly democratic spaces.

Our work also relies on another kind of bravery. In addition to protecting access to books that appear frequently on banned books lists, we must also protect teens' right to access works that have fallen out of favor in liberal circles. Rising above the discomfort created from partisan viewpoints allows library workers to set an authentic example of freedom of information.

To continue this work, we need to become better at mobilization—connecting not only with one another and our supporters, but also with those who may not yet understand the importance of libraries. We must focus on common goals, set aside our egos, and invite everyone in.

This requires action and empathy—coming together to build, struggle, and create truly free spaces. If libraries are to survive in this century and beyond, we must also include people who may not regularly visit libraries but share our democratic values. It is time to connect beyond our walls, reaching out to those who want to build a society based on true American values.

Books in the hands of young readers can change their lives. That's why *Books Unbanned* ensures that they have unrestricted access to anything they want to read. But providing books alone isn't enough. It takes human connection to turn that access into a meaningful movement. Libraries foster these connections in shared spaces, giving everyone a place where their curiosity is seen and supported.

As library workers, we must show up in solidarity with young people who are advocating for their rights. Speak up for them, for your community, and for your library—even when the voices against you seem loud and intimidating. Let's act with intention and help secure the future of our libraries and the young people we serve.

Intellectual Freedom: The Law in Flux

The law regarding minors' First Amendment rights to access information has been changing. For more information, refer to "Intellectual Freedom: The Law in Flux" in part I, chapter 3.

II., Ch. 6 Children & Youth

CHAPTER 7
Collection Development and Management

BIG IDEA BREAKDOWN

Key Concepts

- Library collections should reflect the diversity of people and ideas in society. When selecting resources, library workers should include a range of viewpoints, including those that are controversial or that some may find offensive. They should also select a variety of formats, languages, and publishers.
- A well-balanced collection does not need to represent every viewpoint in equal amounts. Instead, it should aim for equitable representation of ideas and perspectives.
- The presence of an item in the library's collection does not mean the library endorses its contents or guarantees its accuracy.
- Collection development, including the selection and removal of materials, should follow professional standards and the library's collection development policy.
- The policy should include clear procedures and guidelines for weeding, to prevent it from being used as a form of censorship.
- Viewpoint-neutral directional aids can help users locate materials. However, labels and rating systems that try to influence users' choices are inappropriate and can become tools of censorship.

What Does the Law Say?

- Ratings given to movies, video games, and music are not law. They are voluntary rating systems created by private organizations to offer guidance. Courts have struck down laws and ordinances that try to enforce these ratings to deny minors access to materials, ruling that such restrictions violate minors' First Amendment rights.

- Hate speech is protected by the First Amendment. This protection is based on the belief that freedom of speech requires the government to allow strong debate on public issues—even if the speech is offensive, hurtful, or hateful. Under current law, hate speech can only be criminalized if it directly incites imminent criminal activity or contains a specific threat of violence aimed at a person or group.

Creating Policy for Your Library

- Adopt the *Library Bill of Rights* (part I, chapter 2) as policy for your library. It contains statements about the importance and value of providing materials and information that present all points of view.
- Be sure that your collection development policy covers resources in all formats (part I, chapter 3).

For Academic Libraries

- Don't use the excuse of material being "unscholarly" to avoid adding it to the collection. Academic libraries often include holdings that are considered "unscholarly," "pseudoscience," or offensive to groups (e.g., Holocaust denial literature) for the purpose of studying the controversy or for the historical record.
- Academic libraries may collect and keep controversial titles in children's and young adult literature. These materials serve as historical artifacts and examples of past cultural norms, supporting research and the study of children's literature over time.
- Refer to "Intellectual Freedom Principles for Academic Libraries" (part II, chapter 4).

For Public Libraries

- The library collection should reflect the interests of the entire community, not just the majority.

For School Libraries

- A school library must serve the entire student body, supporting not only the formal curriculum, but also students' personal research and recreational reading needs.
- Providing a broad range of materials on controversial issues helps students develop analytical skills and learn to make informed decisions based on information from multiple points of view.
- Reading-level labels are prejudicial and should not be used to limit students' use of resources.

To Learn More

- "Selection & Reconsideration Policy Toolkit for Public, School, & Academic Libraries," ala.org/tools/challengesupport/selectionpolicytoolkit.
  - "Basic Components of a Selection Policy," for links to guidance about collection development.
- "Religion in American Libraries Q&A," ala.org/advocacy/intfreedom/religionfaq.
- "Hate Speech and Hate Crime," ala.org/advocacy/intfreedom/hate.

Reflection Questions

- What's the difference between selection and censorship?
- A prominent local politician offers to donate a selection of religiously themed materials to your library. What's your response?
- When should materials be weeded from collections?
- A teen librarian wants to add rainbow flag labels to all LGBTQIA+ fiction to help teens more easily find books they relate to. The librarian's goal is to support teens who share these identities. What do you do?

OFFICIAL ALA POLICY STATEMENT

Diverse and Inclusive Collections: An Interpretation of the *Library Bill of Rights*

Adopted July 14, 1982, by the ALA Council; amended January 10, 1990; July 2, 2008; July 1, 2014 (under previous name "Diversity in Collection Development"); and June 24, 2019 (under previous name "Diverse Collections"); and May 29, 2025.

A diverse and inclusive collection reflects everyone in the community. Article I of the *Library Bill of Rights* states:

> Books and other library resources should be provided for the interest, information, and enlightenment of all people of the community the library serves. Materials should not be excluded because of the origin, background, or views of those contributing to their creation.[1]

This means the collection should include content by and about people from different backgrounds, cultures, and viewpoints. It should reflect many ideas, stories, and experiences.

Library workers must select, maintain, and support access to materials from diverse authors and creators. This helps the collection serve the community's needs, interests, and abilities. Libraries should include materials that are popular, diverse, or both, to ensure a well-rounded and inclusive collection. Library workers have a professional and ethical duty to be inclusive when developing collections. Libraries should offer interlibrary loan whenever possible to give users access to a broader and more diverse range of materials.

A well-balanced collection doesn't need to include every viewpoint in equal amounts. Instead, it should aim for equity in content and ideas. This means considering structural inequalities and the availability of accurate, timely materials. A diverse and inclusive collection should have a wide range of works. Library workers should choose these works based on the library's selection policy and review them regularly.

Collection development, cataloging, and classification follow professional standards and procedures. Building a diverse and inclusive collection means:

- selecting content in multiple formats;
- considering resources from self-published, independent, small, and local producers;
- looking for content created by or about marginalized and underrepresented groups;
- checking how metadata reflects diverse resources in the collection;
- reviewing how diverse materials are labeled, shelved, and displayed;
- including content in all the languages used in the community, for all age groups; and
- offering materials in accessible formats.[2]

Library workers shouldn't exclude materials just because others find the content or creator offensive or controversial. They also shouldn't let their own personal beliefs or objections influence their decisions. Refusing to add resources due to potential controversy is censorship. Removing materials for these reasons is also censorship. Libraries must defend against challenges that limit the diversity of the collection.

People often challenge library materials they think are improper, offensive, or disputed. These challenges cover a wide range of concerns, such as:

- Prejudicial language
- Political ideas
- Economic theories
- Age appropriateness
- Educational value
- Social philosophies
- Religious beliefs
- Marginalized groups
- Scientific research
- Sexual content
- Diverse sexual orientations, gender identities, and expressions

Library workers shouldn't let the fear of a challenge stop them from adding diverse and inclusive materials to the collection.

Intellectual freedom is the foundation of equitable library services. This means libraries provide free access to all kinds of ideas so people can explore a question, cause, or movement. Library workers have a professional and ethical duty to defend each user's right to read, view, or listen to content protected by the First Amendment. They must defend this right, regardless of the creator's viewpoint or personal history. Professional ethics and standards—not personal opinions or biases—should guide collection decisions. This commitment helps library workers build diverse and inclusive collections for their communities.[3,4,5]

NOTES

1. American Library Association, "Library Bill of Rights," adopted June 19, 1939, by the ALA Council; amended October 14, 1944; June 18, 1948; February 2, 1961; June 27, 1967; January 23, 1980; January 29, 2019. Inclusion of "age" reaffirmed January 23, 1996. https://www.ala.org/advocacy/intfreedom/librarybill.
2. American Library Association, "Services to People with Disabilities: An Interpretation of the *Library Bill of Rights*," adopted January 28, 2009, by the ALA Council, *under the previous name* "Services to Persons with Disabilities"; amended June 26, 2018; and June 29, 2025. https://www.ala.org/advocacy/intfreedom/librarybill/interpretations/servicespeopledisabilities.
3. American Library Association, "ALA *Code of Ethics, Article VII,*" adopted at the 1939 Midwinter Meeting by the ALA Council; amended June 30, 1981; June 28, 1995; January 22, 2008; and June 29, 2021, https://www.ala.org/tools/ethics.
4. American Library Association, "Diverse and Inclusive Collections," adopted July 14, 1982, by the ALA Council; amended January 10, 1990; July 2, 2008; July 1, 2014 under the previous name "Diversity in Collection Development"; and June 24, 2019 under the previous name "Diverse Collections"; and May 29, 2025, https://www.ala.org/advocacy/intfreedom/librarybill/interpretations/diversecollections.
5. American Library Association, "ALA Core Competencies," adopted by the ALA Council January 28, 2023, https://www.ala.org/educationcareers/careers/corecomp/corecompetences.

PERSONAL STORY

Intellectual Freedom and Indigenous Knowledge

SARAH R. KOSTELECKY

I grew up in a tribal community in New Mexico. That experience taught me that some cultural traditions are meant to be known by certain people and not by others. Zuni Pueblo lifeways continue because of this way of sharing knowledge.

Intellectual freedom means being able to freely form your own beliefs. My beliefs come from my tribe's teachings. Like other Indigenous groups, Zuni Pueblo people have systems for sharing information based on age, gender, clan, and a family's role in the community. Information is shared when you are ready for it, when you need it, or when you are responsible enough to know it. Guided by respect for my cultural teachings, I know that some library materials are not meant for me to access.

However, we know that libraries have books about Native people written by non-Natives. Some of these authors took information they didn't understand and removed it from its original context. This led to inaccurate, inappropriate, and offensive depictions of Indigenous people and culture. Reading these descriptions can spiritually harm members of the community.

Some of these books may be the only record of a language. I advocate managing these materials using Indigenous knowledge protocols. This helps balance the professional value of access while also honoring the information-sharing systems created by Native people.

I led a project at the University of New Mexico Libraries to digitize language learning materials from my Pueblo while respecting community information practices. The materials were donated by the publisher, the school district, which made the final decisions about what would be digitized. The goal was to make Zuni-language books and posters available to tribal members anywhere, without log-ins or controlled access.

This open-access model meant that anyone, even non-Zuni people, could find the resources. This challenged traditional information-sharing norms. By collaborating with the tribal community, we balanced the need for access with the tribe's knowledge of which cultural materials were appropriate to share widely online. This had not been done before. Any library can take time to build relationships with its local tribal communities as a way to respectfully manage that library's Indigenous materials.

Indigenous people have the right to intellectual freedom. We have the right to see ourselves accurately represented in library books and collections while freely seeking information. As a Native librarian, I want to research my community without the distress of realizing that a photo I found is one I shouldn't have seen (true story). I also want others to experience the joy of discovering a historic photo of a relative in a library digital collection (also a true story).

Libraries should aim to describe Indigenous items thoroughly. Ideally, they will collaborate with the affiliated tribe to help users make informed decisions about accessing an item. Libraries can continue to support intellectual freedom by managing Indigenous materials using Indigenous knowledge-sharing practices. This approach upholds our values of equitable access for all.

OFFICIAL ALA POLICY STATEMENTS

Evaluating Library Collections: An Interpretation of the *Library Bill of Rights*

Adopted February 2, 1973, by the ALA Council; amended July 1, 1981; June 2, 2008; and June 25, 2019.

Libraries continually develop their collections by adding and removing resources to maintain collections of current interest and usefulness to their communities. Libraries should adopt collection development and maintenance policies that include criteria for evaluating materials. Reasons for inclusion or removal of materials may include but are not limited to accuracy, currency, budgetary constraints, relevancy, content, usage, and community interest. The collection-development process is not to be used as a means to remove materials or deny access to resources on the grounds of personal bias or prejudice or because the materials may be viewed as controversial or objectionable. Doing so violates the principles of intellectual freedom and is in opposition to the *Library Bill of Rights*.

Some resources may contain views, opinions, and concepts that were popular or widely held at one time but are now considered outdated, offensive, or harmful. Content creators may also come to be considered offensive or controversial. These resources should be subject to evaluation in accordance with collection-development and collection-maintenance policies. The evaluation criteria and process may vary depending on the type of library. While weeding is essential to the collection-development process, the controversial nature of an item or its creator should not be the sole reason to remove any item from a library's collection. Rather than removing these resources, libraries should consider ways to educate users and create context for how those views, opinions, and concepts have changed over time.

Failure to select resources merely because they may be potentially controversial is censorship, as is withdrawing resources for the same reason. Library workers should consider the cataloging, classification, and display of resources to ensure that they are discoverable and readily available to the populations they are meant to serve.

The American Library Association opposes censorship from any source, including library workers, faculty, administration, trustees, and elected officials. Libraries have a profound responsibility to encourage and support intellectual freedom by making it possible for the user to choose freely from a variety of offerings.

Labeling and Rating Systems: An Interpretation of the *Library Bill of Rights*

Adopted July 13, 1951, by the ALA Council; amended June 25, 1971; July 1, 1981; June 26, 1990; January 19, 2005; July 15, 2009; and July 1, 2014. Divided into two interpretations, "Labeling Systems: An Interpretation of the *Library Bill of Rights*," and "Ratings Systems: An Interpretation of the *Library Bill of Rights*," both adopted June 30, 2015; "Rating Systems" amended June 25, 2019. "Labeling Systems" and "Ratings Systems" merged into a single document, "Labeling and Rating Systems: An Interpretation of the *Library Bill of Rights*," adopted May 29, 2025.

The American Library Association (ALA) affirms that everyone has the right to form their own opinions about the things they read, listen to, or watch. Libraries do not support, endorse or promote the ideas found in the materials or resources they provide. Offering access to a book or digital resource doesn't mean the library agrees with its contents. Labeling and rating systems can conflict with the principles of intellectual freedom.

Labeling Systems

Sometimes, libraries use labels to organize materials or help users find resources. Labels can be simple—like a colored dot to indicate a reference book, or genre labels (such as "mystery" or "western") for fiction. They can also be more complex, such as the Dewey Decimal System or Library of Congress call numbers. Libraries may also add subject headings from professional sources to guide users in making selections. Classification systems and subject headings are meant to label information in a fair and neutral way. They help users find and use resources more easily and save time. Users can choose to use these labels or ignore them. They are different from labels that try to influence or to restrict access to certain resources.

While classification and subject heading systems try to be viewpoint-neutral, many of these systems reflect outdated or limited views. These systems should be regularly reviewed and updated to address biases, use current language, and better reflect a diverse, multicultural society.

Prejudicial labels are used to try to influence opinions or behaviors and restrict access, which is a form of censorship. The ALA opposes using labels to bias people's views about library resources. These types of labels might be based on a value judgment about:

- the content;
- language;
- themes; or
- the background or views of the creator.

These labels often mark materials as inappropriate or offensive for certain groups of users. They are used to warn, discourage, or block access. Sometimes, libraries use these labels to move materials to restricted areas. This may mean making materials harder to find by separating them from other similar items in the collection or requiring staff assistance to use them.

Directional aids can have the same effect as prejudicial labels when they make it more difficult to access materials. Directional aids should be used to help users locate items. If they are used to restrict access or imply moral or doctrinal approval, they function as prejudicial labeling. Even labels with good intentions can have this effect.

Libraries that use prejudicial labeling assume they know what is appropriate for users. They also assume people need guidance in deciding what ideas to explore. The ALA opposes prejudicial labeling. Everyone has the right to form their own opinions about what they choose to read, listen to, or watch.

Rating Systems

Rating systems are tools or labels designed to guide people on whether materials are suitable or appropriate. The creators of these systems assume there is someone who can decide what is right for others. They also assume that people want or need help choosing what to access.

While creating and publishing rating systems is protected by the First Amendment's right to free speech, the ALA believes everyone has the right to form their own opinions about the content they use.

Using, enforcing, or approving of rating systems violates the *Library Bill of Rights*. It may also be unconstitutional if it restricts someone's access to library materials or resources. If a law requires libraries to enforce rating systems, the library leadership should seek legal advice to understand how it will affect library operations.

Libraries often acquire items with ratings, such as DVDs, CDs, and video games. Library workers should not approve or endorse these rating systems. However, removing or destroying ratings placed on the original item by the publisher, distributor, or copyright holder could be considered censorship.[1]

Libraries should resist policies that restrict access based on a user's reading or age level. When libraries rate or label materials based on assumed age-appropriateness or readability levels, that may be perceived as restricting access. These systems can stop users from choosing materials that interest them. It can also limit access to the library's full collection.

Some libraries add ratings in their bibliographic records because they accept standard records that include them. Others do so to provide as much information about the resource as possible. Including rating systems in library catalogs can conflict with intellectual freedom principles. Cataloging best practices do not require libraries to include ratings. If ratings are included, the source of the rating should be clear to users. Including ratings without proper attribution is a violation of the *Library Bill of Rights*. The library should not endorse rating systems and rating systems should never be used to restrict access to materials based on the age of a user. Such restrictions may violate the First Amendment rights of minors.[2]

Libraries can answer questions about rating systems without endorsing them. Library workers can share resources about rating systems to help users find the information they need. Staff may also guide users to review sources, which can help them form their own opinions about what to read, listen to, or watch.

NOTES

1. "Censorship by Altering Library Resources: An Interpretation of the *Library Bill of Rights*," adopted February 2, 1973, by the ALA Council; amended July 1, 1981; January 10, 1990; July 2, 2008; and July 1, 2014, under the previous name "Expurgation of Library Resources"; and June 29, 2025.
2. *Engdahl v. City of Kenosha*, 317 F. Supp. 1133 (E.D. Wis. 1970); *Motion Picture Ass'n of Am. v. Specter*, 315 F. Supp. 824 (E.D. Pa. 1970); *Swope v. Lubbers*, 560 F. Supp. 1328 (W.D. Mich. 1983); and *Rosen v. Budco*, 10 Phila. 112 (1983).

User-Generated Content in Library Discovery Layers

Adopted January 12, 2016, by the ALA Council; amended June 24, 2019 (under previous name "User-Generated Content in Library Discovery Systems"); and June 29, 2025.

Libraries offer a variety of systems that provide access to the resources in their collections. Examples of such systems include, but are not limited to:

- the library catalog;
- institutional repositories;
- digital collections; and
- discovery layers.[1]

Some of these systems also let users add their own comments, reviews, or ratings. This makes the library experience more engaging by allowing people to share their thoughts. Creating this shared knowledge can show the value of libraries as places for information and learning.

Discovery layers may let users add commentary, reviews, and ratings (e.g., one star to five stars), or participate in discussions. When users add content, the library should clearly show the difference between user-generated content and library-generated content. Libraries should avoid giving the impression that they endorse or disapprove of any content. User-generated content can influence search results (e.g., content with higher ratings may appear first). Such search features should not be turned on by default. Users should have the option to enable such features.

Libraries do not have to allow user-generated content. A publicly funded library can set rules to limit who can add content and what content they can add. These rules can't be based on the users' views, beliefs, or affiliations.[2] For example, the library may require users to have a valid library card or an online account to add content through the discovery layer.

Commenting systems in publicly funded libraries may be considered limited public forums. Libraries that allow users to add content should have policies that explain when, where, and how people can contribute. Any restrictions must be reasonable and not based on users' views, beliefs, or affiliations.[3] Libraries should:

- regularly review policies with legal counsel;
- share policies with staff; and
- make the policies available to the public in the main languages spoken in the community.

Libraries must protect the privacy of users who add content to discovery layers. They should review the privacy policies of any vendors that manage or store user-generated content. Libraries should encourage users to review these policies. Users should give consent before personal information is collected and shared with third-parties. Lastly, libraries have a duty to keep all library-use data safe and private.[4]

NOTES

1. "Library Privacy Guidelines for Library Websites, OPACs, and Discovery Systems," Intellectual Freedom Committee, June 24, 2016. "A discovery service provides a single web-based user interface to search across multiple resources such as library catalogs, periodical databases, institutional repositories, and digital collections."
2. *Knight First Amendment Inst. at Columbia Univ. v. Trump,* 302 F. Supp. 3d 541 (S.D.N.Y. May 23, 2018).
3. "Social Media Guidelines for Public and Academic Libraries," approved by the Intellectual Freedom Committee, June 2018.
4. *Library Bill of Rights,* adopted June 19, 1939, by the ALA Council; amended October 14, 1944; June 18, 1948; February 2, 1961; June 27, 1967; January 23, 1980; January 29, 2019; "Privacy: An Interpretation of the *Library Bill of Rights,*" adopted June 19, 2002, by the ALA Council; amended July 1, 2014; June 24, 2019; and June 29, 2025.

A DEEPER LOOK

The Law Regarding Rating Systems

This chapter was written by a legal expert in the field. The author's name has been withheld by mutual agreement.

Content ratings often appear on library materials. These ratings are created by private organizations such as:

- the Motion Picture Association (MPA)
- the Entertainment Software Ratings Board (ESRB)
- the Recording Industry Association of America (RIAA)

A common question is whether a library has a legal duty to enforce these ratings to limit youth access to materials. The answer is no.

An item's rating is only meant to help parents decide if the material is suitable for their child. A rating like the MPA's "R" rating is not, and has never been, a legally enforceable restriction on youth access to a movie. Ratings are not a determination that a motion picture is inappropriate or obscene for minors. Only a court of law can make that decision. Libraries have no legal duty to enforce ratings assigned to films, games, or other materials.

Trade associations assign content ratings. These private nonprofit organizations represent members who create and distribute movies, games, and music. They are not government agencies. They do not act on behalf of local, state, or federal governments.

Ratings systems are strictly voluntary. No law requires filmmakers, game designers, or musicians to submit their work for a rating. Likewise, no law requires theaters and retailers to follow the ratings guidelines when selling movie tickets, DVDs, games, or music. Those businesses that choose to enforce ratings do so voluntarily as a service to parents.

Publicly funded libraries face First Amendment concerns when ratings are used to restrict minors' access to films, games, or other media. Courts have overturned laws and ordinances that enforce ratings systems to deny minors access to films, games, and other content, ruling that such restrictions violate their First Amendment rights.

Case Examples

- *Engdahl v. City of Kenosha:* The court struck down a city ordinance that used MPA ratings to ban minors from seeing R-rated films.[1]
- *Motion Picture Association of America v. Specter:* The court invalidated a city's criminal ordinance that penalized any theater allowing minors to view films rated "not suitable for children" by the MPA.[2]
- *American Amusement Mach. Association v. Kendrick* and *Interactive Digital Software Association v. St. Louis County:* Federal appellate courts overturned

state and local laws that used the ESRB's private ratings system to restrict minors' access to video games.[3]

- *Brown v. Entertainment Merchants Association:* The Supreme Court held that a California law barring minors from buying video games rated "M" without their parents' written permission violated their First Amendment rights, stating: "even where the protection of children is the object, the constitutional limits on governmental action apply."[4]

Trade associations are not the only private organizations that assign ratings to media. Nonprofits and websites now provide ratings based on their beliefs about the suitability of materials for children and young adults. These ratings are applied to:

- books;
- films;
- video games;
- television shows; and
- computer applications.

For example, Common Sense Media claims to provide objective reviews by detailing a book, film, or game's content and assigning a precise age level to it.[5] Similarly, Lexile scores and Accelerated Reader assign books an age, grade, or developmental level. Like MPA ratings for films, these ratings only reflect the reviewer's opinion. They are not a legal determination that a book or other media is unsuitable for minors.

Many websites now rate books and other library materials written for children and young adults based on a group's moral or religious beliefs. These beliefs can include broad disapproval of any discussion or reference to:

- gender identity;
- sexual orientation;
- sex education; or
- race.

These ratings disregard the material's literary or educational value for youth.[6]

Websites like BookLooks.org and RatedBooks.org often use legal-sounding language to falsely imply that certain books that do not comply with their moral or religious beliefs are illegal and "harmful to minors." They claim that libraries should restrict access to these books or remove them from library collections.[7] Their claims are false and have no basis in law. Libraries should not use ratings from these sites to justify removing books from their collections, limiting access to library resources, or making decisions about what books to purchase for library collections. Federal courts have warned that "even where the protection of children is the object, the constitutional limits on governmental action apply."[8] Because of this, publicly funded libraries should not use private content ratings systems to restrict access to materials. This policy should apply to all users, including children and young adults.

Instead, libraries should provide information to help users and parents make their own choices. They should also offer programs that teach young people critical thinking and media literacy. These skills will help them make informed decisions about the films, music, and games they view and use.

Genre Labels and Religious Fiction

Sometimes, even a simple genre spine label can raise significant constitutional concerns. One example is using a cross to mark Christian fiction.

Using these labels, especially when fiction from other religions is not labeled, can appear to show a preference for Christianity by the library. This violates the First Amendment's requirement that public libraries and schools remain neutral toward religion and not favor religion over nonbelief.

The cross as a genre label is especially problematic. Federal courts have ruled that the cross is the foremost symbol of Christianity. It is so widely recognized that its use or display by a government agency can violate the separation of church and state under the Establishment Clause of the First Amendment.

Labeling only Christian books raises challenges for libraries trying to serve the whole community through reference and readers' advisory services. When only one religion's fiction is labeled, it gives visibility to that religion alone. People of other faiths may feel unwelcome or underrepresented. It may also create tension between different Christian denominations.

Using a cross as a genre label may suggest that the library has reviewed or approved the book's religious content and found it "safe." Libraries must avoid anything that looks like they are endorsing or favoring a particular viewpoint or belief.

Libraries that want to identify religious fiction as a genre can use neutral labels, such as "inspirational fiction." This avoids legal concerns, especially if the classification is used for books with and without religious viewpoints and includes books from faiths other than Christianity.

NOTES

1. *Engdahl v. City of Kenosha*, 317 F. Supp. 1133 (E.D. Wis. 1970).
2. *Motion Picture Ass'n of America v. Specter*, 315 F. Supp. 824 (E.D. Pa. 1970).
3. *Am. Amusement Mach. Ass'n v. Kendrick*, 244 F.3d 954 (7th Cir. 2001) and *Interactive Digital Software Ass'n v. St. Louis County*, 329 F.3d 954 (8th Cir. 2003).
4. *Brown v. Entertainment Merchants Association*, 131 S. Ct. 2729, 2741 (2011).
5. Brian Kenney, "Fear Factor: Kids' Lit Style: Common Sense Media Gives Censors a New Tool," *School Library Journal*, July 1, 2010; Pat Scales, "Weighing In: Three Bombs, Two Lips, and a Martini Glass," *Booklist*, August 2010.
6. J. Spering and K. Kedley, "From Book Rating to Book Bans: A Critical Content Analysis of BookLooks.org's Report Cards on LGBTQIA+ Titles," *Journal of Intellectual Freedom and Privacy* 3, no. 4 (2024): 22–35, journals.ala.org/index.php/jifp/article/view/8142/11594; E. Siegel and E. Rubin, "Inside the Book Ban Machine: The Rise of Parental Rights Groups," Stacker, September 23, 2023, stacker.com/art-culture/inside-book-ban-machine-rise-parental-rights-groups-and-their-efforts-ban-books.
7. *Siegel and Rubin, "Inside the Book Ban Machine."*
8. *Brown*, at 2741.

INTELLECTUAL FREEDOM TOPICS AND BEST PRACTICES

CHAPTER 8
Copyright

BIG IDEA BREAKDOWN

Key Concepts

- Copyright law is essential to library operations. It supports learning and the sharing of information by giving creators an economic reason to produce new works. These works, along with those in the public domain, make up library collections.
- Libraries often get copyrighted materials through licenses instead of buying them outright. In these cases, libraries should negotiate for the same rights that copyright law gives them, like lending through interlibrary loan.
- Library workers should understand the legal doctrine of "fair use," which includes four factors to help decide how copyrighted materials can be used:
  - the purpose of the use;
  - the nature of the work;
  - the amount of work used; and
  - the potential effect on the market.
- Most copyright decisions should be based on these fair use factors.
- Library workers should also educate users about copyright law—especially its exceptions and limits. They should know the special rights that libraries have under the law, as well as the limits to those rights.

What Does the Law Say?

- The Copyright Act of 1976 is the basis of U.S. copyright law. It appears in Title 17 of the U.S. Code and has been updated by later laws like the Digital Millennium Copyright Act and the Copyright Term Extension Act. These laws affect how libraries work with materials in both physical and digital formats.

- Because copyright law can be unclear and doesn't spell out every situation libraries and users may face, expert interpretation is often needed.
- Copyright law includes exceptions and limitations that let users and libraries use copyrighted materials in ways that don't break the law.
  - One example is the "first sale" doctrine. It limits a copyright holder's control after something is legally sold. It lets libraries lend out materials without paying the copyright holder again after the first purchase.

Creating Policy for Your Library

- Adopt the *Code of Ethics of the American Library Association* (part I, chapter 2) as policy for your library. It contains statements related to intellectual property, which copyright is part of.
- When creating copyright policies and procedures for things like interlibrary loan and preservation, get advice from legal counsel or librarians with copyright expertise. They can help ensure your policies are sound and may offer useful examples.

For Academic Libraries

- The widespread adoption of learning management systems has made it easier for faculty members to post and share copyrighted material in the digital environment. Consider hosting regular workshops on using the library's online reserves system and educating faculty about the policies and procedures at your institution.
- Consult the Association of Research Libraries' "Code of Best Practices in Fair Use for Academic and Research Libraries," arl.org/code-of-best-practices-in-fair-use-for-academic-and-research-libraries/.

For Public Libraries

- While library workers may be knowledgeable about what's allowable with copyrighted material in print, the variety and complexity of licenses for digital resources make it difficult to have standard policies and procedures. Make sure the staff is aware of restrictions and permissions for both licensed and purchased resources.

For School Libraries

- The Creative Commons website (creativecommons.org) offers a search tool you can use to help students and teachers find creative works that require no permission or license fees to be used and adapted in projects.

To Learn More

- Refer to "Copyright," ala.org/advocacy/copyright.
- Consult with the copyright specialist at the ALA Public Policy and Advocacy Office, (202) 628-8410, who can direct you to additional educational tools.

Reflection Questions

- Many libraries have posted signs warning against violation of copyright at photocopiers. Should there also be signs on computers regarding copyrighted digital content?
- A teacher wants to distribute multiple copies of articles or short excerpts from a text to students for educational purposes. What would you advise?
- A faculty member wants to show a movie in their class using a Blu-ray they borrowed from the library. Is this a problem? What if the faculty member wants to stream the movie in their online course instead?
- A librarian wants to read a picture book during a virtual storytime. How would you proceed?

OFFICIAL ALA POLICY STATEMENT

Copyright: An Interpretation of the *Code of Ethics*

Adopted by ALA Council on July 1, 2014; amended January 29, 2019; and June 30, 2025.

Article IV of the ALA's *Code of Ethics* states that library workers "respect intellectual property rights and advocate balance between the interests of information users and rights holders." In libraries, copyright is the most important part of intellectual-property law. U.S. Copyright law, as established by the U.S. Constitution and the Copyright Act, grants creators rights over their work, but also puts limitations on those rights.[1,2]

Copyright law was established to encourage people to share their created works by giving them specific exclusive rights such as reproduction, distribution, and public performance.[3] There are limits to those rights, like fair use or the length of copyright term. These limitations are necessary to protect creators' rights while also preserving freedom of information and freedom of expression.

Copyright and libraries both aim to benefit the public by creating and sharing information and creative works. Copyright law should balance the public's access to these works with the economic interests of rights holders. Libraries represent the very best of this balance in U.S. copyright law. Libraries are the economic engine of both copyright law and information sharing by spending billions of dollars on copyrighted materials, such as books, journals, movies, art, music, etc. Libraries serve the "use and access" purpose of copyright when users borrow billions of copyrighted items each year.

Libraries have both the opportunity and the duty to maintain this balance. They do this by:

- acquiring information resources;
- curating and preserving cultural heritage;
- offering services and programs that improve access to information; and
- lending books or other resources.

Copyright law gives rights holders the exclusive legal right to:

- make copies of the work;
- create derivative works;
- distribute the work to the public; and
- perform or display the work in public.

Copyright law also gives the public the right to make fair use of copyrighted works.[4] There are also restrictions to the exclusive rights of copyright holders. For example, the First Sale Doctrine allows the public to borrow, loan, sell, or transfer a purchased, particular copy of a work. The public has unlimited use of the work when the copyright term expires.[5]

Copyright law provides a specific exception for libraries, archives, and nonprofit educational institutions.[6] This exception may allow institutions to:

- make limited copies for users;
- preserve and make replacement copies;
- create copies for accessibility purposes; and
- perform or display works for educational purposes.

This exception sets boundaries to ensure that libraries can carry out their mission while following copyright law.

Libraries and their parent institutions have a responsibility to promote and maintain policies and procedures that align with their ethical duties, missions, and the law. This includes copyright law. These policies and procedures should carefully weigh legal risks and respect the rights of both copyright holders and users of those copyrighted works. Libraries also need to ensure that all staff know about the copyright laws that impact their library's services.

Library workers serve a critical role in providing copyright information to their communities. They must be informed about copyright updates and understand the law, its purpose, and its relevance to library activities. This includes understanding and analyzing various copyright scenarios, such as fair use and other limitations, with good judgment and strategies to reduce risk.

Library workers should use these skills to identify their rights and the rights of their users. They should do outreach about copyright topics and refer users with questions to reliable resources. However, library workers should avoid providing legal advice. They may provide information about the law and copyright but should recommend users consult an attorney for legal advice.

Library workers should be able to explain to users any restrictions on how they can use content based on digital-licensing agreements that may exceed those covered by copyright law. This includes digital content like e-books, databases and streaming services.

Libraries have a proud history of advocating for the public interest. They recognize that copyright law must balance the rights of creators with the needs of the public. If there is an unfair balance between the rights holders and the public's access to information, library workers should speak up. They should engage with rights holders and legislators to advocate for laws and practices that protect users' right to access information and ensure broad public access to information.

NOTES

1. Copyright protects "original works of authorship fixed in any tangible medium of expression." Copyright Act of 1976, 17 U.S.C. § 102 (2011).
2. Article 1, Section 8 of the U.S. Constitution empowers Congress to pass laws "to promote the Progress of Science and useful Arts, by securing for limited Times to Authors and Inventors the exclusive Right to their respective Writings and Discoveries."
3. The exclusive rights of a copyright owner include reproduction, the creation of derivative works, distribution, public performance, public display, and the public performance of sound recordings by means of digital audio transmission (Copyright Act of 1976, 17 U.S.C. § 106).
4. Fair use applies when considering these four factors: the purpose and character of the use, the nature of the copyrighted work, the amount and substantiality used, and potential effects on the market for the work (Copyright Act of 1976, 17 U.S.C. § 107).
5. Copyright Act of 1976, 17 U.S.C. § 109.
6. Copyright Act of 1976, 17 U.S.C. § 108.3.

A DEEPER LOOK

The Law Regarding Copyright

KATHERINE ROTH

Copyright and intellectual freedom are both essential in libraries. However, they often seem to be at odds with one another. Copyright restricts access to information, while intellectual freedom promotes its free flow. Despite this tension, libraries can actively support both through a thoughtful use of copyright law.

Recognizing the tension between copyright and intellectual freedom, the law has been modified to include exceptions for libraries, schools, and other cultural institutions. Libraries play an essential role in maintaining this balance and advocating for the public's right to access information.

The Constitutional Basis for Copyright

The constitutional basis for copyright law is found in Article I, Section 8, Clause 8. Congress wanted to promote "the Progress of Science and useful Arts" by granting creators "exclusive rights" in their works. In other words, Congress encouraged creators to produce useful works. However, Congress also recognized that these "exclusive rights" could lead to monopolies. To prevent this, it placed limits on how long the rights would last.

Today, these "exclusive rights" still exist, but exceptions have been added for libraries. These exceptions help libraries follow copyright law while supporting intellectual freedom.

If a work is still protected by copyright, it cannot be used without the creator's permission. Using it without permission goes against their exclusive rights and is considered copyright infringement. The creator would then have grounds to sue for copyright violation. Without exceptions to these exclusive rights, libraries would not be able to engage in activities that promote information access and support intellectual freedom, such as:

- lending books;
- photocopying and scanning materials for users;
- providing interlibrary loan (ILL) services; or
- offering other similar services.

Exceptions for Library Workers and Libraries

There are several exceptions in copyright law that permit libraries to use copyrighted materials without a creator's permission. These exceptions can be used for limited times under specific circumstances.

17 U.S. Code Section 108 allows libraries to reproduce copyrighted materials for ILL, archival preservation, or to replace damaged and deteriorating works.

The *"First Sale"* doctrine (17 U.S.C. Section 109(a)) allows anyone who legally owns a physical copy of a work to resell, lend, donate, or give it away without needing the creator's permission. This applies to both individuals and libraries. For example, a professor can donate a legally obtained book to the library for students to borrow from the Reserves desk. Libraries can also use this doctrine to loan, donate, or resell physical materials in their collection. However, the first sale doctrine does not apply to digital materials, which are usually covered by licenses and contract law.

The *"Fair Use"* doctrine (17 U.S.C. Section 107) lets people use limited portions of copyrighted work without permission in certain situations. To decide if a use is "fair," four factors must be considered:

1. the purpose and character of the use (for example, whether it's for education or commercial use);
2. the nature of the copyrighted work (such as whether it's more factual or more creative);

3. the amount and importance of the part used; and
4. the effect on the market for the original work (whether the use could hurt the original work's sales).

While courts decide what counts as fair use, library workers should understand the four factors and how they apply. For example, a librarian may want to use a few pages from a textbook in a LibGuide. If the use is educational (factor 1) and the material is factual, not creative (factor 2), the use might qualify as fair use. But the librarian must also consider how much of the book is used (factor 3) and whether it harms the book's market value (factor 4). Again, the final determination would be made by a court of law.

Creative Commons Licenses

Creative Commons (CC) licenses are a different kind of copyright. They were created in 2002 by the nonprofit group Creative Commons. Unlike traditional copyright, which says, "all rights reserved," CC licenses use a "some rights reserved" approach.

These licenses let creators share their work and give permission in advance for others to use and build on it, with some limits. Creators can also choose to give up their copyright entirely. This puts the work in the public domain, where anyone can use it freely without asking for permission. The CC licenses are used around the world. They are simple to use, legally binding, and permanent.

CC licenses can also be used as tools to promote intellectual freedom. By allowing and encouraging people to share and use information, they support collaboration and innovation. In libraries, CC licenses can be used to openly license library LibGuides, institutional repositories, and open educational resources (OERs). This helps more people access these materials.

Why Library Workers Should Care About Copyright Law

Library workers have a unique role in balancing copyright law and intellectual freedom. They need to understand the values and details of both. Copyright law is changing, and library workers must know the law and exceptions to help users get the most access to information. They also need to understand the practical parts of copyright law, like licensing, so they can recognize everyday situations that may raise copyright concerns.

For example, a librarian needs to understand a license to know what uses of a work are allowed, if permission is needed, and whether a copyright exception applies. They must also know if copying, scanning, or sharing materials is allowed or qualifies as fair use.

Library workers need to be familiar with the fair use doctrine. They should understand when courts have found certain uses fair and how this doctrine is changing. This includes recent court opinions about using AI training data and whether its use to train generative chat models is fair.

Library workers should be able to advise faculty and students on how to legally share and build on existing works. CC licenses are ideal for this. Lastly, library workers should ensure that any recommendations are clearly stated as not providing legal advice and should advise users to consult an attorney if professional legal advice is required.

Conclusion

Copyright law is a foundation for how libraries operate. That's why it's essential for library workers to understand its basic principles. With this knowledge, they can make informed decisions that enhance user access while protecting their institutions from copyright violations.

While legal counsel may be needed for complex issues, library workers who know copyright law and support intellectual freedom are a major asset to the institution and its stakeholders. By staying up to date, they can follow the law and still promote open access to knowledge. This helps create a library that supports learning, research, and the free flow of information while staying legally compliant.

Copyright Law and Library Operations

Many common library operations have copyright implications. Libraries should be mindful of potential copyright concerns and should consult with legal counsel or a copyright specialist about:

- Interlibrary loan
- Course reserves
- Digitization of documents and other materials
- Posting of faculty articles in institutional repositories
- Film exhibitions
- Streaming media

What Are Trade Secrets, Trademarks, and Patents?

Trade secrets, trademarks, and patents are other intellectual property laws that are used to protect original works.

- Patents protect inventions and unique ways of doing things, such as how to make a particular type of doorknob.
- Trademarks are used to ensure the singular "identity" of a product so rights holders can ensure that customers will not confuse it with a similar but competing product. Both slogans ("Just do it!") and logos (the Nike swish) are trademarks.
- Trade secrets are the unique "know-how" required to create a product, such as the secret recipe for a popular soft drink.

Some creative processes, logos, or expressions can be protected by more than one intellectual property right. Mickey Mouse is a long-standing example.

CHAPTER 9
Meeting Rooms, Exhibit Spaces, and Programming

BIG IDEA BREAKDOWN

Key Concepts

- Libraries do not necessarily endorse the viewpoints of authors in their collections. The same is true for the viewpoints shared in public meetings, exhibits, or programs held in the library.
- If a library offers meeting rooms or exhibit spaces to the public, it must do so equitably. Decisions should not be based on the beliefs or affiliations of the individuals or groups making the request. A room or space should not be denied just because some may find the content offensive.
- Programs should not be canceled because of the ideas, topics, or views expressed by participants or speakers. Likewise, library workers should not censor or remove displays just because someone disagrees with the content.
- Libraries may choose to limit the use of meeting rooms or exhibit spaces to library-sponsored activities only.
- Libraries that use social media should understand why they are using it, be aware of the legal risks, and have a written policy that guides its use.

What Does the Law Say?

- Libraries are not required to make meeting rooms or exhibit spaces available for public use. If they do, any restrictions must be neutral and not based on the content or viewpoint of the user. Limits can only be based on the time, place, or manner of use.
- Hate speech is protected by the First Amendment. This protection is based on the belief that freedom of speech requires the government to allow strong debate on public issues—even if the speech is offensive, hurtful, or hateful. Under current law, hate speech can only be criminalized if it

directly incites imminent criminal activity or contains a specific threat of violence aimed at a person or group.

Creating Policy for Your Library

- Adopt the *Library Bill of Rights* (part I, chapter 2) as policy for your library. It contains a statement about providing meeting rooms and exhibit spaces on an equitable basis.
- If you offer meeting rooms or exhibit spaces to the public, make sure to have a written policy. The policy should define any restrictions based on the time, place, and manner of use. Restrictions must be neutral and not based on the content or viewpoint of the user (part I, chapter 3).
- Collection development policies should include a process for users to request the library to reconsider a program or exhibit.

For Academic Libraries

- Refer to "Intellectual Freedom Principles for Academic Libraries" (part II, chapter 4).

For Public Libraries

- Parents and guardians are the only ones who can decide whether their own children can participate in library programs. No other person or organization may interfere with another person's access or participation.

To Learn More

- "Meeting Rooms, Exhibit Spaces, and Programs," ala.org/advocacy/intfreedom/spaces.
- "Religion in American Libraries Q&A," ala.org/advocacy/intfreedom/religionfaq.
- "Hate Speech and Hate Crime," ala.org/advocacy/intfreedom/hate.
- "Hateful Conduct in Libraries: Supporting Library Workers and Patrons," ala.org/advocacy/hatefulconduct.
- "Social Media Guidelines for Public and Academic Libraries," ala.org/advocacy/intfreedom/socialmediaguidelines.

Reflection Questions

- A church group asks to reserve your meeting room for a program on the biblical path to prosperity. What do you do?
- A local women's group sponsors an exhibit related to the impacts since the *Dobbs v. Jackson Women's Health Organization* court decision. How do you respond to complaints from a member of the library board?

- An anti-immigration group wants to schedule regular meetings in your library. What's your response?
- The children's librarian wants to host a Drag Story Hour event. What issues should you consider?
- A university librarian allows a local Black Lives Matter chapter to put up a display in the library. Several students have complained to the dean. How should you proceed?
- A local nonprofit is requiring users to give their name and email address to attend its program in the library's meeting room. What do you tell the nonprofit?

OFFICIAL ALA POLICY STATEMENTS

Exhibits, Displays, and Bulletin Boards: An Interpretation of the *Library Bill of Rights*

Adopted July 2, 1991, by the ALA Council; amended June 30, 2004; and July 1, 2014 (under the previous name "Exhibit Spaces and Bulletin Boards"); amended June 25, 2019 (under the previous name "User-Initiated Exhibits, Displays, and Bulletin Boards"); and May 29, 2025.

Libraries may offer physical or digital spaces for exhibits, displays, and bulletin boards to benefit the community.

Libraries are not required to make space available to community groups or individuals for:

- exhibits;
- public displays;
- notices;
- pamphlets; or
- flyers.

If they do offer space, they should post a permanent notice stating that the spaces are a public service and do not reflect the library's viewpoint.

Libraries should have written policies that:

- are content neutral (restrictions are not based on the display's content or the identity, beliefs, or affiliations of the sponsors);
- are clearly defined;
- are applied equally; and
- address any time, place, and manner restrictions.

Policies should be inclusive rather than exclusive. For example, a policy that the library's space is "open to organizations engaged in educational, cultural, intellectual, or charitable activities" is an inclusive statement about the limited uses of the space.

If someone objects to the content, they should be able to request reconsideration, just like challenging any library resource. Library workers should not censor or remove materials from exhibits, displays, or information areas because someone may disagree with the content or the identity, beliefs, or affiliations of the sponsors.

Library initiated displays help users discover library resources and raise awareness of programs and services. They use library worker expertise to highlight:

- community interests;
- collections;
- services;
- facilities; and
- information resources.

Library workers should actively include a diverse range of genres, formats, ideas, and expressions in their displays. These displays should represent many viewpoints and cultural perspectives to reflect the diversity of their communities. Library-initiated displays can help users discover resources and access information by crossing language and cultural barriers. Libraries serving multilingual communities should include information in languages other than English to meet the needs of all users

Displays should not be taken down because of the ideas, topics, or views of participants or speakers.

Library-Initiated Programs as a Resource: An Interpretation of the *Library Bill of Rights*

Adopted January 27, 1982, by the ALA Council; amended June 26, 1990; July 12, 2000; June 26, 2018 (under previous name "Library-Initiated Programs as a Resource"); June 24, 2019 (under previous name "Library-Initiated Programs and Displays as a Resource"); and June 29, 2025.

Library-initiated programs support the mission of the library. They do this by giving users extra ways to access information, education, and recreation. Article I of the *Library Bill of Rights* states, "Books and other library resources should be provided for the interest, information, and enlightenment of all people of the community the library serves."

These programs may take place on-site at the library, off-site at other locations, or online. They may be provided by library workers, volunteers, or partners.

Library workers use their expertise to highlight:

- community interests;
- collections;

- services;
- facilities; and
- information resources.

These programs help users discover library resources and the library's role in providing access to information. Libraries may work with other agencies, organizations, institutions, or individuals to create programs that serve the community.

"Socially excluded, marginalized, and underrepresented people, not just the mainstream majority, should be able to see themselves reflected in the resources and programs that libraries offer."[1] Programming options should represent a diversity of genres, formats, ideas, and expressions. Programming options should provide a variety of viewpoints and cultural perspectives that reflect the diversity in communities. Libraries serving multilingual communities should make efforts to accommodate the needs of those who speak and read languages other than English, including advertising for such events.

Library-initiated programs should comply with all applicable laws. This includes the standards and requirements of the Americans with Disabilities Act and state and local disability accessibility guidelines.[2] Program spaces should be safe and accessible for all users (e.g., ramps, pathways, and emergency exit routes). Reasonable accommodation should be made to have interpretation, voice amplification, and/or real-time captioning when needed or requested by library users.

Concerns, questions, or complaints about programs should follow the same policies and procedures used to reconsider other library resources. These policies should apply equally to everyone, including, but not limited to, library users, staff, and members of the governing body. They should also emphasize the library's commitment to free and open access to information and ideas for all.

Sponsoring a program does not mean the library endorses the content or the views of the participants or speakers. Similarly, adding materials to the collection or curating a display doesn't mean the library supports the creator or resources' views. Libraries should vigorously defend the First Amendment right of speakers and participants to express themselves.

Article V of the *Library Bill of Rights* states, "A person's right to use a library should not be denied or abridged because of origin, age, background, or views." The right to use a library includes all the resources offered, including programming.

Libraries may create programs for:

- specific age groups;
- educational suitability; or
- audience interest.

However, restrictions based solely on gender, age, or educational level violate this right. These restrictions should only be enforced if not doing so would have a negative impact on the safety of the participants or the intended purpose of the program.

Parents and guardians may decide whether their own children can participate in library programs. They should discuss these decisions with their children. However, no person or organization may interfere with another person's access or participation, including decisions about other people's children.

Users should not be denied access to programs because they owe overdue fines or other fees. If libraries charge for supplies, they should make every effort to reduce economic barriers to participation.[3]

Libraries should only collect and keep participants' personal information if they choose to opt-in. Attendees may need to show a library card or student ID to prove eligibility, but their information should not be recorded as a condition for attending the program.

NOTES

1. "Services to People with Disabilities: An Interpretation of the *Library Bill of Rights,*" adopted January 28, 2009, by the ALA Council, under the previous name "Services to Persons with Disabilities"; amended June 26, 2018; and June 29, 2025.
2. "Equity, Diversity, Inclusion, and Belonging: An Interpretation of the *Library Bill of Rights,*" adopted June 27, 2017, by the ALA Council, under the previous name "Equity, Diversity, Inclusion"; amended May 29, 2025.
3. "Economic Barriers to Library Access: An Interpretation of the *Library Bill of Rights,*" adopted June 30, 1993, by the ALA Council; amended June 25, 2019, under the previous name "Economic Barriers to Information Access"; and June 29, 2025.

Meeting Rooms: An Interpretation of the *Library Bill of Rights*

Adopted July 2, 1991, by the ALA Council; amended June 26, 2018; amended version rescinded August 16, 2018; amended January 29, 2019; and June 29, 2025.

Many libraries offer meeting rooms and other spaces for public use as a community service. Article VI of the *Library Bill of Rights* states, "Libraries which make … meeting rooms available to the public they serve should make such facilities available on an equitable basis, regardless of the beliefs or affiliations of individuals or groups requesting their use."

Article V of the *Library Bill of Rights* states, "A person's right to use a library should not be denied or abridged because of origin, age, background, or views." This applies to meeting rooms and spaces designated for public use just as it does to the library collections and services.

Libraries do not support or endorse the views of meeting room users, just as they do not endorse the viewpoints of materials in their collections. Some groups may engage in activities that, while legally protected, can cause fear and discomfort for library users and staff. Libraries should create and enforce user behavior policies that protect users and staff from harassment while upholding free speech rights.[1] This interpretation provides general guidelines for meeting room use and is not legal advice.

Publicly funded libraries are not required to offer meeting rooms for public use. However, if they do, these spaces are considered designated public forums.[2] This means libraries cannot exclude groups based on the topics they discuss or the ideas they support.[3] The First Amendment's Establishment Clause allows religious groups to use library meeting rooms and spaces.[4]

Libraries can enforce their behavior policies if a group disrupts or harasses others in the library. Libraries may face legal and financial consequences if their policies seem to unfairly limit controversial groups' access to meeting rooms.

Libraries should work with legal counsel to create policies in advance for using meeting rooms and public spaces. These policies should explain when, where, and how the space can be used. However, they should not restrict access based on the content of a meeting or to the beliefs or affiliations of the sponsors. Libraries should also be transparent about the privacy and confidentiality policies regarding use of meeting rooms as a library resource.

Policies should be available to the public in the community's most commonly used languages. Library staff should also review them regularly.

Library policies should be inclusive, not exclusive. An inclusive policy may state:

Our library's meeting rooms are open to groups for activities related to:

- education;
- culture;
- charity;
- advocacy;
- civic engagement;
- religion; or
- politics.

For example, if a library allows a charity or sports club to use its space, then political or religious groups should also be allowed. If meeting rooms are open to a variety of civic organizations, then the library may not deny access to a religious group.

Policies may set limits on how often a space can be used. They may also require users to follow the library's behavior policy.[5] The policy should state whether meetings must be open to the public or if private events are allowed.

Libraries may offer space for public or private events unless restricted by state or local laws. The same rules should apply to all meeting room users. Libraries should also have a process for users to appeal if their meeting room request is denied.

If meeting rooms and spaces are open to the public, library policies should clearly state any fees. Fees for meeting rooms may limit or deny access for some users.[6] Charging fees does not change the status as a designated public forum. Libraries that charge fees should review:

- local and state laws;
- the American Library Association's *Code of Ethics*; and
- the *Library Bill of Rights*.

Meeting rooms may be offered as a resource to all members of a community. While prioritizing the safety of library users and workers, libraries must also uphold the First Amendment rights of all users—including those with ideas that other members of the community may disagree with. Strong policies, approved in advance, are the best way to ensure both safety and freedom of speech for all.

NOTES

1. "Resolution on Libraries as Responsible Spaces," adopted June 26, 2017, by the ALA Council.
2. *Concerned Women for Am. v. Lafayette Cnty.*, 883 F.2d 32 (5th Cir. 1989).
3. *Hale v. Schaumburg Twp. Dist. Library, et al.*, 01-cv-2220 (N.D. Ill. 2001); *Hale, et al., v. Schell and the Martin Library Bd. of Dirs.*, 1:02-cv-1156 (M.D. Pa. 2002); "White Supremacist Wins Library Venue in Schaumburg," *American Libraries*, August 20, 2001, https://web.archive.org/web/20181212231846/https://americanlibrariesmagazine.org/white-supremacist-wins-library-venue-in-schaumburg/; "White Supremacists to Meet after Library Changes Policy," *Library Journal*, November 25, 2002, https://web.archive.org/web/20150407153623/http://lj.libraryjournal.com/2002/11/ljarchives/white-supremacists-to-meet-after-library-changes-policy/.
4. *Concerned Women for Am. v. Lafayette Cnty.*, 883 F.2d 32 (5th Cir. 1989).
5. "Guidelines for the Development of Policies and Procedures Regarding User Behavior and Library Usage," adopted January 24, 1993, by the ALA Intellectual Freedom Committee; amended November 17, 2000; January 19, 2005; March 29, 2014; August 16, 2019; and August 5, 2025.
6. "Economic Barriers to Library Access: An Interpretation of the *Library Bill of Rights*," adopted June 30, 1993, by the ALA Council; amended June 25, 2019, under the previous name "Economic Barriers to Information Access"; and June 29, 2025.

PERSONAL STORY

Intellectual Freedom, Meeting Rooms, and Owl Ears

MARCELLUS TURNER

My long career in library administration across several systems has given me "owl ears." Owl ears perk up when awareness of your surroundings is critical—when there's potential danger. And so it is with meeting rooms, public spaces, and intellectual freedom. I know danger.

Now before I go too far, I will acknowledge that all libraries have a love-hate relationship with meeting rooms. We love and need them. Our users love them too. Big or small, with or without whiteboards, someone, somebody, some group, somewhere wants a space where they can gather, focus, or retreat and be by themselves.

But these rooms come with problems, such as:

- people overstaying their time limits;
- locking and unlocking the room;
- keeping the lights on;
- dealing with payments;
- verifying nonprofit status;
- managing food policies;
- and on and on.

These are everyday problems, and they're part of why we have such a complicated relationship with these rooms. But sometimes, a problem becomes an issue. Then we are forced to think about the bigger picture and what it means to offer meeting spaces for public use. When meeting rooms and public spaces turn into public forums, we bump up against intellectual freedom.

This was the case when an organization, with views that clashed with many in a liberal and proud city, correctly rented the auditorium (for a private-ticketed event) in an iconic public library. You can google the rest of the story because the specifics are not what I want to talk about here. What matters is what it represented.

And it starts with intellectual freedom.

Intellectual freedom is not an issue in and of itself. Every library, no matter its size or number of meeting rooms, is built on a foundation of intellectual freedom. This extends to every corner of our buildings. We defend the right to access information and to share ideas—even when those ideas challenge us.

When someone books a meeting room, in this case, a public auditorium, we recognize we may not agree with their views. We issue a disclaimer that "The views of Group ABC do not reflect those of XYZ Library." But that doesn't always help because some believe that allowing controversial speech means endorsing it. That by providing a space, we enable harm and foster hate.

In this case, many didn't see the issue as one of intellectual freedom. They saw it as freedom of speech—and felt the library was giving a platform to hate. They wrote letters, came to board meetings, and called for the firing of the chief librarian. The group's presence was seen as everything wrong, egregious, and harmful. Many believed that allowing the group a space to speak could potentially hurt the people their message targeted.

Some called it hate speech. But hate speech is hard to define legally or defend against, even when you know and can hear how hateful it is.

Then things escalated. People across the country, some who didn't even live in the city or state, chimed in. Some asked that the library's recent national award be rescinded. Others vowed to return the same award in protest. The criticism created even more public outcry, misunderstanding, and distraction.

And then it got worse. Someone whispered "discrimination." Legal experts said that if we denied the group access based on its views, we could (and would) face legal action. Thankfully, we never considered denying them their right to use the space; instead, we looked for ways to make the best of the situation for both sides while maintaining our neutrality.

But all of this just skims the surface of what is at the heart of the matter: This was about values.

Many in that community believed the library shared their values. These values were reinforced by the staff who suggested a great book to read, helped them find the answer to a trivia question, led their kids' storytimes, opened the doors and greeted them each day, and participated in the festivals and parades in the community. Many in the community assumed that the library had the same values as they did. By our allowing this group to use the space, they felt betrayed. They thought it meant we agreed with the group's message, that we shared its values. And that wasn't true at all.

It was all about shared values. The community thought the library's values mirrored their own. And because the group's values didn't, they should not be allowed to rent the space and share their views and beliefs with others, even those who paid to attend.

But that is unreasonable.

As a library, our very tenets, principles, and practices support access to all information for everyone. We uphold these principles with our collections, programs, and spaces. Intellectual freedom means respecting the fact that our views on the topic might be different, and that has to be okay.

Intellectual freedom doesn't stop at the printed word or what is on the shelves. If a person or group wants to use a space to speak, and we deny them based on their viewpoint, we risk violating the principles we stand for.

I can only imagine what my director colleagues in more conservative states must fight for, or against, in the name of intellectual freedom each day. Their meeting rooms are just as busy, just as contested, and just as important.

I am sure these directors have owl ears too.

OFFICIAL ALA POLICY STATEMENT

Visual and Performing Arts in Libraries: An Interpretation of the *Library Bill of Rights*

Adopted February 13, 2018 by ALA Council; amended May 29, 2025.

Visual and performing arts transform how people see and appreciate the world's cultural diversity. The American Library Association (ALA) believes these arts are essential parts of library collections and services. They play a vital role in sharing a wide range of ideas to everyone. Understanding and valuing the arts builds artistic literacy. Libraries should create opportunities for the community to experience and engage with art.

Art serves many purposes. It can be personal, political, or purely aesthetic. It can:

- convey social, historical, or political messages;
- enhance daily life;
- create visual delight; or
- challenge the status quo.

In this interpretation of the *Library Bill of Rights*, art means work created or chosen by a person to evoke an emotional response or engage the senses. In the end, art combines the artist's creativity, the viewer's perception, and a reflection of the culture and time in which it was created.

Humans make visual art with intention. Visual art includes:

- painting
- drawing
- sculpture
- photography
- printmaking
- textile and decorative arts
- digital art and design
- architecture and installation art

All visual art includes formal elements such as line, shape, color, form, and texture.

Performance art includes traditional forms like theater, dance, and music. It also includes modern live artistic expressions that use body, voice, or actions to convey meaning. Like visual art, performance art can reflect or challenge cultural understanding. By providing access to the arts, libraries uphold Article I of the *Library Bill of Rights*, supporting the "interest, information, and enlightenment"[1] of all community members.

Libraries may provide in-person and digital spaces for users to experience, interact with, and create art. Visual and performing art pieces may be:

- temporary exhibits;
- permanent installations;
- programs;
- performances; and
- viewable or archived collections.

When creating arts exhibits and programs, libraries should include diverse opinions and viewpoints. They should not avoid controversial content or exclude art because of the artists' beliefs or affiliations. Libraries don't endorse the views of artists, artwork owners, or exhibit organizers. This applies to both internal and external contributors.[2]

Libraries that allow the community to use gallery or performing space should create clear policies about when, where, and how the spaces can be used. They may consider criteria such as the:

- size of the artwork;
- space needed for an audience;
- length of display or performance time;
- frequency of use by the same group or person; and
- eligibility for submitting work.

Policies should use inclusive language and ensure that space is provided equitably. Policies and outreach should encourage a wide range of groups and people to use library display, exhibit, and performance spaces.[3] However, libraries can choose to limit the use of these spaces to "strictly 'library-related activities.'" If they do, the policy must be clearly defined and viewpoint neutral.[4]

These policies should be easy for the community to access. Behavior policies should not be used to limit access to art or performances in the library. Users should have a clear process to voice concerns about a work of art or performance, such as through a reconsideration policy.

Art in the library's permanent or exhibit holdings are an integral part of the collection. It is just as important as books, movies, and digital materials. When possible, collection development policies should include art. Libraries should create welcoming, engaging spaces where users can explore, experience, and create art. They should actively include diverse voices in creative projects, performances, and exhibits. This allows art to reflect many cultural traditions. When planning exhibits, programs, and performances, the library should consider all the communities it serves and provide a variety of viewpoints.

Laws may require libraries to use internet filters. These filters can block moving and still images—an issue for users seeking information on the visual arts. Library policies should encourage users to ask for unfiltered online access that respects their privacy. Libraries should consult the "Internet Filtering" interpretation for more information on the Children's Internet Protection Act.[5]

Visual and performing arts should be accessible to all, without content-based restrictions. This includes ensuring equitable access for children and teens. Library workers should actively seek out a wide variety of art, with limits only due to space, budget, and technical constraints. The same access standards for books and other library materials apply to the visual and performing arts.

NOTES

1. *Library Bill of Rights,* adopted June 19, 1939, by the ALA Council; amended October 14, 1944; June 18, 1948; February 2, 1961; June 27, 1967; January 23, 1980; and January 29, 2019; inclusion of "age" reaffirmed January 23, 1996.
2. "Politics in American Libraries: An Interpretation of the *Library Bill of Rights,*" adopted June 27, 2017, by the ALA Council; amended June 29, 2025.
3. "Exhibits, Displays, and Bulletin Boards: An Interpretation of the *Library Bill of Rights,*" adopted July 2, 1991, by the ALA Council; amended June 30, 2004; and July 1, 2014, under the previous name "Exhibit Spaces and Bulletin Boards"; amended June 25, 2019 under the previous name "User-Initiated Exhibits, Displays, and Bulletin Boards"; and May 29, 2025.
4. "Meeting Rooms: An Interpretation of the *Library Bill of Rights,*" adopted July 2, 1991, by the ALA Council; amended June 26, 2018; amended version rescinded August 16, 2018; amended January 29, 2019; and June 29, 2025.
5. "Internet Filtering: An Interpretation of the *Library Bill of Rights,*" adopted June 30, 2015, by the ALA Council; amended June 29, 2025.

A DEEPER LOOK

The Law Regarding Access to Meeting Rooms and Exhibit Spaces

STEPHANIE "COLE" ADAMS

What Is a "Public Forum"?

This essay uses the term "public forum." To learn more about what that means and how it applies to libraries, refer to "The Law Regarding Access to the Library: Public Forums and User Behavior Rules" (part II, chapter 4).

Allowing people and groups to use a library's physical space is a key service libraries can provide. But meeting rooms and exhibit spaces can also become sites of civil rights disputes, personal injury claims, or conflicts over limited resources. These issues often overlap, creating risks not only to intellectual freedom but also to safety and property. Libraries can take many steps to ensure that their policies and practices maximize equal access while also keeping staff safe and limiting legal risk to the institution.

Understand Property Ownership

It is important to know who owns the property where the meeting room or exhibit space is located. Does the library or its parent institution own it, or does another entity? If a library is a tenant, there should be a lease or other contract that clearly shows how much control the library has over the space.

Whether the space is owned or rented, the library should have a map or floor plan that shows which areas belong to the library. This should include where the property line ends and where public meeting space is located.

If a library owns its property, a survey or public tax map can confirm the boundaries. If a library rents its space, the lease should include a description of the leased property. From there, the floor plans of rooms that are rented or borrowed by the public should be included in the contracts and room use policies.

Have a Safety Plan

Libraries should have a safety plan for any events held in meeting rooms or exhibit spaces, whether allowed by policy or contract. The plan should cover the types of events that might take place, and the specific safety needs of those spaces.

Policies and contracts should require that anyone using the space must follow the safety plan. Good resources for developing a safety plan include:

- a local health department;
- the state department of labor; and
- insurance carriers, which may have guidance and template materials.

Know Your Insurance Coverage

It is critical to know what insurance covers the space, and what is required for the coverage to apply. These requirements should inform the policies and contracts for using the space. For example, some insurance policies for art galleries don't allow red wine in rooms with art.

Find out what coverage the institution has by contacting the insurance carrier directly—not the broker. While property insurance policies can be lengthy, it is important to *review the full policy*. This helps the library assess what is covered and what isn't. For example, a policy might cover damage caused by employees but not by volunteers or third-party contractors.

Create a Clear Policy

Libraries need to have a clear policy about different types of access to meeting rooms and exhibit spaces. Is access through a per diem rental, a standing contract, or a policy that makes access free to cardholders and certain types of organizations? Each approach should have a separate policy or contract.

This is particularly important for public institutions and 501(c)(3) nonprofit organizations. For-profit businesses usually must pay a fair market value to use the space, unless the free use is carefully managed so it doesn't provide an unfair benefit.

Have Written Contracts

If the space is available to rent, there should be a written contract. This contract allows the library to:

- control how the event is advertised, stressing that it is not a library-sponsored program; and
- manage risk by requiring the renter to have their own insurance.

Be Content-Neutral

If access is free only to certain people or groups, it must be based on objective criteria. Avoid broad bans like "no religious activity," "no loud activity," or "no commercial activity"—as these can pose risks of a legal claim. Instead, use clear, content-neutral criteria such as:

- "Access to the Meeting Room is free to all charitable organizations serving people in the library's service area."
- "Use of the Gallery Walls is reserved for artists living in the library's service area."

Clearly State Reasons for Prohibitions

When a type of conduct or content must be prohibited, clearly state the reason. Examples include:

- "To comply with the Internal Revenue Code, free access to the Meeting Room cannot be used for 'political activity' (supporting candidates for public office)."
- "To comply with the fire code, cooking over an open flame is not allowed in the Social Hall."

Have Flexible Access

The library can make use of a combination of access types. These could include rentals, free access, and affiliate access. Here are policy examples about these different approaches:

- Rental access: "Any group that pays the rental fee and meets the criteria can use our Meeting Room. Such groups are required to clarify in all event advertisements that their event is not sponsored by the library."

- Free access: "Any group that meets our criteria for service to our community can use our Meeting Room. Such groups must use the space according to our policies, which include the event being free and open to the area served by the library."
- Affiliate access: "This event is being put on in affiliation with our library."

There is no "right" way to combine these approaches. Some libraries avoid activities that might distract from their space, and so they choose not to offer rentals. Others use the "rental" model to control how the space is used and to offset cleaning costs. Some prefer a "free" approach, with clear criteria so only groups with some formality and legal accountability can use the space. For others, the "affiliate" model works well because it limits use to programs that support the library's mission and strategic plan.

Libraries should ensure that any approach they take is applied consistently across the community. For example, if commercial activities are prohibited in meeting rooms, they must be denied to everyone—from time-share salespeople to Girl Scouts selling cookies.

Conclusion

Why is it important to consider property boundaries, safety, insurance, and rental terms when considering the intellectual freedom implications of a room use or exhibit space policy? It is important because these factors often influence key civil rights factors, such as:

- content neutrality;
- equal access;
- limited public forum status;
- due process prior to loss of privileges; and
- compliance with the Freedom of Information Act or equivalent state laws.

For example, if a library doesn't know where its property begins, it can't determine where its limited public forum obligations start. If it doesn't have a safety plan, it can't manage its First Amendment responsibilities during a noisy or disruptive protest. Without a clear meeting-room rental policy, the library can't show that it followed legal requirements if access is denied. And if leadership doesn't understand the library's insurance coverage, they can't fully assess the risks of hosting a potentially controversial program.

What does this mean for policy development? Because every library is unique—as is the risk of liability—libraries should work with a lawyer who understands premises liability, contracts, and the First Amendment to help draft room-use policies and contracts.

Libraries can develop clear policies and contracts for meeting rooms and exhibit spaces by:

- starting with a solid knowledge of the property;
- considering safety and insurance plans; and
- focusing on how to make resources accessible to the public.

This holistic approach ensures that the library not only considers—but actively prioritizes—intellectual freedom while providing vital access to the public.

Concerns About Controversial Groups

Some groups may have a constitutional right to use the library, but their presence can still cause fear or discomfort for library users and staff. Libraries can take steps beyond just setting and enforcing behavior policies to remain welcoming and inclusive.

One option is to close meeting rooms to all outside users. This allows the library to fully control the messages shared in its spaces.

Another option is for the library to use its own First Amendment rights as a government agency. This could include offering programs that actively counter messages of bias, hate, and discrimination.

For more information, check out "Hate Speech and Hate Crime," ala.org/advocacy/intfreedom/hate.

Libraries do not have to make their spaces, such as meeting rooms, available to the public. In *Lehman v. City of Shaker Heights*, 418 U.S. 298 (1974), the Supreme Court said that a city's public transit vehicles did not have to provide advertising space to the public. However, once a library makes a space available to some members of the public, the library must make it available to everyone.

Libraries may restrict the use of their spaces when the restrictions are content-neutral and pertain to time, place, and manner. For instance, libraries could prohibit uses of library space that would disrupt or interfere with general use of the library, per *Concerned Women for America, Inc. v. Lafayette County*, 883 F.2d 32 (5th Cir. 1989).

Restrictions based on content are only allowed if the state has a compelling interest and the restrictions are narrowly tailored to achieve those interests. Viewpoint-based restrictions are never allowed. See, for example, *Hopper v. City of Pasco*, 241 F.3d 1067 (9th Cir.), *cert. denied*, 534 U.S. 951 (2001). In another example, the Supreme Court has found that church groups can use public school facilities to show religious films, per *Lamb's Chapel v. Center Moriches Union Free School District*, 508 U.S. 384 (1993). Public libraries cannot craft restrictions to exclude groups and activities that would cause controversy or espouse offensive views. The Supreme Court has held that avoiding controversy is not a valid ground for restricting speech in a public forum, per *Cornelius v. NAACP Legal Defense and Educational Fund, Inc.*, 473 U.S. 788 (1985).

The Law Regarding Social Media

STEPHANIE "COLE" ADAMS

"Social media" is a big category, but for this section the definition is "a generally accessible electronic publication of interactive content conducted via an account on a third-party platform." The key elements of this definition are:

- *Generally accessible*: the content is not meant to be private.
- *Electronic*: the content is not a physical or printed copy.
- *Publication*: the content is duplicated and shared with others.
- *Interactive content*: viewers can respond or engage with the content.
- *Conducted via an account on a third-party platform*: the content is shared through a third-party host (like YouTube or Facebook).

As such, this section does not cover non-interactive or closed electronic media, like static websites, texting, and teleconferencing.

What legal issues should libraries consider when using a "generally accessible electronic publication of interactive content conducted via an account on a third-party platform"?

There are quite a few such issues. To sort through them, it helps for a library to first ask why it uses social media. From there, the library should write a short summary of what it uses the media for. Examples include:

- "The Library uses social media to alert users to new materials, programs, and how to donate to our Foundation."
- "The Library uses social media to get feedback on our collections and programs, and to help our community get to know our staff and volunteers."
- "The Library uses social media to share our hours, announce emergency closures, support emergency response, and livestream board meetings."

Once a library knows what it uses social media for—and just as critically, what it *doesn't* use it for—it can identify legal issues and put policies and safeguards in place.

The legal risks of the typical examples listed above, and the policies and safeguards that can limit them, follow.

Alerting Users About New Materials

Social media posts with book cover images can trigger a Digital Millennium Copyright (DMCA) Act "notice and takedown" demand. This demand may be automatically sent by a bot or by an actual human. To receive the "safe harbor" protection of the DMCA, make sure your library has a registered agent for receiving DMCA notices (for more information on this, visit copyright.gov/dmca-directory/). When posting book covers and other proprietary content, follow the library's policy for fair use, per Section 107 of the Copyright Act. Make sure the library's insurance policy covers claims of copyright infringement.

Promoting Library Programming

Promoting the library's programs requires the same caution as when creating "real-world" promotional materials. It is especially important to not accidentally violate copyright and trademark rights online. This is because copyright enforcement agents use technology to seek out violations and are not shy about threatening libraries with legal action. If the library gets a notice of violation, they should not respond before sending the threat to their lawyer or insurance carrier. This is true even if the threat seems shaky or spammy. Some legal threats can seem bogus but are real, while others that seem real can be a scam. Let the lawyer or the carrier decide.

Asking for Donations

This requires careful planning because each state has very specific laws about asking for donations. Because of this, every library should have a policy about asking for donations, and that policy should be based on guidance from both the IRS and your state attorney general's office. If the library uses social media to ask for donations, the social media "ask" should follow that library's policy, just like print and in-person solicitations.

Requesting Feedback on Collections and Programming

This is risky for public libraries that operate as a part of government because the library cannot remove or limit critical feedback. Comments that contain threats, abuse, or that violate clear rules can be restricted—but that is a risky First Amendment game. A safer option is to invite users to submit reviews separately and ask for their permission to share selected ones. This is a way to channel feedback without making it an open forum and to make the best use of positive feedback.

Help the Community Get to Know Library Workers

Sharing favorite books and highlighting library workers is a great way to connect with the community. However, it's important to protect staff safety and privacy. If not handled properly, social media posts featuring employees can raise safety, labor law, and privacy concerns. If there is an employee union, it may also violate the contract. No staff member should be required to appear on social media unless it is in their job description and state laws about image rights have been considered.

Notifying the Community of Hours of Operation and Emergency Closure

If the library uses social media to inform the public about when it is open, one person—and a backup—should be assigned to keep the page current. This responsibility should be included in a specific social media policy or put in job descriptions.

Contributing to Your Community's Emergency Response

Many libraries are important resources for their communities during floods, fires, or pandemics. Social media can be a vital part of coordinating emergency services. If your library uses social media during emergencies, it is critical to include that in the library's emergency response plan. Staff using social media for this purpose should have backup technology available for updating resources.

Livestreaming Board Meetings

For taxpayer-funded libraries, sharing board meetings on social media is a powerful transparency tool. If a library does this, choose a social media platform that meets Americans with Disabilities Act (ADA) requirements. All libraries must follow state and local open meeting laws. This includes quasi-governmental libraries, such as:

- Library districts of authorities created by special legislation
- Nonprofit libraries that receive public funding or are chartered by a government agency
- Joint public-private library partnerships

It is best to include these legal and accessibility considerations in the board's meeting policy. That policy can also cover:

- how to handle public comment made on social media;
- sharing meeting materials on social media;
- recording and posting meetings; and
- retaining and sharing records of livestreams.

General Requirements for Any of the Above

1. Even if your library doesn't use social media, it should still have insurance that covers claims of copyright or trademark infringement, and defamation. This coverage is important because libraries work with content and often promote materials to the public. If someone threatens legal action, notify insurance carriers right away.

2. While many of the risks above can be handled in stand-alone policies (like for donations), it is wise to have a dedicated social media policy. This policy should explain how the library uses social media and which staff position is responsible for managing it. These employees should be trained to understand the risks and policies that apply to the library's use of social media.
3. Social media accounts should be in the name of the library, not in the name of an individual employee or linked to their personal account. Account names and passwords should be stored in a secure, need-to-know file that is accessible to more than one person—but only to those who need access.
4. The library should clearly require that account information is saved only on library-owned devices. This might be inconvenient—no one wants to carry two phones—but it helps prevent accidental posts and protects the library if an employment relationship turns sour.
5. It is important to read the platform's "terms of use" to understand what services they provide and to use these with care. One platform might be great for promoting events, while another is better for emergency updates. As has been seen in recent years, a platform that works well one year may not be effective the next. Social media accounts should be reviewed each year to ensure they are being used as intended.

"Social media" is a big category, but when used with intent, awareness, and caution, it is a powerful tool for outreach. Libraries making use of it should have a clear policy, adequate insurance, and a well-developed sense of why they are using it.

Social Media and the First Amendment

When public libraries have social media accounts, the same public forum rules that apply to physical meeting rooms apply to those digital spaces. If a library opens its social media account to public comments, it may only restrict the public's participation using content-neutral restrictions that pertain to time, place, and manner.

In 2019, a federal court held that the U.S. president could not block people's speech on his public Twitter account, per *Knight First Amendment Institute v. Trump*, 928 F.3d 226 (2nd Cir. 2019). A county board supervisor similarly engaged in unconstitutional viewpoint discrimination when she blocked one of her critics from posting on her Facebook page, per *Davidson v. Randall*, 912 F.3d 666 (4th Cir. 2019). For this reason, it is not unusual for libraries to keep their comments closed. These libraries opt to use their social media spaces as platforms for communicating library news and advertising library events, rather than opening the page up to public commentary. If you do decide to open your social media to comments, make sure you have a social media policy in place to communicate the content-neutral time, place, and manner restrictions that apply.

CHAPTER 10
Politics, Religion, and Free Expression

BIG IDEA BREAKDOWN

Key Concepts

- Libraries are institutions that welcome and promote freedom of expression. They should encourage open discussion among library workers and administrators about nonconfidential professional and policy matters.
- The principles in the United Nations' "Universal Declaration of Human Rights" support intellectual freedom in libraries. These principles uphold:
  - access to information;
  - resisting censorship;
  - protecting privacy; and
  - protecting against government intrusion and oppression.
- Libraries are critical to helping their communities learn and grow. Access to education and information through the library forms the foundation of intellectual freedom.
- Libraries that offer public spaces may not restrict access to them based on political or religious affiliation.

What Does the Law Say?

- Because the relationship between an employee and employer is based on a contract, employee speech is governed by the terms of that contract. The First Amendment's protection of free expression generally does not apply to employee speech in the workplace.
- The doctrine of "employment at will," which applies in most states, means that employees can resign at any time, and employers can dismiss employees at any time—unless the reason for dismissal is illegal (such as discrimination based on race or age).

- Federal and state laws may protect employees from retaliation for "whistleblowing," or reporting certain types of employer misconduct.
- Public employees may have limited First Amendment protection if their speech addresses a matter of public concern. However, that protection only applies if the speech does not disrupt discipline or workplace harmony or interfere with the employer's ability to provide public services. The Supreme Court has ruled that when public employees speak as part of their official duties, they are not speaking as private citizens and may be disciplined for that speech.
- Favoring one religious tradition over others may violate the Establishment Clause of the First Amendment.

Creating Policy for Your Library

- Adopt ALA Policy B.9.21 on "Workplace Speech" to help promote free speech in the workplace (ala.org/aboutala/governance/policymanual).
- Adopt the *Code of Ethics of the American Library Association* (part I, chapter 2) as policy for your library. It contains statements about treating coworkers with respect and fairness.

For Academic Libraries

- Adopt the American Association of University Professors' "1940 Statement of Principles on Academic Freedom and Tenure" (aaup.org/report/1940-statement-principles-academic-freedom-and-tenure). It examines the question of an employee's right to speak as a citizen while balancing the responsibilities of representing an academic institution.

For School Libraries

- Consult with your union to ensure that whistleblowing and reporting wrongdoing are covered by your collective bargaining agreement. Also, consult the National Education Association's resources on free speech for teachers (nea.org/resource-library/first-amendment-protections-educators).

To Learn More

- Questions about speech in the workplace may be directed to the Office for Intellectual Freedom at oif@ala.org or (312) 280-4221.
- "Professional Ethics," ala.org/tools/ethics, which includes "Ethics and Social Media Q&A," "Conflicts of Interest Q&A," and "Speech in the Workplace: An Explanatory Statement of the ALA *Code of Ethics*."
- "Religion in American Libraries Q&A," ala.org/advocacy/intfreedom/religionqa.

- Visit the websites of the National Whistleblower Center (whistleblowers.org) and the Whistleblowers Protection Program (whistleblowers.gov).

Reflection Questions

- Should libraries allow their employees to speak freely about all library-related matters, or should some aspects of library operations be out of bounds for public discussion? If so, what aspects and why?
- What are effective ways to address concerns about policy decisions, equity issues, conflicts between coworkers, or ethical concerns about materials or programming in the workplace?
- What role do libraries play in supporting the principles of the United Nations' "Universal Declaration of Human Rights"?
- Many people do not feel it is right to discuss religion and politics in public settings. How does this societal resistance to exploring these topics impact a library's collections, programming, and other resources and services related to religion and politics?

OFFICIAL ALA POLICY STATEMENTS

Education and Information Literacy: An Interpretation of the *Library Bill of Rights*

Adopted July 15, 2009, by the ALA Council (under previous name "Importance of Education to Intellectual Freedom"); amended July 1, 2014 (under previous name "Advocating for Intellectual Freedom"); June 25, 2019; and May 29, 2025.

Everyone has the right to seek and receive information from all viewpoints. Being able to do so freely, without barriers, is called intellectual freedom. Education and information literacy are the foundation of intellectual freedom.[1] They are a core part of every library's mission. Libraries support this mission by providing access to information and ideas through their facilities, resources, and services.

Libraries teach people how to use resources through educational programs. In 1948, the United Nations showed the importance of intellectual freedom and education in the "Universal Declaration of Human Rights." These principles align with the American Library Association's *Library Bill of Rights.*

Both documents stress the importance of intellectual freedom. Article 26 of the "Universal Declaration of Human Rights" highlights the essential role of education in developing intellectual freedom:

1. Everyone has the right to education. Education shall be free, at least in the elementary and fundamental stages.

2. Education shall be directed to the full development of the human personality and to the strengthening of respect for human rights and fundamental freedoms. It shall promote understanding, tolerance and friendship among all nations, racial, or religious groups, and shall further the activities of the United Nations for the maintenance of peace.[2]

The *Library Bill of Rights* "affirms that all libraries are forums for information and ideas." Libraries foster education, spark curiosity, support learning, and expand the principles of intellectual freedom.

Articles I and II of the *Library Bill of Rights* stress the need for access to information from many viewpoints. Libraries should provide a variety of resources that allow users to evaluate content and context:

> Article I: Books and other library resources should be provided for the interest, information, and enlightenment of all people of the community the library serves. Materials should not be excluded because of the origin, background, or views of those contributing to their creation.
>
> Article II: Libraries should provide materials and information presenting all points of view on current and historical issues. Materials should not be proscribed or removed because of partisan or doctrinal disapproval.

Library workers promote lifelong learning by encouraging free expression and supporting the exchange of ideas among users.[3] Libraries use resources, programming, and services to strengthen access to information. This usage builds the foundation of intellectual freedom. As educators, library workers nurture intellectual freedom by:

- developing collections and services that represent many viewpoints and empower people to explore broadly;
- providing programming in many formats to support different types of learning;
- leading instruction in information literacy and critical thinking;
- building skills needed to identify false or misleading information; and
- advocating for diverse voices and using the library to explore contested concepts.

Libraries provide education services that help people to:

- explore ideas and discover new perspectives;
- find, access, and evaluate information;
- understand information presented in different formats;
- develop thoughtful and informed conclusions; and
- express their own new ideas.

By offering these services, libraries make information accessible and highlight how important it is for people to be able to think and learn freely. They also show how crucial libraries are in helping people in their communities learn and grow.

NOTES

1. "To be information literate, a person must be able to recognize when information is needed and have the ability to locate, evaluate, and use effectively the needed information." ALA Presidential Committee on Information Literacy, "Evaluating Information: Information Literacy," report, January 10, 1989, https://libguides.ala.org/InformationEvaluation/Infolit.
2. United Nations General Assembly, "Article 26," in "Universal Declaration of Human Rights," United Nations, December 10, 1948.
3. "Freedom of expression is an inalienable human right and the foundation for self-government. Freedom of expression encompasses the freedoms of speech, press, religion, assembly, and association, and the corollary right to receive information without interference and without compromising personal privacy."

Politics in American Libraries: An Interpretation of the *Library Bill of Rights*

Endorsed by the ACRL Professional Values Committee in June 2017. Adopted June 27, 2017, by the ALA Council; amended June 29, 2025.

The U.S. Constitution's First Amendment states that "Congress shall make no law ... abridging the freedom of speech, or of the press..." The *Library Bill of Rights* says that library materials should include "all people" and "all points of view." There are no restrictions on viewpoint, origin, or politics. Libraries should not exclude opinions just because they are unpopular or offensive to some. This applies even when those opposing views are loud or influential in society.

Associate Justice William J. Brennan, Jr. observed in *New York Times Co. v. Sullivan (1964)*:

> [There exists a] profound national commitment to the principle that debate on public issues should be uninhibited, robust, and wide-open, and that it may well include vehement, caustic, and sometimes unpleasantly sharp attacks on government and public officials.

This means libraries should collect, maintain, and provide access to a wide range of materials. Within budget limits and community needs, they should include diverse views on political topics.

A balanced collection does not need to have an equal number of resources for every possible viewpoint. Instead, it should offer a variety of perspectives around each issue.[1]

Libraries that have designated space for community use must make it available to all community organizations and groups, no matter their views or affiliations.[2] This includes political organizations. To guarantee access and to avoid misuse, libraries should have time, place, and manner rules. These rules may include how often a meeting can happen, meeting length, and behavior policies.[3] Libraries should create similar rules if they have space for public exhibits or the public distribution of literature.[4] Policies about use of the library and its resources should be available to all library users.

A healthy democracy must have a robust exchange of ideas and opinions. American libraries play a key role by providing free, unrestricted access to these ideas. Libraries should support civic engagement by encouraging political discussion in designated forums. They should not avoid these discussions out of fear of offense or controversy.

Library workers may have limitations on workplace speech, including political advocacy.[5]

When libraries serve as polling places, state or local laws may temporarily limit political expression. These rules can apply to the public, poll workers, and library workers while the polling place is open.

Libraries should implement these guidelines in accordance with their institutional mission and state and local laws.

NOTES

1. "Diverse and Inclusive Collections: An Interpretation of the *Library Bill of Rights*," adopted July 14, 1982, by the ALA Council; amended January 10, 1990; July 2, 2008; July 1, 2014, under the previous name "Diversity in Collection Development"; and June 25, 2019, under the previous name "Diverse Collections"; and May 29, 2025.
2. "Meeting Rooms: An Interpretation of the *Library Bill of Rights*," adopted July 2, 1991, by the ALA Council; amended June 26, 2018; amended version rescinded August 16, 2018; amended January 29, 2019; and June 29, 2025.
3. "Guidelines for the Development of Policies and Procedures Regarding User Behavior and Library Usage," adopted January 24, 1993, by the ALA Intellectual Freedom Committee; amended November 17, 2000; January 19, 2005; March 29, 2014; August 16, 2019; and August 5, 2025.
4. "Exhibits, Displays, and Bulletin Boards: An Interpretation of the *Library Bill of Rights*," adopted July 2, 1991, by the ALA Council; amended June 30, 2004; and July 1, 2014, under the previous name "Exhibit Spaces and Bulletin Boards"; amended June 25, 2019, under the previous name "User-Initiated Exhibits, Displays, and Bulletin Boards"; and May 29, 2025.
5. "Speech in the Workplace Q&A," adopted by the Committee on Professional Ethics, July 2001; amended January 2004; June 26, 2006; January 24, 2007; July 1, 2014; April 30, 2019; and March 25, 2025.

Religion in American Libraries: An Interpretation of the *Library Bill of Rights*

Adopted June 28, 2016, by the ALA Council; amended June 29, 2025.

The First Amendment of the U.S. Constitution guarantees freedom of the press and speech. Courts have held that these rights are meaningful only if people also have the right to receive information—allowing them to read, view, hear, or access what they choose.

The First Amendment also protects religious freedom through two key clauses:

- The "free exercise" clause guarantees the right to believe and practice any religion or none at all.
- The "establishment" clause prohibits the government from creating or endorsing a religion.

These provisions ensure each person's freedom to practice any religion, to live according to their religious beliefs and customs, and to live without being forced to adopt or participate in any religious beliefs or activities.

Legal issues involving religion and libraries are usually not about the "free exercise" or "establishment" clauses. Instead, most cases involve freedom of expression—the right to share ideas—and the right to access the expression of others. For example, most challenges to materials with religious content do not restrict the challenger's beliefs or religious practices. Rather, they try to infringe on the rights of others to access constitutionally protected speech.

Library Collections

Library workers have a duty to build inclusive collections. Within budget limits, libraries should meet the information needs of all community members, including religious needs. Collections should include diverse religious materials without promoting any specific belief. They should offer both fiction and nonfiction materials in multiple formats.

Libraries should take care when selecting, shelving, and labeling religious fiction. This is especially important when labeling items with religious symbols. Article I of the *Library Bill of Rights* states, "Materials should not be excluded because of the origin, background, or views of those contributing to their creation." Excluding religious fiction would violate this principle. Libraries need to balance providing access to religious fiction without appearing to endorse a specific viewpoint.

Check out "The Law Regarding Rating Systems" (part II, chapter 7).

Religious content has the same legal protections as any other type of speech. While library workers should respect the diverse religious traditions of their communities, their primary role is to serve the information needs of all users.

Library policies should not treat the following differently from other topics:

- the shelving of religious materials;
- the storage or display of religious objects; or
- providing access to religious websites.

Favoring one religious tradition over others could violate the First Amendment's Establishment Clause. Libraries should follow their cataloging system to help users find religious materials. Giving special treatment to or limiting access to a specific sacred text or object may violate the *Library Bill of Rights*. This includes the categorization of religious documents, particularly of marginalized religions, into folklore or mythology sections.

Libraries can add religious materials to the collection to meet community needs. However, they should not remove or limit access based on religious affiliation or content. All religious materials should be treated fairly and respectfully.

Libraries may set aside shelving for scripture if they also have designated areas for other specialized materials such as:

- atlases;
- directories;
- college guides;
- dictionaries; or
- local history.

All scriptures should be treated equally, including texts that occupy a similar status among other groups (e.g., the Humanist Manifesto II).

Libraries should not remove or restrict access to resources based on an individual's objections based on personal religious belief. A library's review procedure and policies should ensure that one person's religious beliefs do not affect another person's access to library resources.[1]

Meeting Rooms

Libraries do not have to provide meeting room space to community groups. Courts have held that if libraries provide meeting room space for community use, they may not exclude religious groups solely because the group is religious or is hosting religious activities.[2]

Courts have also ruled that libraries are limited public forums for receiving information. This means libraries can designate areas for community use and create rules for how those spaces are used. Libraries should provide equal access and apply the same rules to everyone. These rules should be content neutral and only regulate time, place, and manner. Libraries must be consistent, ensuring all groups follow the same rules, such as:

- rental fees;
- use restrictions;
- conduct and safety policies; and
- food bans.[3]

Displays

Libraries do not have to open display or exhibit spaces to community groups. However, if they do, all groups must have equal access, regardless of their beliefs or affiliations.

The *Library Bill of Rights* states, "Materials should not be proscribed or removed because of partisan or doctrinal disapproval." Denying or restricting access to these spaces based on religious beliefs or content would violate this principle.

Religious groups should also have the same access to community literature distribution spaces as other groups. Library policies about literature distribution should cover:

- how many items can be distributed;
- size limits for materials; and
- how long items will be left out.

For more guidance, see "Exhibit Spaces and Bulletin Boards: An Interpretation of the *Library Bill of Rights*."

Policies about use of the library and its resources should be available to all library users.

Conclusion

Because religion is a sensitive and sometimes controversial topic for library users, it should receive the full protections guaranteed in the U.S. Constitution and the *Library Bill of Rights*.

For more information about staff and users' religious beliefs in libraries, see "Religion in American Libraries Q&A."[4]

NOTES

1. "Challenged Resources: An Interpretation of the *Library Bill of Rights*," adopted June 25, 1971 by the ALA Council; amended July 1, 1981; January 10, 1990; January 28, 2009; July 1, 2014; January 29, 2019; and May 29, 2025. https://www.ala.org/advocacy/intfreedom/librarybill/interpretations/challenged-resources
2. "Meeting Rooms: An Interpretation of the *Library Bill of Rights*," adopted July 2, 1991, by the ALA Council; amended June 26, 2018; amended version rescinded August 16, 2018; amended January 29, 2019; and June 29, 2025. https://www.ala.org/advocacy/intfreedom/librarybill/interpretations/meetingrooms

3. "Hateful Conduct in Libraries: Supporting Library Workers and Patrons," https://www.ala.org/advocacy/hatefulconduct
4. Intellectual Freedom Committee, "Religion in American Libraries: Questions and Answers," American Library Association, originally created 2010, revised 2020, https://www.ala.org/advocacy/intfreedom/religionqa

The Universal Right to Free Expression: An Interpretation of the *Library Bill of Rights*

Adopted January 16, 1991, by the ALA Council; amended on July 1, 2014; and May 29, 2025.

Freedom of expression is a basic human right and the foundation for self-government. It includes the right to free speech, press, religion, assembly, and association. It also means having the right to receive information without interference and to keep personal information private.

The American Library Association (ALA) endorses this principle. It is also in the Universal Declaration of Human Rights, adopted by the United Nations General Assembly.[1] The preamble states that:

> ... recognition of the inherent dignity and of the equal and inalienable rights of all members of the human family is the foundation of freedom, justice, and peace in the world ... [and] ... the advent of a world in which human beings shall enjoy freedom of speech and belief and freedom from fear and want has been proclaimed as the highest aspiration of the common people. ...

Article 12 of this document states:

> No one shall be subjected to arbitrary interference with his privacy, family, home or correspondence, nor to attacks upon his honor or reputation. Everyone has the right to the protection of the law against such interference or attacks.

Article 18 states:

> Everyone has the right to freedom of thought, conscience and religion; this right includes freedom to change his religion or belief, and freedom, either alone or in community with others and in public or private, to manifest his religion or belief in teaching, practice, worship and observance.

Article 19 states:

> Everyone has the right to freedom of opinion and expression; this right includes freedom to hold opinions without interference and to seek, receive and impart information and ideas through any media regardless of frontiers.

Article 20 states:

1. Everyone has the right to freedom of peaceful assembly and association.
2. No one may be compelled to belong to an association.

In 2013, the UN General Assembly reaffirmed that the right to privacy applies to digital communications and records. They require governments of member nations to "respect and protect" peoples' privacy rights.

The ALA believes that every person has these rights, no matter their origin, age, background, or views. The ALA shows its commitment to these principles in the *Library Bill of Rights* and *Code of Ethics*. These principles should be upheld by libraries and library workers worldwide. The ALA's "International Relations" policy reflects these objectives, "... to encourage the exchange, dissemination, and access to information and the unrestricted flow of library materials in all formats throughout the world."

Censorship, ignorance, and manipulation are the tools used by those in power. The ALA actively supports net neutrality, transparency, and accountability. Governments and companies that block, control, or monitor personal communications without consent or oversight is unfair and unjust. These same entities also collect large amounts of personal information without due process or transparency. This abuse of public trust threatens privacy and harms the right to free expression. Everyone benefits when people are treated with respect. This allows ideas and information to be freely shared, debated, and tested in the public sphere.

The ALA is deeply committed to human rights, especially the rights to privacy and free expression. These rights are essential to the practice of librarianship. The rights of privacy and free expression are not tied to politics, race, economics, or culture. These rights are inherent in every person. They cannot be taken away, reduced, or denied by governments or businesses. True justice and equality depend on protecting and using these rights every day.

Information and ideas have power. They can:

- inspire justice;
- restore freedom and dignity to the exploited and oppressed;
- change the hearts and minds of the oppressors; and
- offer opportunities for a better life to all people.

Throughout history, courageous people have defended the right to speak freely, even when faced with threats, slavery, captivity, torture, exile, and death. Their actions demonstrate that free expression is a basic human right and that it demands justice. Their bravery inspires ALA. Their deeds challenge library workers to stay committed to promoting and defending the rights of privacy and free expression.

There is no such thing as good censorship. Restricting free expression and the flow of information leads to discrimination and oppression. Using censorship to fight oppression only causes more harm. People can't truly be free without personal privacy. A society that does not respect personal privacy will fail to see when its rights and freedoms are taken away.

Threats to the privacy and freedom of expression of any person anywhere are threats to the privacy and freedom of all people everywhere. Violations of these human rights have been recorded in nearly every country and society around the world. Vigilance in protecting these rights is our best defense.

In response to these violations, the ALA:

- Opposes any government action that prevents people from exercising their rights. Everyone should be free to seek, receive, and share information and ideas without interference. Libraries and library workers must actively resist these abuses and support those affected by them.
- Condemns any government effort to use libraries and library workers to restrict people's rights. Libraries exist to help people seek, receive, and share information and ideas. Laws, contracts, or agreements that limit these rights go against the mission of libraries. They also violate the professional responsibilities of library workers.
- Rejects censorship in any form. Actions that deny basic human rights weaken the will to resist oppression. They also empower oppressors and undermine the cause of justice.

Censorship harms justice and destroys freedom. As such, the ALA will not stand down from these principles.

NOTE

1. United Nations General Assembly, "Universal Declaration of Human Rights," United Nations, December 10, 1948.

Resolution on Workplace Speech

Adopted June 26, 2005, by the ALA Council.

WHEREAS, The American Library Association is firmly committed to freedom of expression (Policy 53.1.12); and

WHEREAS, The library is an institution that welcomes and promotes the expression of all points of view; and

WHEREAS, Library staff are uniquely positioned to provide guidance on library policy issues that is informed by their experience and education; now, therefore, be it

RESOLVED, That ALA Council amends Policy 54 (Library Personnel Practices) by adding:

> 54.21 Workplace Speech
> Libraries should encourage discussion among library workers, including library administrators, of non-confidential professional and policy matters about the operation of the library and matters of public concern within the framework of applicable laws.

Note: A new numbering system for the ALA Policy Manual was developed after the adoption of this resolution. ALA Policy Manual, 54.21; "Workplace Speech" is now Policy Manual B.9.21.

Speech in the Workplace: An Explanatory Statement of the ALA *Code of Ethics*

Adopted July 2001 by the Committee on Professional Ethics,; amended January 2004, June 26, 2006, January 24, 2007, July 1, 2014; April 30, 2019; and March 25, 2025.[1]

This document is intended to provide general guidance for employees, administrators, governing authorities, and volunteers of libraries of all types regarding common questions about Speech in the Workplace, and is not intended as a comprehensive statement of requirements or legal advice. Legal counsel should be consulted for definitive guidance and for the approval of policy statements. All libraries should have board or administration-approved policies addressing speech in the workplace. It is the responsibility of all employees to be aware of and adhere to such policies. Employees should use professional judgment regarding speech in the workplace, including via social media platforms.

Through the *Library Bill of Rights* and its Interpretations, the American Library Association supports freedom of expression and the First Amendment in the strongest possible terms. However, the freedom of expression guaranteed by the First Amendment does not always apply to employee speech in the workplace. Since the relationship between employee and employer is a contractual one, employee speech is governed by the employment contract. It is the responsibility of the employer to have clear policies and procedures regarding expressions of viewpoints not necessarily in line with the employer, and it is the employee's responsibility to be familiar with these policies and procedures. Note that speech may include more than just verbal statements. Speech may also include but not be limited to buttons, t-shirt slogans, posters, stickers or trending symbols of political or social activism.

The speech environment in a library as a workplace may vary according to the organizational hierarchy and an employee's place in it, the organizational culture, and the personalities that make up that culture. It is your obligation to know the policies regarding what you are permitted to say professionally in that setting and to find out if there are restrictions on what you say in the workplace.

Related Case Law

As noted above, First Amendment protections for speech activities in the workplace are generally not available to employees of private companies or institutions. As one court explained, "the First Amendment free speech provision fails to establish public policy against terminations by private employers for speech-related activities because this provision applies only to government actions and expresses no public policy regarding terminations by private employers."[2] In *George v. Pacific-CSC Work Furlough*, the court noted that "the First Amendment protects individuals only against government, not private, infringements upon free speech rights."[3]

In *Pickering v. Board of Ed.*, the Supreme Court crafted a balancing test intended to protect the constitutional rights of an employee speaking as a citizen on matters of public concern while preserving the government employer's interest in ensuring that its employees do not undermine its operations or interfere with the accomplishment of its objectives.[4] In brief, if your speech addresses a matter of public concern, and does not interfere with your employer's ability to provide public services or does not impair discipline or harmony in the workplace, the courts may side with you. Note, however, that the courts often give great deference to an employer's conclusion that an employee's speech has been disruptive or damaging.

In *Garcetti v. Ceballos*, the Supreme Court held that public employees who make statements pursuant to their official duties are not speaking as citizens for First Amendment purposes and may be disciplined by their employer for that speech.[5]

Financial Assistance

While the ALA does not provide mediation, direct financial aid, or legal aid in response to workplace disputes, ALA does administer the LeRoy C. Merritt Humanitarian Fund, which provides financial assistance for librarians who have been discriminated against or denied employment rights because they defended intellectual freedom including freedom of speech.[6]

Some state library associations offer professional liability insurance for members that can help with reimbursement of legal fees related to termination. Check with your state association to see if this is available to you.

(See the "Enforcement of the *Code of Ethics* Q&A" in part I, chapter 2 for a history of past efforts related to mediation.)

More Information

Questions about speech in the workplace can be directed to the Committee on Professional Ethics c/o the ALA Office for Intellectual Freedom by phone at (312) 280-4221 or by email at oif@ala.org.

The National Whistleblower Center (NWC), a non-profit, tax-exempt, non-partisan organization, is the leading whistleblower legal advocacy organization with an almost 30-year history of protecting the right of individuals to report wrongdoing without fear of retaliation.[7]

Through the Whistleblower Protection Program, the Occupational Safety and Health Administration (OSHA) enforces the whistleblower provisions of more than twenty whistleblower statutes protecting employees who report violations.[8] Rights afforded by these whistleblower protection laws include, but are not limited to, worker participation in safety and health activities, reporting a work-related injury, illness, or fatality, or reporting a violation of the statutes herein.

The American Institute of CPAs provides tips for staying professional on social media.[9]

NOTES

1. Some of the citations in this statement have been moved into endnotes in this book.
2. *Grinzi v. San Diego Hospice Corp.*, 120 Cal. App. 4th 72, 79 (2004).
3. *George v. Pacific-CSC Work Furlough*, 91 F.3d 1227 (1996).
4. *Pickering v. Board of Ed.* 391 U.S. 563 (1968).
5. *Garcetti v. Ceballos*, 547 U.S. 410 (2006).
6. "LeRoy C. Merritt Humanitarian Fund," American Library Association, accessed July 25, 2025, ala.org/aboutala/affiliates/relatedgroups/merrittfund/merritthumanitarian.
7. National Whistleblower Center, Whistleblower, accessed July 25, 2025, whistleblowers.org.
8. U.S. Department of Labor, Whistleblower Protection Program, WhistleBlowers.gov, accessed July 25, 2025, whistleblowers.gov.
9. Association of International Certified Professional Accountants (AICPA & CIMA), AICPA & CIMA, accessed July 25, 2025, aicpa-cima.com.

CHAPTER 11
Privacy and Confidentiality

BIG IDEA BREAKDOWN

Key Concepts

- Privacy is essential for true intellectual freedom. It allows library users to choose, access, and use information without fear of embarrassment, judgment, punishment, surveillance, or rejection.
- Libraries should minimize the collection of personally identifiable information (PII) and store it securely and locally whenever possible.
- Library practices should not expose user information or make it publicly visible (for example, self-service hold shelves that display users' full names).
- Libraries should not share PII with third parties—including vendors, Friends of the Library groups, or law enforcement—unless the user gives permission or there is a valid court order or search warrant.
- Users should not be required to give their identity or personal details to vendors or publishers in order to access library resources.
- Vendor contracts and licenses should:
  - state that the library owns and controls user PII;
  - require vendors to follow all laws and the library's privacy policies; and
  - prohibit the sharing or selling of user data without the library's explicit permission.

What Does the Law Say?

- Courts have upheld the right to privacy based on the First and Fourth Amendments of the U.S. Constitution. Many court decisions have defined and expanded these rights. In addition, many states guarantee privacy through their constitutions and laws.

- All states and the District of Columbia have either laws or attorney general opinions that protect the confidentiality of library records, including the records of minors in many cases. Check your state law to see how it applies to your library.
- The rights of parents or guardians to access their minor children's public library records vary by state. Check your state law for guidance. In schools, parents' and guardians' access to their children's library records is governed by the Family Educational Rights and Privacy Act (FERPA).

Creating Policy for Your Library

- Adopt the *Library Bill of Rights, Libraries: An American Value,* and the *Code of Ethics of the American Library Association* (part I, chapter 2) as policy for your library. They contain statements about protecting library users' privacy and confidentiality.
- Have a written privacy policy that outlines the way your library:
  - limits the collection of personally identifiable information;
  - deletes personal information when no longer needed;
  - avoids placing personal information on public view; and
  - responds to third-party requests for user information (part I, chapter 3).
- Depending on state law, it may not be illegal to reveal that someone is in the library. However, libraries may choose to adopt a policy against doing so. Library workers often don't know if a user is experiencing domestic violence, harassment, or a custody dispute.
- Photography and recording in the library can threaten user privacy and discourage people from using the library. Because libraries are limited public forums, they may set rules that restrict photography and recording. For example, a policy might allow photos or videos of the library building and collections, but not of library users.

For Academic Libraries

- Faculty members may mistakenly assume that their right to monitor student coursework includes the right to monitor their use of library resources and services. Library workers should educate faculty about students' privacy rights.
  - It's helpful to educate colleagues in the campus Information Technology (IT) department about librarians' ethical obligation to promote access and protect privacy. The IT community often operates under a different set of professional values that may lean more toward the protection of campus digital resources.

- Special collections libraries often keep circulation records long-term to deter theft. Such records should be secured and only consulted when needed to trace a missing item. Special collections librarians who know their users' research interests well should keep this information confidential unless the user gives explicit permission to share it with others working on a similar topic.
- Academic libraries should treat data about students' use of online learning objects and tutorials with the same care as other library user information.
- Refer to "Intellectual Freedom Principles for Academic Libraries" (part II, chapter 4).

For School Libraries

- To help protect student privacy, libraries should have a privacy policy that clearly states who may access minors' library records and under what conditions.
- Teachers may want to know what their students are reading or what resources they're using, but it is never appropriate for library workers to share this information. Teachers should ask students directly.
- Refer to "Library Privacy Guidelines for Students in K–12 Schools," ala .org/advocacy/privacy/guidelines/students.

For Public Libraries

- Create policies for public access computers, including:
  - allowing users to log in to computers without showing any identification;
  - deleting log-in records by the end of the day;
  - clearing all data from a previous session; and
  - providing privacy screens.
- Have a method for users to register for library programming without being required to give their name or other PII.

To Learn More

- "Privacy," ala.org/advocacy/privacy: including "Privacy and Confidentiality Q&A" and "Privacy Field Guides."
- "Library Privacy Guidelines," ala.org/advocacy/privacy/guidelines, and "Library Privacy Checklists," ala.org/advocacy/privacy/checklists.
- "Visits and Requests from Law Enforcement" (part II, chapter 12).
- "The Universal Right to Free Expression: An Interpretation of the *Library Bill of Rights*" (part II, chapter 10).

- "Libraries and Immigration Enforcement," ala.org/advocacy/privacy/lawenforcement/guidelines#immigration.
- "State Privacy Laws Regarding Library Records," ala.org/advocacy/privacy/statelaws.

Reflection Questions

- Your library wants to offer self-service holds. What's the best procedure for labeling user holds without compromising the users' identity?
- A user asks to see what their thirteen-year-old daughter has checked out. One of the books is about alcoholic parents. What do you do? What if it was a book about witchcraft?
- Your meeting rooms have a schedule that's posted on the door. What information should you post on the schedule? How long do you keep the reservation information, and why?
- A vendor requires users to give their email address to access a resource provided by the library. How would you address this with the vendor?
- A teacher has asked the school librarian to give a list of all students with overdue items, listing their name and the item checked out. What would you do?
- Your library wants to use a new product that uses behavioral data surveillance to assign users to various categories for marketing purposes. How do you proceed?

OFFICIAL ALA POLICY STATEMENT

Privacy: An Interpretation of the *Library Bill of Rights*

Adopted June 19, 2002, by the ALA Council; amended July 1, 2014; June 24, 2019; and June 29, 2025.

Everyone has the right to privacy and confidentiality in their library use, no matter their origin, age, background, or views.[1] When users recognize or fear that their privacy is at risk, they lose the freedom to explore ideas.

Privacy is essential for free speech, free thought, and free association. Courts recognize the First Amendment right to access information in publicly funded libraries.[2] Courts have also upheld privacy rights under the U.S. Constitution. Many states guarantee privacy in their constitutions and laws.[3] Many court decisions have defined and extended these rights to all.[4]

The right to privacy means being able to seek information in person or online without fear of judgment. Confidentiality is when a library has users' personally identifiable information (PII) and keeps it private.[5] Article III of the American Library Association's (ALA) *Code of Ethics* states that confidentiality covers "information sought or received and resources consulted, borrowed, acquired or transmitted." This includes, but is not limited to:

- reference questions and interviews;
- circulation records;
- digital interactions; and
- records about using library resources, services, programs, or facilities.

Protecting user privacy and confidentiality has long been central to libraries. ALA has recognized the right to privacy since 1939.[6] Current ALA policies affirm that confidentiality is essential for free inquiry. Article VII of the *Library Bill of Rights* clearly states users have rights to privacy and confidentiality.

Rights of Library Users

A lack of privacy and confidentiality has a chilling effect on users' selecting, accessing, and using library resources. Everyone has the right to use the library without unjust surveillance or intrusion. Minors have the same rights to privacy as adults. Library users expect their data to be protected and kept private. In many states, they have legal rights to this protection.

Unless required by law (such as the Family Educational Rights and Privacy Act), libraries should never have policies or practices that limit users' right to privacy based on:

- age;
- ability;
- housing status;
- immigration status;
- involvement with the criminal justice system;
- religion;
- ethnicity;
- sexual orientation;
- gender identity; or
- other forms of identity or status.

If required by law, libraries should consult with legal counsel before limiting privacy rights.

Libraries have a duty to inform users about how their PII and library-use data are collected, secured, and retained. Users should always have the choice to opt in to any nonessential data collection. They should also be able to opt out again at any time. All nonessential data collection should be turned off by default.

Libraries should give users control over as many privacy choices as possible. Privacy options should be clearly displayed, easy to find, and understandable for all.

Library Responsibilities

Libraries have long had an ethical commitment to providing access to information without monitoring its use. They do this by following privacy laws and maintaining clear, updated, and publicly available privacy policies. These policies should state:

- what data is being collected;
- who it is shared with; and
- how long it is kept.

Everyone in the library, including volunteers, has a duty to respect and protect the privacy of users. Libraries should provide ongoing privacy training to library workers, governing bodies, and their users.

The National Information Standards Organization (NISO) Consensus Principles on Users' Digital Privacy in Library, Publisher, and Software-Provider Systems recognizes that:

> [t]he effective management and delivery of library services may require the library user to opt into the provision of personal data in order to access a library resource or receive library services. Users' personal data should only be used for purposes disclosed to them and to which they consent.[7]

Data Protection

Libraries should clearly define any collection of a person's library use. Such data must be:

- transparently disclosed to users;
- retained for the minimum amount of time necessary; and
- anonymized when possible.

Any data collected for analysis should be anonymous or aggregated, it should never be linked to personal information. Biometric technologies, like facial recognition, do not align with the library's mission of facilitating access without unjust surveillance.

No matter what technology is used, anyone who collects or accesses PII, in any format, has a legal and ethical duty to keep it confidential. Library security practices to safeguard personal information should be current and comply with state, local, and national standards. The NISO Consensus Principles on Users' Digital Privacy in Library, Publisher, and Software-Provider Systems requires these practices include:

- encrypting personal data both at rest and in transit;
- promptly updating systems and software to fix vulnerabilities;
- establishing systems, procedures, and policies for controlling access to sensitive data;

- providing security training for those with data access;
- maintaining written procedures for breach reporting and incident response; and
- setting clear policies for system, software, and network security configuration and auditing.[8]

Libraries should follow the principles of purpose limitation, storage limitation, and data minimization when collecting and retaining library-use data.[9] They should only collect and store the PII required for specific, clearly disclosed purposes.

Libraries should regularly review their data collection and retention policies to identify when collecting user data is no longer necessary. When developing data management policies, libraries must follow state, institutional, and other government retention requirements. To meet industry privacy and security standards, libraries should routinely update their procedures for collecting and maintaining user data.

Library Vendors

Libraries should never share users' PII with third parties or vendors unless:

1. they have explicit user permission; or
2. they are required by law or an existing contract.

Libraries or their governing institutions should ensure vendor agreements retain library ownership of user data. These agreements should allow audits of how vendors collect, retain, and access data. They should also state that user data is confidential and cannot be used or shared without the library's permission. Vendors handling user data should have a publicly available privacy policy that follows the NISO Consensus Principles. As contracts near expiration, libraries should negotiate future contracts to include these privacy safeguards.

Law Enforcement

Records should only be shared in response to properly executed court orders or legal processes. Law enforcement may request library records and data they believe are relevant to an investigation. Libraries should have clear procedures for handling these requests. Staff should be regularly trained on following these procedures.

Conclusion

ALA affirms that privacy rights are essential for intellectual freedom and a core value of librarianship. Rapid advances in technology increase the risk of exposing users' PII and library use data. The use of new technologies in libraries may conflict with the *Library Bill of Rights* and library workers' ethics when they rely on:

- collecting;
- using;
- sharing;
- monitoring; and
- tracking user data.

Libraries should prioritize privacy when designing and delivering programs and services. They should carefully review their own policies and procedures and those of their vendors. Privacy is the foundation of libraries and the reason they remain trusted parts of every community.

NOTES

1. Article VII, *Library Bill of Rights,* adopted June 19, 1939, by the ALA Council; amended October 14, 1944; June 18, 1948; February 2, 1961; June 27, 1967; January 23, 1980; and January 29, 2019; inclusion of "age" reaffirmed January 23, 1996.
2. Court opinions establishing a right to receive information in a public library include *Bd. of Educ. v. Pico,* 457 U.S. 853 (1982); *Kreimer v. Bureau of Police for the Town of Morristown,* 958 F.2d 1242 (3d Cir. 1992); and *Reno v. Am. Civil Liberties Union,* 117 S.Ct. 2329, 138 L.Ed.2d 874 (1997).
3. Ten state constitutions guarantee a right to privacy or bar unreasonable intrusions into citizens' privacy. Forty-eight states protect the confidentiality of library users' records by law, and the attorneys general in the remaining two states have issued opinions recognizing the privacy of users' library records.
4. Cases recognizing a right to privacy include: *NAACP v. Alabama,* 357 U.S. 449 (1958); *Griswold v. Connecticut,* 381 U.S. 479 (1965); *Lamont v. Postmaster Gen.,* 381 U.S. 301 (1965); *Katz v. United States,* 389 U.S. 347 (1967); and *Stanley v. Georgia,* 394 U.S. 557 (1969).
5. The phrase "personally identifiable information" was adopted by the ALA in 1991.
6. Article XI of the *Code of Ethics for Librarians* (1939) asserted that "it is the librarian's obligation to treat as confidential any private information obtained through contact with library patrons." Article III of the current *Code of Ethics of the American Library Association* (2021) states: "We protect each library user's right to privacy and confidentiality with respect to information sought or received and resources consulted, borrowed, acquired or transmitted."
7. National Information Standards Organization, "NISO Consensus Principles on Users' Digital Privacy in Library, Publisher, and Software-Provider Systems," Baltimore, MD, December 10, 2015.
8. *Ibid.*
9. These principles, drawn from the European Union's "General Data Protection Regulation" (GDPR; 2016) and reflected in other fair privacy practice principles such as the "NISO Consensus Principles" (see note 7) and "Guidelines

on the Protection of Privacy and Transborder Flows of Personal Data" (Paris: Organisation for Economic Co-operation and Development, 2013), provide sound guidelines for libraries to follow in their data-privacy practices. Libraries in the United States are generally not subject to the GDPR, but should consult with legal counsel to determine whether the GDPR applies.

PERSONAL STORY

Student Privacy Rights: FERPA and SSO

ADAM CHANDLER

Staff in our electronic resources unit received a troubleshooting request from a student who was trying to access a database for a course. For some reason, the student was unable to log in, but other users could. The vendor of the product requires the user to log in through the campus single sign-on (SSO), whether they are on campus or off, and unlike most other library resources, this product was configured in the campus identity management server to release personal data and the student name and email because that is what the vendor insisted on during licensing negotiations. Our library had agreed to that provision because it was the only way to acquire this faculty-requested product. After some back and forth between the vendor and the student, we realized that the cause of the log-in problem was the student's decision to exercise their right to restrict access to their profile information in the campus directory. The university calls this "FERPA (Family Educational Rights and Privacy Act) suppression."[1] By law, universities must provide a mechanism for students to control (to a large extent) how much of their profile information in the campus directory is shared with third parties.

What happened next is indicative of a certain class of library content vendors. Even when notified of the problem that our student was having, and after campus identity management staff offered to rig it so a fake name was sent to the vendor, the vendor representative still insisted that the student's real name be included in the session. After library staff notified the student of the situation, the student did the most expeditious thing available because they needed access in order to complete their assignment. The student toggled off FERPA suppression and allowed their personal information to be shared. This meant their information could be shared with all the other third parties doing business with the university. Library colleagues contacted the vendor and informed them that their practices violated a federal regulation. It seems the vendor lawyers didn't want to take that risk, so they changed their product log-in system so that students who activate FERPA suppression could log in to their product.

FERPA, enacted back in 1974 when print was the norm, is deeply flawed in today's networked environment.[2] For example, FERPA contains language that defines directory information as data that would "generally not be considered harmful or an invasion of privacy if disclosed," and then goes on to include as directory information "student's name; address; telephone listing; electronic mail address; photograph; date and place of birth," and more. Despite the limitations of FERPA, this regulation does provide some protection for proactive students.

It is in the interests of library workers to encourage the use of FERPA suppression. As we discovered in this case, FERPA can provide the library with additional leverage in negotiations with library vendors on matters of student privacy. Some takeaways for academic librarians:

1. Understand how FERPA is connected to federated log-in systems.
2. Develop a working relationship with your campus identity management staff.
3. Educate students about their right to minimize access to their personal information by exercising their right to use FERPA suppression.
4. Advocate for legal protections that match the needs of today's students.

NOTES

1. Family Educational Rights and Privacy Act, 34 C.F.R. § 99 (1974).
2. Sarah Hartman-Caverly, "The Failure of FERPA," Inside Higher Ed, October 26, 2023, insidehighered.com/opinion/views/2023/10/26/harvard-doxing-truck-shows-ferpas-obsolescence-opinion.

OFFICIAL ALA POLICY STATEMENTS

Resolution on the Retention of Library Usage Records

Adopted June 28, 2006, by the ALA Council.

WHEREAS, "PROTECTING USER privacy and confidentiality is necessary for intellectual freedom and fundamental to the ethics and practice of librarianship" (ALA Policy Manual, 53.1.16; "Privacy: An Interpretation of the *Library Bill of Rights*"); and

WHEREAS, Library usage records containing personally identifiable information (PII) are maintained for the sole purpose of effectively managing library resources; and

WHEREAS, The confidentiality of library usage records is protected by law in all fifty states and in the District of Columbia; and

WHEREAS, "The government's interest in library use represents a dangerous and fallacious equation of what a person reads with what that person believes or how that person is likely to behave" (ALA Policy Manual, 52.4.2; "Confidentiality of Personally Identifiable Information About Library Users"); and

WHEREAS, The American Library Association strongly recommends the adoption of policies recognizing "circulation records and other records identifying the names of library users to be confidential" (ALA Policy Manual, 52.4;

"Confidentiality of Library Records"); now, therefore, be it

RESOLVED, That the American Library Association urges all libraries to:

- Limit the degree to which personally identifiable information is collected, monitored, disclosed, and distributed; and
- Avoid creating unnecessary records; and
- Limit access to personally identifiable information to staff performing authorized functions; and
- Dispose of library usage records containing personally identifiable information unless they are needed for the efficient and lawful operation of the library, including, but not limited to data-related logs, digital records, vendor-collected data, and system backups; and
- Ensure that the library work with its organization's information technology unit to ensure that library usage records processed or held by the IT unit are treated in accordance with library records policies; and
- Ensure that those records that must be retained are secure; and
- Avoid library practices and procedures that place personally identifiable information on public view; and
- Assure that vendor agreements guarantee library control of all data and records; and
- Conduct an annual privacy audit to ensure that information-processing procedures meet privacy requirements by examining how information about library users and employees is collected, stored, shared, used, and destroyed; and, be it further

RESOLVED, That the American Library Association urges all libraries to adopt or update a privacy policy protecting users' personally identifiable information, communicating to library users how their information is used, and explaining the limited circumstances under which personally identifiable information could be disclosed; and, be it further

RESOLVED, That the American Library Association urges members of the library community to advocate that records retention laws and regulations limit retention of library usage records containing personally identifiable information to the time needed for efficient operation of the library.

Note: A new numbering system for the ALA Policy Manual was developed after the adoption of this resolution.

- ***ALA Policy Manual*, 53.1.16; "Privacy: An Interpretation of the *Library Bill of Rights*" is now Policy Manual B.2.1.17.**
- ***ALA Policy Manual*, 52.4.2; "Confidentiality of Personally Identifiable Information About Library Users" is now Policy Manual B.8.5.2.**
- ***ALA Policy Manual*, 52.4; "Confidentiality of Library Records" is now Policy Manual B.8.5.**

Resolution to Protect Library User Confidentiality in Self-Serve Hold Practices

Adopted June 28, 2011, by the ALA Council.

WHEREAS, the ALA *Code of Ethics* states, "We protect each library user's right to privacy and confidentiality with respect to information sought or received and resources consulted, borrowed, acquired or transmitted"; and

WHEREAS, the American Library Association affirms that rights of privacy are necessary for intellectual freedom and are fundamental to the ethics and practice of librarianship (ALA Policy Manual, 53.1.16, Privacy: An Interpretation of the *Library Bill of Rights*); and

WHEREAS, the lack of privacy and confidentiality has a chilling effect on users' choices (ALA Policy Manual, 53.1.16, Privacy: An Interpretation of the *Library Bill of Rights*); and

WHEREAS, the American Library Association strongly recommends the adoption of policies recognizing circulation records and other records identifying the names of library users to be confidential (ALA Policy Manual, 52.4, Confidentiality of Library Records); and

WHEREAS, confidentiality extends to (but is not limited to) database search records, reference interviews, circulation records, interlibrary loan records and all other records of personally identifiable uses of library materials, facilities, or services that associate the names of library users with specific materials (ALA Policy Manual, 52.4.2, Confidentiality of Personally Identifiable Information About Library Users); and

WHEREAS, the confidentiality of library records is protected by law or by attorney general opinion in all fifty states and in the District of Columbia; and

WHEREAS, U.S. courts have upheld the right to privacy based on the Bill of Rights of the U.S. Constitution;[1] and

WHEREAS, U.S. courts protect privacy when there is a reasonable expectation of privacy; and

WHEREAS, U.S. courts have ruled that when an individual's personal data is shared with a third party or the public, the individual no longer has an expectation of privacy in that data; and

WHEREAS, keeping a library user's personally identifiable information and circulation record absolutely confidential is essential for preserving the library user's expectation of privacy in his or her reading history; and

WHEREAS, many libraries across the country are instituting self-service hold systems that fail to adequately protect library users' confidentiality because the self-service hold systems reveal personally identifiable information linking specific users to specific items; and

WHEREAS, some methods of truncating user names or other personally identifiable information do not adequately protect library users' privacy, nor preserve the legal expectation of privacy, and may violate a state's library confidentiality law; and

WHEREAS, there are effective solutions that conceal a library user's identity while permitting the library to continue its use of open-shelf, self-service holds, such as the use of pseudonyms, codes, numbers, or other means that mask personally identifiable information; and the use of methods that obscure the identity of library user requests and the items requested through the practice of packaging the items inside an envelope or a reusable bag to hold the item, or wrapping them in a full sheet of paper, or an equivalent option. Now, therefore, be it

RESOLVED, that the American Library Association

1. Urges all libraries that implement self-service holds to protect patron identity by adopting practices and procedures that conceal the library user's personally identifiable information in connection with the materials being borrowed;
2. Urges libraries, librarians, and the responsible bodies of ALA to work with vendors to incorporate applications into integrated library systems that enable libraries to conceal a library user's identity in a cost-effective manner.

Note: A new numbering system for the ALA Policy Manual was developed after the adoption of this resolution.

- ***ALA Policy Manual* 53.1.16, "Privacy: An Interpretation of the *Library Bill of Rights*" is now Policy Manual B.2.1.17.**
- ***ALA Policy Manual*, 52.4, "Confidentiality of Library Records" is now Policy Manual B.8.5.**
- ***ALA Policy Manual*, 52.4.2, "Confidentiality of Personally Identifiable Information About Library Users" is now Policy Manual B.8.5.2.**

NOTE

1. U.S. Constitution, 4th, 5th, and 9th Amendments and case law, including *NAACP v. Alabama*, 357 U.S. 449 (1958); *Griswold v. Connecticut* 381 U.S. 479 (1965); *Katz v. United States*, 389 U.S. 347 (1967); and *Stanley v. Georgia*, 394 U.S. 557 (1969).

Resolution on the Misuse of Behavioral Data Surveillance in Libraries

Adopted January 26, 2021, by the ALA Council.

Whereas the *Library Bill of Rights* states, "All people, regardless of origin, age, background, or views, possess a right to privacy and confidentiality in their library use. Libraries should advocate for, educate about, and protect people's privacy, safeguarding all library use data, including personally identifiable information";

Whereas the American Library Association's (ALA) "Privacy: An Interpretation of the *Library Bill of Rights*" states, "All users have a right to be free from any unreasonable intrusion into or surveillance of their lawful library use";

Whereas the ALA's "Privacy: An Interpretation of the *Library Bill of Rights*" states, "Libraries should not monitor, track, or profile an individual's library use beyond operational needs. Data collected for analytical use should be limited to anonymous or aggregated data and not tied to individuals' personal data";

Whereas ALA Policy Manual B1.2 ("Code of Professional Ethics for Librarians") states, "We do not advance private interests at the expense of library users, colleagues, or our employing institutions";

Whereas ALA has long affirmed that the protection of library users' privacy and confidentiality rights is necessary for intellectual freedom and is fundamental to the ethical practice of librarianship;

Whereas behavioral data surveillance is defined as the collection of data about an individual's engagement with the library that, alone or with other data, can identify the user, for purposes of monitoring, tracking, or profiling an individual's library use beyond operational needs;

Whereas some vendor products require behavioral data surveillance as a condition of use;

Whereas libraries face financial pressure to monetize user data to secure discounts from vendors;

Whereas inequities exist within libraries that may limit those with less scale, money, or power to resist the monetization of user data;

Whereas behavioral data surveillance disproportionately impacts minority and marginalized populations who may be identified or misidentified when utilizing these technologies;

Whereas it is now technologically feasible to use behavioral data surveillance as a mechanism to deny access to library resources; now, therefore, be it

Resolved, that the American Library Association, on behalf of its members

1. stands firmly against behavioral data surveillance of library use and users;
2. urges libraries and vendors to never exchange user data for financial discounts, payments, or incentives;
3. calls on libraries and vendors to apply the strictest privacy settings by default, without any manual input from the end-user;
4. urges libraries, vendors, and institutions to not implement behavioral data surveillance or use that data to deny services;
5. calls on libraries to employ contract language that does not allow for vendors to implement behavioral data surveillance or use that data to deny access to services;
6. calls on libraries to oversee vendor compliance with contractual obligations;
7. calls on library workers to advocate for and educate themselves about library users' privacy and confidentiality rights; and

8. strongly urges libraries to act as information fiduciaries,[1] assuring that in every circumstance the library user's information is protected from misuse and unauthorized disclosure, and ensuring that the library itself does not misuse or exploit the library user's information.

NOTE

1. Martin Garnar and Trina Magi, eds., *Intellectual Freedom Manual, 10th ed.* (Chicago: ALA Editions, 2021), 217.

A DEEPER LOOK

The Law Regarding Privacy and Confidentiality in Libraries

SARAH LAMDAN

There is no single, unitary privacy law in the United States. Instead, U.S. privacy law is piecemeal, made up of hundreds of laws, regulations, court decisions, and constitutional provisions. These rules and legal precedents protect various types of information, including:

- health information;
- financial information;
- school records;
- employment records; and
- business and consumer data.

They also put privacy safeguards on government searches, seizures, and electronic surveillance.[1]

These privacy laws shape how libraries protect users' rights—ensuring that people can read, explore ideas, and form beliefs without surveillance and interference.

Intellectual Freedom and Privacy in the Library

Privacy is essential to the right to read. People cannot freely and securely seek information if their reading, research, and online activities are being monitored or shared with others, including the government, data brokers, or the public. They also cannot explore ideas, weigh arguments, and decide what they believe if they fear criticism, retaliation, or punishment. The fear of surveillance can stifle expression and lead to self-censorship.

Library workers have a long history of protecting library users' privacy. Article VII of the *Library Bill of Rights* states that "all people, regardless of origin, age, background, or views, possess a right to privacy and confidentiality in their library use." Article III of the ALA *Code of Ethics* reinforces this by stating that library workers should protect the confidentiality of "information sought or received and resources consulted, borrowed, acquired, or transmitted."

Libraries apply these privacy protections to:

- reference questions and interviews;
- circulation records;
- digital transactions and queries; and
- records that reflect the use of library resources, services, programs, or facilities.

The Constitution and the Right to Privacy

The U.S. Constitution and the Bill of Rights define people's individual rights. Neither one explicitly guarantees a right to privacy. However, the Supreme Court has held that a right to privacy is implicit in the Bill of Rights, including in the First and Fourth Amendments.

The Supreme Court has held that the First Amendment protects the private exploration and discussion of public issues.[2] The court called such anonymity "a shield from the tyranny of the majority" meant to protect unpopular ideas from suppression.[3]

The Supreme Court has also protected the privacy of people's reading choices.[4] In 1953, the court struck down a contempt conviction after a witness refused to share the names of people who bought political books in bulk.[5] The court also blocked a statute that required the post office to hold "communist political propaganda" mailers until the intended recipients identified themselves.[6] The court found that the statute violated the First Amendment in part because a lack of privacy deters people from seeking information.[7]

Courts have even found that a reader's First Amendment right to receive and explore information privately can outweigh a grand jury's subpoena power.

In one case, a federal court applied a heightened standard of scrutiny to a grand jury's request for records of Monica Lewinsky's purchases from a Washington, D.C. bookstore. The grand jury believed the records would support allegations of an affair with President Bill Clinton.[8] However, the court said that the government failed to show a compelling need for the materials. It also found there was not a strong enough connection between the information and the investigation to justify invading Monica Lewinsky's privacy.[9]

A Colorado court applied a similar legal standard when prosecutors sought a bookstore invoice to support allegations about a suspected illegal drug manufacturer. The court ultimately decided to protect the suspect's book purchase receipts.[10]

Likewise, when a grand jury subpoenaed records from an Amazon bookseller, a court reinforced the idea that "living in the land of the free means that it's none of the government's business what books people are reading."[11]

Courts have interpreted the Fourth Amendment as granting similar privacy rights against government intrusion. That amendment protects people from unreasonable searches and seizures and limits the government's ability to access a person's private records and data.

Before searching or seizing private information, government actors (including law enforcement and national security agents) must get a warrant. To obtain one, they must show "probable cause" in a court. This means proving a reasonable belief that a crime is about to happen or that the search will uncover evidence of a crime.

The Fourth Amendment protects a person's privacy when that person has a reasonable expectation of privacy in the information the government seeks.[12]

Laws Protecting the Privacy of Library Users' Records

Forty-eight states and the District of Columbia have laws that protect the confidentiality of library records.[13] Kentucky and Hawaii do not have such laws. Instead, their attorneys general have issued binding opinions declaring that library records must be confidential.[14]

Library privacy laws vary from state to state. At a minimum, they protect a person's library circulation records from being shared under the state's open records law.[15]

Many states go further by limiting when libraries can release records to third parties or law enforcement. In most cases, law enforcement must get a valid court order before a library can be compelled to share user records.

A few states make it a crime to share library records in violation of that state's library privacy laws.

Three states—California, Missouri, and Arizona—include specific privacy protections for digital or online resources. These laws also require third-party vendors that manage, store, or send users' data to follow privacy rules.

A state's library privacy law may not apply to every library or every library user. It may exclude privately funded libraries, K–12 school libraries, or academic libraries. Some laws allow parents to access their minor children's library records. However, many states choose to protect all library users' records regardless of age. Many states also apply these privacy laws to all libraries, regardless of their funding, ownership, or type.

Even if a library is not subject to its state's privacy law, it can point to the state's law as evidence of the state's intent to protect library users' privacy.

Library privacy laws provide a legal basis for requiring law enforcement to show probable cause before obtaining a court order to access user records. They also provide grounds for requiring anyone with access to or control of library users' information to keep it private unless the user gives consent.

Library workers should be informed about their state's library privacy law and how to comply with it.

Law Enforcement and Third-Party Demands for Library Records

The confidentiality of library records is not an absolute privilege. Law enforcement, prosecutors, and third parties can compel libraries to produce records if the facts and circumstances of an investigation or lawsuit justify their disclosure.

To protect First Amendment rights, the law allows for judicial review of subpoenas, warrants, and other legal processes before a library must release user information.

A library can ask a court to quash a subpoena or withdraw a court order that demands a user's records. They can do this if they believe the order will chill a person's right to receive information.

The party seeking the information must show a compelling need for it and prove a substantial and legally sufficient connection between the requested information and the government's investigation.[16] If the government meets this standard, the court will uphold the order, and the library must provide the records as required. However, if the government or agency fails to provide sufficient evidence, the court will quash or set aside the subpoena or court order.

Libraries and bookstores have successfully challenged subpoenas and search warrants in state and federal courts. In one case, investigators looking into an abandoned infant issued a subpoena to a public library. The subpoena demanded the names, addresses, and phone numbers of people who had borrowed books on childbearing. A Texas court quashed the subpoena, calling the overbroad request a "fishing expedition."[17]

Federal Privacy Laws Impacting Library Users' Privacy and Confidentiality

Some federal laws protect certain types of information and records and prohibit certain information uses. However, there is no comprehensive federal privacy law, and no federal laws protect the privacy and confidentiality of library users' records and information. Some federal laws may affect a library user's privacy rights, however. Among these laws are the following:

- *The Video Privacy Protection Act (VPPA)*—Forbids sharing personally identifiable loan or rental records for "prerecorded video cassette tapes or similar audiovisual material."[18] Video rental records can only be shared with third parties if the borrower consents or if a court order requires disclosure. The VPPA also establishes rules for how long rental records can be kept and when they must be destroyed.
- *The Electronic Communications Privacy Act*—Regulates the disclosure of electronic communications.[19] The following major sections of the act may apply to libraries and other institutions that provide electronic communications services to users:

  - *The Wiretap Act*—Prohibits the intentional interception, use, or disclosure of wire and electronic communications unless a statutory exception applies.[20]
  - *The Stored Communications Act*—Prohibits the disclosure of stored communications and records held by communication service providers unless a statutory exception applies.[21]
  - *The Pen Register Act*—Limits the use of pen registers (devices that record routing and signal information from phones and computers) and trap-and-trace devices (devices that record incoming signals to a phone or computers).[22]

- *The Family Educational Rights and Privacy Act (FERPA)*—Governs how students' educational records and information are shared.[23] It requires educational institutions to adopt policies that allow parents or students to inspect and correct the student's educational records. It also prohibits the disclosure of a student's education records without written permission from the parent or student. Records that are directly related to a student and that are maintained by an educational agency or institution are considered "education records" according to FERPA.[24] Circulation and similar records kept by school or university libraries would likely be subject to FERPA according to the Department of Education's criteria. School and academic library workers should consult with their institution's legal counsel to understand their rights and responsibilities under FERPA.
- *The Children's Online Privacy Protection Act (COPPA)*—Limits how commercial websites and online services collect, use, or share personal information from children under thirteen.[25] COPPA applies to operators of websites or services directed at children. It also applies to general websites and services that knowingly collect, use, or share personal data from children under thirteen. Websites must get verifiable parental consent before collecting or using a child's personal information online. COPPA generally does not apply to noncommercial websites, such as:
  - public libraries;
  - nonprofits;
  - schools; and
  - universities.

- However, libraries may need to comply with the act if their websites include third-party apps, plug-ins, ads, or social media that collect personal information from children, or if children are visiting and using the website.

Perhaps one of the most concerning laws impacting library privacy was Section 215 of the USA PATRIOT Act, a surveillance law passed after 9/11. It allowed the Foreign Intelligence Surveillance Court (FISC) to issue classified, secret court orders in an effort to prevent and investigate international terrorism and clandestine intelligence activities.[26] These orders authorized the

II., Ch. 11 Privacy

Federal Bureau of Investigation (FBI) access to "any tangible thing," which includes physical and digital records. Section 215 expired on March 15, 2020.[27]

Section 702 of the Foreign Intelligence Surveillance Act (FISA) allows U.S. intelligence agencies to collect electronic communications from non-U.S. persons. This includes phone calls, texts, and emails.[28] The law only authorizes surveillance of foreigners outside of the United States. However, these searches usually include Americans' communications. These "backdoor searches" give the government access to private information without a warrant.[29]

State Laws Governing Data Privacy and Security

Without a comprehensive federal privacy law, states have adopted their own laws to address a range of privacy risks and harms.[30] California was the first state to pass its own comprehensive data privacy law.[31] The California Consumer Privacy Act (CCPA) gives Californians the right to:

- know what personal data is collected about them;
- know if their data is being sold or shared and with whom;
- refuse the sale of their personal data; and
- request that businesses delete their data.

Other states have passed laws that address data security, identity theft, data brokering, and the collection of certain types of data. For example, Illinois's Biometric Information Privacy Act (BIPA) requires private entities to get written consent before collecting, storing, or using biometric identifiers, such as fingerprints and facial scans. The law also bans sharing biometric data with third parties.[32] People whose data is collected without consent may sue for substantial damages.

Most states have student data privacy laws. These laws control how schools and their vendors collect, use, and share K–12 students' personal data.[33] California's Student Online Personal Information Protection Act (SOPIPA) is an example. It regulates websites, apps, and platforms that provide online educational services to California's K–12 students.[34] The act:

- prohibits targeting advertising to students;
- limits the sharing of student data;
- bans the sale of student data; and
- prevents operators from creating student profiles for commercial use.

A full review of state privacy and data security laws is beyond the scope of this essay. Library workers should consult with legal counsel or privacy experts to understand how their state's privacy laws apply to their libraries. Most data privacy laws govern the commercial use of personal data. However, some may control the library's collection, use, and storage of personal data. It is also helpful to know what data privacy rules and regulations apply to library vendors and their products.

International Data Privacy Law: The EU General Data Protection Regulation

The European Union's General Data Protection Regulation (GDPR) is a comprehensive law that governs how personal data is processed.[35]

The GDPR bans processing personal information without user consent, a contract, or other legal grounds. It requires organizations handling personal data to follow "privacy by design" and "privacy by default" standards to protect people's privacy rights. The GDPR also requires prompt reporting of data breaches. All EU residents have the right to data privacy, including the right to review, correct, and demand the deletion of their personal data.

One part of the GDPR has raised concerns for libraries and archives: the right to request that personal data be deleted, often called "the right to be forgotten." This rule allows individuals to require a data-processing entity, like Google, to de-index or remove their personal information from search results so it can no longer be found.[36] The right to be forgotten creates ethical conflicts between protecting individual privacy and the public's right to access information. Removing information can:

- limit research;
- hinder historical understanding; and
- conflict with libraries' mission to preserve historical records.

The European Commission has clarified that there is no absolute right to deletion under the GDPR. It also emphasized that this rule does not impact historical research or the freedom of the press.[37]

As with state privacy laws, a full examination of the GDPR's requirements is beyond the scope of this essay. Library workers should consult with legal counsel or privacy experts to understand how the GDPR may apply to their libraries.

The Future of Privacy and Confidentiality in Libraries

Privacy law in the United States falls into two categories. One set of laws limits government surveillance based on the Constitution and other civil rights laws. The other set regulates certain types of personal information, like health, finance, credit, and education, in select situations.

Outside of these two areas, U.S. law places few limits on how nongovernmental organizations collect and use personal data. Once a business or other third party obtains someone's personal information, the person has little or no means to control how it is used. These entities collect large amounts of personal data, often keeping it forever. They may use the data in ways the owner cannot predict. Unless fraud or misrepresentation is involved, the law offers few or no legal remedies for people harmed by the use of their data.

This gap in the law directly affects library users' privacy. More and more libraries are using digital content, networked services, and complex platforms and databases to serve their users. While these digital tools may enhance the library experience, they also create opportunities for governments, businesses, and individuals to track what people read and research.[38]

Vendors that provide digital content and services are a specific concern. Current laws give them a lot of freedom to collect and exploit data about a person's library use.[39] This is especially concerning because many vendors do not share library workers' ethical commitment to preserving user privacy. Also, they are often not required to follow state laws that keep library user data confidential.[40]

Library workers must also address the fact that most users do not have enough familiarity with library vendors or power to make informed choices about their privacy. They are not able to control how vendors, digital platforms, or even the library itself use their data.[41]

For example, few library users will stop to carefully evaluate the privacy policies of a vendor providing the library's integrated library system. They may also not be able to identify all the possible future harms that might result from their school's use of learning analytics tools. The same is true for a self-service hold system that displays their full name and other identifying data in public.

In an era of unregulated data use, library workers must go beyond the requirements of state library confidentiality laws. They must uphold the duties of trust and loyalty, like those of physicians and lawyers. They must follow the professional and ethical duties in Article VII of the *Library Bill of Rights* and Article III of the ALA *Code of Ethics*.

In brief, libraries and library workers must act as *information fiduciaries*. In every circumstance, libraries must protect a user's information from misuse and unauthorized disclosure. They must also ensure that the library itself does not misuse or exploit user information.[42]

Library Policy and Practice

To act in the best interests of users, libraries must make privacy a core part of their missions. They can do this by following the principles of "privacy by design," such as:

- being transparent about when library users' data will be collected and how it will be used;
- minimizing data collection and use; and
- empowering users to opt out of data collection and use.[43]

Libraries should also ensure they comply with privacy laws and professional standards.

Examples of Privacy Practices

Transparency

- Provide public statements that explain users' legal right to privacy and how the library protects their information.
- Disclose how the library and third-party vendors collect and use library users' data.

Data Minimization

- Avoid labeling self-service holds with users' names.[44]
- Limit the collection of user data to only what is necessary for the library's circulation services, and keep the data for only as long as necessary to ensure that materials are properly disseminated and collected.
- Avoid setting up digital library services in ways that require library users to create individual accounts and passwords. Substitute generic library log-in accounts when possible.

Empowerment

- Offer privacy education to help users understand how to protect their information.
- Provide tools and procedures that allow for anonymous use of the internet and electronic resources.

Complying with Laws and Standards

- Follow an "opt-in" approach to data collection instead of requiring users to opt out.
- Do not reuse library users' data beyond the purpose for which the library collected it. For instance, do not use circulation records for fundraising purposes or unsolicited emails unrelated to circulation.
- Evaluate all library services, platforms, and practices for privacy risks before adopting them.
- Conduct regular privacy audits to ensure that library practices align with privacy goals.[45]
- Include all applicable state library confidentiality laws in policies about privacy, access, and technology.

Third-Party Vendors

Libraries must actively protect users' rights to privacy when third-party vendors have access to user data. The library and its staff must take steps to keep this data secure from disclosure and misuse by vendors and their agents. A written contract provides the legal foundation for this protection.[46]

Negotiating written contracts with third-party content and service providers requires the library to review the vendor's privacy policies and data management practices before entering into agreements. The contract terms can then be changed to address gaps in the vendor's policies and procedures, striking an appropriate balance between the need to protect user privacy and the vendor's need to access user data to provide content and services.[47] Such terms should do the following:

- Acknowledge library users' right to privacy and the confidentiality of library users' data.
- Bar the further use, sharing, storage, or sale of library users' data for non-library purposes.
- Require the vendor to conform its policies to the library's privacy policy and professional standards like the ALA's "Library Privacy Guidelines" and the NISO Consensus Principles on Users' Digital Privacy in Library, Publisher, and Software-Provider Systems.[48]
- Require compliance with any or all data-protection laws regulating the vendor's activities, including the GDPR, CCPA, COPPA, and student-data privacy laws.
- Require that subcontractors follow the privacy and data security protection terms in contracts between the library and its vendors and require vendors to notify the library whenever a subcontractor, like a cloud services provider, is employed by the vendor to process or store user data.
- Require that vendors notify the library as soon as they learn of data or security breaches, a breach of the contract's terms, or whenever a government agency demands access to user information.
- Additionally, specify the information security controls the library requires, such as the encryption of stored and transmitted data.

A vendor's refusal to negotiate or to provide information about its data collection and data management practices may signal that the library should find a different vendor or alternative means of delivering the content or service.

Advocacy

Library workers act in the best interests of users by advocating for stronger privacy rights. This includes defending existing protections and pushing for new ones. Legal changes are needed because the United States lacks a comprehensive data protection law. Privacy protections should not rely only on library workers' professional values.

The most critical advocacy for libraries is promoting legislation that would amend or adopt library confidentiality laws. These changes could ensure that the law's requirements apply equally to any public or private entity that manages, stores, or uses library users' data and information.[49]

Updating these laws would require third-party vendors that handle users' data to share the same legal obligations as libraries. They would have to protect user records from unauthorized disclosure to law enforcement or other third parties. Updates could also regulate any future uses of library users' data that could harm users' privacy. Missouri and California have updated their laws to achieve these goals. Both laws provide a model for achieving this kind of legislative change.

Improving library confidentiality laws is not the only change needed to protect user privacy and freedom of thought and expression. Library workers should also advocate for comprehensive data protection laws that prevent the misuse of emerging technologies, such as artificial intelligence and algorithmic decision-making. These measures are essential to safeguarding library users' privacy and confidentiality. In the end, securing greater legal protections for civil liberties may be the best defense for library users' privacy.

NOTES

1. Neil M. Richards, Andrew B. Serwin, and Tyler Blake, "Understanding American Privacy," in *Research Handbook on Privacy and Data Protection Law: Values, Norms and Global Politics*, ed. Gloria González Fuster, Rosamunde van Brakel, and Paul De Hert (Cheltenham, UK: Edward Elgar, 2018).
2. In *McIntyre v. Ohio Elections Commission*, 514 U.S. 334 (1995) (holding that the First Amendment protects people's rights to hand out anonymous leaflets on political issues).
3. McIntyre at 357.
4. *Stanley v. Georgia*, 394 U.S. 557, 564 (1969) (upholding a First Amendment right to receive information and ideas free from "unwanted governmental intrusions into one's privacy").
5. *United States v. Rumely*, 345 U.S. 41 (1953). In his concurring opinion, Judge William O. Douglas wrote, "Fear of criticism goes with every person into the bookstall. ... Some will fear to read what is unpopular, what the powers-that-be dislike. When the light of publicity may reach any student, any teacher, inquiry will be discouraged." 345 U.S. 41, 57.
6. *Lamont v. Postmaster General*, 381 U.S. 301 (1965).
7. *Id.*
8. In re Grand Jury Subpoena to Kramerbooks & Afterwords, Inc., 26 Med. L. Rptr. 1599 (D.C. 1998).
9. *Id.*
10. *Tattered Cover, Inc. v. City of Thornton*, 44 P.3d 1044 (Colo. 2002). The court opined that "the First Amendment embraces the individual's right to purchase and read whatever books she wishes to, without fear that the government will take steps to discover which books she buys, reads, or intends to read."
11. In re Grand Jury Subpoena to Amazon.com, 246 F.R.D. 570 (W.D. Wis. 2007).
12. *Katz v. United States*, 389 U.S. 347 (1967).
13. The ALA maintains a web page listing all of these laws: "State Privacy Laws Regarding Library Records," ala.org/advocacy/privacy/statelaws.

14. Steven L. Beshear, Kentucky Attorney General Opinion 82-149 (March 12, 1982), ala.org/sites/default/files/advocacy/content/privacyconfidentiality/statelibraryprivacy/kentucky_OAG_Opinions.pdf; Hugh R. Jones, Hawaii Attorney General Opinion Letter 90-30 (October 23, 1990), oip.hawaii.gov/wp-content/uploads/1990/10/90-30.pdf.
15. A federal court in New York refused to compel the production of library users' records and data, holding that the state's library confidentiality statute barred the disclosure of library records under the New York Freedom of Information Act. *In the Matter of Quad/Graphics, Inc., v. S. Adirondack Library Sys.*, 174 Misc. 2nd 291 664 N.Y.S. 2d 225 (N.Y. Sup., 1997).
16. *In re Grand Jury Subpoena to Kramerbooks & Afterwords, Inc.*, 26 Media L. Rep. 1599, 1601 (D.D.C. 1998).
17. *Decatur Pub. Library v. Dist. Attorney of Wise Cty.*, No. 90-05-192, 271st Judicial Court (Texas, 1990) (slip opinion on file with the Office for Intellectual Freedom).
18. 18 U.S.C. § 2710 (2025).
19. 18 U.S.C. §§ 2510 et seq. (2025).
20. 18 U.S.C. §§ 2510–2522 (2025).
21. 18 U.S.C. §§ 2701–2712 (2025).
22. 18 U.S.C. §§ 3121–3126 (2025).
23. 20 U.S.C. § 1232g; 34 C.F.R. pt. 99 (2025).
24. 34 CFR § 99.2; Department of Education, "Protecting Student Privacy," https://studentprivacy.ed.gov/faq/what-education-record.
25. 5 U.S.C. §§ 6501–6506 (2025).
26. ALA spoke out against Section 215, which was referred to as the "library records provision." See American Library Association, "ALA Council Continues Opposition to Use of Section 215 of Patriot Act and Use of National Security Letters to Violate Reader Privacy," August 16, 2011, ala.org/news/press-releases/2011/08/ala-council-continues-opposition-use-section-215-patriot-act-and-use-national. Four Connecticut librarians successfully challenged a National Security Letter gag order, protecting the privacy of their patron data from the PATRIOT Act provision. Sanhita SinhaRoy, "Defenders of Patron Privacy," *American Libraries*, September 1, 2021, americanlibrariesmagazine.org/2021/09/01/defenders-of-patron-privacy/.
27. Electronic Frontier Foundation, "Yes, Section 215 Expired. Now What?" April 16, 2020, eff.org/deeplinks/2020/04/yes-section-215-expired-now-what.
28. 50 U.S. Code § 1881a (2025).
29. ALA coalition letter urging the House Judiciary Committee to close the "backdoor search loophole" in Section 702 of the FISA Amendments Act (November 6, 2017), ala.org/sites/default/files/advocacy/content/privacyconfidentiality/Coalition_Supports_Poe-Lofgren_-Shut_the_Backdoor-_Amdt_to_USA_Liberty.pdf.
30. The International Association of Privacy Professionals tracks state privacy legislation; see "U.S. State Privacy Legislation Tracker," iapp.org/resources/article/us-state-privacy-legislation-tracker/.
31. The California Consumer Privacy Act (CCPA) was passed in 2018. California Civil Code § 1798.100 et seq. (2025).
32. 740 ILCS § 14/1 et seq. (2025).
33. The Student Privacy Compass tracks state educational privacy laws; see studentprivacycompass.org/state-laws/.

34. Cal. Bus. & Prof. Code § 22584.
35. Regulation (EU) 2016/679 of the European Parliament and of the Council of 27 April 2016 on the protection of natural persons with regard to the processing of personal data and on the free movement of such data, and repealing Directive 95/46/EC (General Data Protection Regulation) (2016).
36. Case C-131/12, Google Spain SL v. Agencia Española de Protección de Datos (2014). The court's decision required Google Spain to de-index and take down search results identifying a newspaper article concerning an individual.
37. European Commission Press Release IP/14/60, Data Protection Day 2014: "Full Speed on EU Data Protection Reform" (January 27, 2014).
38. Michael Zimmer, "Patron Privacy in the '2.0' Era: Avoiding the Faustian Bargain of Library 2.0," *Journal of Information Ethics* 22, no. 1 (2013): 44–59.
39. B. J. Ard, "Confidentiality and the Problem of Third Parties: Protecting Reader Privacy in the Age of Intermediaries," *Yale Journal of Law & Technology* 16, no. 1 (2013): 12–18.
40. Trina J. Magi, "A Content Analysis of Library Vendor Privacy Policies: Do They Meet Our Standards?" *College & Research Libraries* 71, no. 3 (2010): 254–72; A. D. Lambert, M. Parker, and M. Bashir, "Library Patron Privacy in Jeopardy: An Analysis of the Privacy Policies of Digital Content Vendors," *Proceedings of the Association for Information Science & Technology* 52, no. 1 (2015): 1–9.
41. Fred H. Cate, "The Failure of Fair Information Practice Principles," chap. 15 in *Consumer Protection in the Age of the Information Economy*, ed. Jane K. Winn (London: Routledge, 2006).
42. Jack M. Balkin, "Information Fiduciaries and the First Amendment" (February 3, 2016), *UC Davis Law Review* 49, no. 4 (2016); posted as "Yale Law School Public Law Research Paper No. 553" (2016); Kyle M. L. Jones, Alan Rubel, and Ellen LeClere, "A Matter of Trust: Higher Education Institutions as Information Fiduciaries in an Age of Educational Data Mining and Learning Analytics," *Journal of the Association for Information Science and Technology* (2019), doi.org/10.1002/asi.24327.
43. Ann Cavoukian, "Privacy by Design in Law, Policy, and Practice," white paper, Office of the Information and Privacy Commissioner, Ontario, Canada, 2011, p. 28.
44. "Practices," adopted 2011 by the ALA Council, ala.org/advocacy/intfreedom/statementspols/ifresolutions/selfserveholds.
45. The ALA provides resources for conducting library privacy audits; see "Privacy Audits," ala.org/advocacy/privacy/audits.
46. William Marden, "Third Party Services in Libraries," in *Protecting Patron Privacy: A LITA Guide*, ed. Bobbie Newman and Bonnie Tijerina (Rowman and Littlefield, 2017), 64, 75–77.
47. Marden, "Third Party Services," 76.
48. "Library Privacy Guidelines," adopted 2016 by the ALA Intellectual Freedom Committee, ala.org/advocacy/privacy/guidelines; National Information Standards Organization, "NISO Consensus Principles on Users' Digital Privacy in Library, Publisher, and Software-Provider Systems," white paper, December 10, 2015.
49. Ard, "Confidentiality and the Problem of Third Parties," 46–51.

The Law Regarding First Amendment Auditors

SARAH LAMDAN

A First Amendment audit is when a person or group records their interactions with government officials or employees to test whether the government will respect their First Amendment right to film and record in public. The people recording will often ask provocative questions or behave in ways that are meant to provoke altercations. These confrontations typically follow a uniform process, in which the individual:

- *records* the encounter;
- *provokes* the employee to respond negatively;
- *posts* the video of the employee's reaction on social media; and then
- *claims* their First Amendment rights were violated and threatens or files a lawsuit.

The people undertaking these "audits" claim that they have a right to film in any place that is accessible to the public, including libraries. They argue that they are entitled to do so as taxpayers and "citizen journalists."

The Legal Limits of First Amendment Audits in Libraries

When deciding if the First Amendment applies to activities like filming, the law distinguishes traditional public forums from limited public forums. Traditional public forums, such as town squares, are open for a wide range of speech. These spaces can only be limited by viewpoint-neutral time, place, and manner restrictions. Limited public forums, including libraries, are only open to First Amendment activities that align with the forum's purpose. This is true even if the facility is open to the public.

Courts have found that a library is a limited public forum meant "for inquiry, study, learning," and "for "reading, writing, and quiet contemplation."[1] First Amendment protections in libraries apply only to activities that support receiving information and accessing library materials and programs.[2] Filming and recording in a library may be regulated using reasonable viewpoint-neutral, time, place, and manner rules that reflect the library's purpose and function.[3]

Best Practices for First Amendment Audits

Filming and recording can have a chilling effect on library use and pose potential threats to intellectual freedom and privacy. Given these concerns, libraries can regulate filming and recording with viewpoint-neutral policies and procedures that apply to all library visitors, including:

- Banning the filming or recording of library users.
- Establishing rules for media, including procedures that media must follow before filming or recording in the library. This is often done through a Media Relations Policy.

- Requiring advance approval from a library supervisor for anyone using cameras or recording equipment.
- Limiting photography and filming to places and collections that do not invade library users' privacy.
- Clearly identifying nonpublic spaces where third-party filming and recording are not permitted. These spaces may include:
  - washrooms;
  - reservable private study spaces;
  - staff offices;
  - break rooms; and
  - work areas.

If a First Amendment audit occurs at your library, follow these steps to uphold your policies and protect library privacy. Best practices include:

- Not engaging with auditors who follow library policies. Allowing auditors to film without incident prevents them from creating videos for their social media accounts.
- Contacting your immediate supervisor or director.
- Staying calm if an auditor approaches you. Do not touch the auditor, their camera, or their phone. Whenever possible, continue with your regular activities.
- Referring to the library's behavior and use policies if an auditor harasses staff or users. A First Amendment right to record does not give them a right to harass or interfere with public employees doing their jobs.
- Firmly and politely directing an auditor to stop if they try to enter a nonpublic area.

If you do not react to the auditor's provocations, they will likely leave. Keep in mind that nobody has a right to harass library visitors or library workers. You may enforce your behavioral policies to ensure people's safety and their right to read.

NOTES

1. *Tronsen v. Toledo-Lucas Cnty. Pub. Library,* No. 3:08CV148, 2008 WL 2622939, at *2 (N.D. Ohio June 30, 2008); *Hill v. Derrick,* No. 4:05-CV-1229, 2006 WL 1620226, at *6 (M.D. Pa. June 8, 2006).
2. *Kreimer v. Bureau of Police for Town of Morristown,* 958 F. 2d 1242 (3rd Cir. 1992).
3. *Sheets v. City of Punta Gorda,* 415 F. Supp. 3d 1115 (Dist. Ct. MD FL 2019); *Kushner v. Butha,* No. 18-2099 (8th Cir. 2019).

CHAPTER 12
Visits and Requests from Law Enforcement

BIG IDEA BREAKDOWN

Key Concepts

- Libraries should not share personally identifiable information (PII) about users with law enforcement unless the user gives permission or the library receives a subpoena, search warrant, or other court order.
- Most law enforcement officers understand that libraries have the right to consult legal counsel before responding to these requests.
- Libraries can cooperate with law enforcement by identifying relevant records or computers and preserving them until a court order is served.
- Libraries are not required to collect or keep information about users for law enforcement. However, if library workers believe a crime has been committed in the library, they should contact law enforcement and make reasonable efforts to preserve direct evidence. That evidence should be given to law enforcement in accordance with the law, which may require a court order before they can view or copy library records.

What Does the Law Say?

- All states and the District of Columbia have either laws or attorney general opinions that protect the confidentiality of library records, including the records of minors in many cases. Check your state law to find out how it applies to your library.
- Federal agents and law enforcement cannot demand access to library records unless they provide legal documentation, such as a subpoena, search warrant, or other court order.
- It's not unusual or burdensome for law enforcement to get a court order. Judges are available to issue them, even outside regular business hours. In rare cases, law enforcement may take records without a warrant. This may happen if they believe:

  - someone's life or public safety is in immediate danger;
  - there isn't enough time to get a warrant; and
  - they have probable cause to seize the records.

- If officers proceed without a court order, they take on any legal risk involved.
- In some states, it may be illegal to share surveillance footage with law enforcement—even if it doesn't show someone using specific library materials or services. Always check your state law and consult legal counsel before disclosing this kind of information.

Creating Policy for Your Library

- Adopt the *Library Bill of Rights, Libraries: An American Value,* and the *Code of Ethics of the American Library Association* (part I, chapter 2) as policy for your library. They contain statements about protecting library users' privacy and confidentiality.
- All libraries, public or private, should have written procedures for handling requests from law enforcement, including subpoenas, search warrants, National Security Letters, and orders issued pursuant to the Foreign Intelligence Surveillance Act and the Electronic Communications Privacy Act.
- Have a written privacy policy that outlines the way your library:
  - limits the collection of personally identifiable information;
  - deletes personal information when no longer needed;
  - avoids placing personal information on public view; and
  - responds to third-party requests for user information (part I, chapter 3).

- Depending on state law, it may not be illegal to reveal that someone is in the library. However, libraries may choose to adopt a policy against doing so. Library workers often don't know if a user is experiencing domestic violence, harassment, or a custody dispute.
- Refer to "Libraries and Immigration Enforcement," ala.org/advocacy/privacy/lawenforcement/guidelines#immigration.

For Academic Libraries

- The Family Education Rights and Privacy Act (FERPA) may also govern how requests for student records from law enforcement must be managed. Consult with your institution's legal counsel about the necessary policies and procedures.

For School Libraries

- FERPA may also govern how requests for student records from law enforcement must be managed. Consult with your institution's legal counsel about the necessary policies and procedures.

For Public Libraries

- Have written procedures and provide training to staff on what to do if Immigration and Customs Enforcement (ICE) officers come to the library seeking information or to detain users.

To Learn More

- "Privacy," ala.org/advocacy/privacy, which includes "Privacy and Confidentiality Q&A."
- "Library Privacy Guidelines," ala.org/advocacy/privacy/guidelines; and "Library Privacy Checklists," ala.org/advocacy/privacy/checklists.
- "Privacy and Confidentiality" (part II, chapter 11); and "The Universal Right to Free Expression: An Interpretation of the *Library Bill of Rights*" (part II, chapter 10).

Reflection Questions

- A police officer approaches the desk and says they're looking for a missing child. They want to review library activity records to see if the child had been in the library that day. What do you do?
- The sheriff asks to install monitoring software on the library's network to look for attempts to access bomb-making websites. They promise that all other internet usage will be ignored. What's your response?
- A group of teenagers comes in every day after school and tends to be loud and energetic. Your coworker is frustrated and wants to call law enforcement. How would you respond?
- During rounds, you notice that a library user is looking at a website that appears to feature young children in sexual situations. What do you do?

Need to Talk to an Attorney?

If your library has received a subpoena, search warrant, or other demand for records and you do not have access to an attorney, contact the ALA Office for Intellectual Freedom at (312) 280-4221 or oif@ala.org, to request a legal referral.

If an agent for the Federal Bureau of Investigation presents an order and informs you that it is issued as part of a terrorism or espionage investigation and is subject to a "nondisclosure order" or "gag order," do not disclose the existence of the order. Simply say, "I need to speak to an attorney."

OFFICIAL ALA POLICY STATEMENT

Policy on Government Intimidation

Adopted February 2, 1973, by the ALA Council; amended July 1, 1981; June 30, 2024 (under previous name "Policy on Governmental Intimidation"); and May 29, 2025.

The American Library Association opposes any government actions that intimidate people or groups, making them afraid to exercise their right to read, learn, or express themselves freely. These rights are protected by the First Amendment to the U.S. Constitution. Government intimidation weakens democracy and can occur at any level of government, targeting individuals, groups, government workers, or elected officials. This abuse of governmental power is especially harmful to those who already face discrimination or economic hardship. ALA encourages active resistance to such misuse of power and stands with those affected, advocating for policies and actions that protect intellectual freedom and democracy.

A DEEPER LOOK

How to Respond to Law Enforcement Requests for Library Records and User Information—Suggested Guidelines

These suggested guidelines will help you prepare for and respond to requests from law enforcement. Libraries should have policies that uphold First and Fourth Amendment rights, professional ethics, and state law. State and local jurisdictions may have different laws that apply to privacy, confidentiality, and library records. Review these guidelines with your legal counsel and adapt them for your library. These guidelines are not meant to be legal advice. If legal advice or expert aid is required, seek out a legal professional.

Before Any Visit

- Decide who will handle law enforcement requests. Most often, it will be the library director and the library's legal counsel, if available. Create a contact list that includes their home or cell phone numbers for use if they are not at the library.
- Review the library's privacy policy and your state's confidentiality law with library counsel. Communicate these policies and the requirements of the law to both staff and volunteer workers in the library.

- Train all library workers, *including volunteers*, on the library's procedure for handling law enforcement requests. They should understand that it is lawful to refer the officer to an administrator and that they generally do not need to respond immediately to any request.
- A court order may require the removal of a computer workstation or other computer storage device from the library. Have plans in place to address service interruptions and any necessary backups for equipment and software.

During a Visit

Procedures for Library Workers

A law enforcement officer requests library records or information about a user or library worker:

1. Ask for the officer's identification. Record the information that appears on the identity card.
2. Inform the officer that the library director or legal counsel is the person authorized to respond to requests for information. Tell them that library policy requires you to refer them to the specified person in the policy.
3. Attempt to reach the library director, their designee, or the library's legal counsel using the contact list.
4. If you can't reach anyone, give the officer their contact information.
5. Write down the officer's request. Provide the written report to the designated person as soon as possible.

Procedures for the Library Director or Their Designee

In all cases:

1. Ask for the officer's identification. Record the information that appears on the identity card. If possible, verify the information with the appropriate law enforcement agency.
2. Have a colleague present during the interview with the officer. One person should take notes. These should be included in an internal incident report.
3. If possible, have the library's legal counsel join the meeting.
4. Ask to see the court order or subpoena.
5. Comply as required by the library's policy, legal guidance, and applicable laws.

A law enforcement officer requests *voluntary assistance* or *warrantless searches*. The officer does *not* present a subpoena or court order:

1. Explain the library's privacy policy. Inform the officer that the records and information about library users and staff are not available to law enforcement without a proper court order.
2. Without a court order, law enforcement can't make someone comply with an investigation. They can only collect the name and address of the person speaking to them. If the officer persists, explain that you are acting as a good citizen and following professional ethics. Let them know that state law and First Amendment rights do not allow information to be disclosed without a court order.
3. If the officer claims that an emergency or other circumstance requires the library to turn over records or provide information without a court order, call the library's legal counsel and ask for assistance. (Go to: "What if It's an Emergency?" later in this chapter.)
4. If the officer employs force to take possession of library records or property, do not obstruct the search in any way. Keep a written record describing the incident. Ask any witnesses to prepare a written record of the interaction between the officer and library employees or volunteers.
5. Provide all notes and records to the library's legal counsel. If a library worker is required to respond to a voluntary request or a warrantless search in the absence of the library director or their designee, all materials should be turned over to the library director as soon as possible.

A law enforcement officer presents a *subpoena* or similar request for information:

1. Accept the subpoena. Inform the officer that the library's legal counsel responds to subpoenas on behalf of the library. A subpoena does not require an immediate response from the library.
2. Turn the subpoena over to the library's legal counsel. If a library worker accepts service of the subpoena in the absence of the library director or a designated alternate, the subpoena should be turned over to the library director for coordination with legal counsel.
3. Work with the library's legal counsel to respond to the subpoena. Examine the subpoena for any legal defect. If a defect exists, legal counsel will advise on the best method to resist the subpoena. Defects may include:
    a. how the subpoena was served on the library;
    b. the breadth of its request;
    c. its form; or
    d. an insufficient showing of good cause.
4. Through legal counsel, insist that any defect be fixed before records are released. Ensure that the subpoena is strictly limited to require the release of specific records. If there does not appear to be a good cause, or if the request for information seems too broad or intrusive, ask counsel to file

a motion to quash the subpoena. Require that the party requesting the information submit a new subpoena in good form and without defects.

5. If you decide to comply with the subpoena after consulting legal counsel, review the information before releasing it. Follow the subpoena strictly and do not provide any information that is not specifically requested.
6. If disclosure of the information requested is required, ask the court to enter a protective order. Legal counsel will draft this to keep the information confidential and limit its use to the particular case. Ask that access be restricted to the people working directly on the case.

A law enforcement officer presents a *search warrant*:

1. Immediately ask the library's legal counsel to provide advice and assistance.
2. Unlike a subpoena, a search warrant may be executed immediately. Ask to have library counsel present before the search begins. This allows legal counsel to examine the warrant and ensure the search follows its terms.
3. If the officer refuses to delay the search, read the warrant and any attached documentation. If you have questions about the validity of the warrant, call the issuing court to verify. Verify that it is:
    a. signed by a judge;
    b. is issued by a local, state, or federal court in your state or county; and
    c. is current and not expired.
4. Identify the items or records specified in the warrant. If the officer will not wait for legal counsel to arrive, you may assist the officer in locating the items or records identified in the search warrant. This will prevent the review of other users' records or items not named in the warrant.
5. Do not agree to any additional searches or volunteer information about the items or records in the warrant. Do not sign any documents on behalf of the library without the advice of the library's legal counsel.
6. Record and keep an inventory of the records or items seized from the library. Ask if it is possible to provide copies to the officer or to make copies for the library's own records.
7. Do not obstruct the search in any way.
8. If the law enforcement officer is unwilling to cooperate with you, simply step aside and do not interfere with the officer. Continue your attempts to notify legal counsel, and make every effort to keep a written record of the incident. Ask any witnesses to keep a written record of the interaction between the officer and library workers.
9. Request that the officer sign an inventory receipt for the materials, with a specific list of all materials seized.
10. Provide all notes and records to the library's legal counsel. If a library worker is required to respond to a search warrant in the absence of the library director or a designated alternate, all materials should be turned over to the library director for coordination with legal counsel.

What If U.S. Immigration and Customs Enforcement (ICE) Officers Come to My Library?

ICE is the law enforcement division of the Department for Homeland Security (DHS). They must follow the Constitution, the Bill of Rights, and the laws of the United States. The federal statute 8 U.S.C. § 1357 defines the powers of immigration officers and employees. The statute allows ICE agents to interrogate undocumented immigrants or people believed to be undocumented about their right to remain in the United States. The agents can do this without a warrant. The statute also allows officers to arrest any person when there is "reason to believe" they are in the United States in violation of federal immigration law.

Types of Warrants

- Administrative warrants: ICE officials and agents can issue these based on Section 287(g) of the Immigration and Nationality Act (INA). These warrants are not reviewed or issued by a court of law. As such, they do not allow ICE agents to enter residences or nonpublic areas of a business without express consent.
- Court-issued subpoenas and warrants: These are issued by a judge or magistrate and have the same force and effect as any other court-issued warrant. They may authorize ICE agents to enter nonpublic spaces without consent. ICE agents may:
  - enter places open to the public;
  - question people in public spaces; and
  - carry out investigations based on their legal authority under 8 U.S.C. § 1357.

What About Library Privacy Laws?

When ICE agents ask questions about library users, state laws and library policies still apply. This includes provisions that require law enforcement to present court-issued subpoenas, court orders, or warrants to get user information.

If an ICE agent shows up without a warrant or subpoena and does not assert their authority to act without one, there is generally no legal obligation to turn over any information or records.

Exception: Libraries must comply with the federal law requiring employers to verify the identity and employment authorization of each person they hire. This includes the requirement that employers retain a Form I-9 (Employment Eligibility Verification) for each employee. ICE agents may ask to inspect an employer's I-9 forms without a subpoena or court order. Libraries that get this request should notify legal counsel and ask for assistance. They should allow the agent to inspect the I-9 forms in accordance with the library's human resources policies and guidance from its legal counsel.

What If It's an Emergency?

Sometimes law enforcement may ask you to voluntarily provide records immediately. They may give you the impression that it's not possible for them to obtain a court order.

Getting a court order is not unusual or burdensome. Law enforcement officers have access to judges even after normal business hours. You can offer to preserve the requested records while the officer seeks a court order. This may mean keeping a computer turned on or downloading a user log.

There is a limited legal exception to the warrant requirement when "exigent circumstances" exist. Law enforcement may take records over the library's objection if they believe:

- an emergency truly exists;
- there isn't enough time to obtain a warrant; and
- they have probable cause for the seizure of records.

If records are taken, you should indicate that you are not giving permission. This is needed so that law enforcement and not the library will bear the responsibility and any legal risks that come with the decision to proceed without a warrant.

A number of states allow for exigent circumstances in the state's library confidentiality statute. If so, precisely follow the law's requirements. For example, one state requires any law enforcement officer asking for library records under exigent circumstances to provide a written affidavit to the library affirming that such circumstances exist. Legal counsel should help the library in interpreting state and local laws on exigent circumstances for inclusion in the policy.

The Law Regarding Law Enforcement Requests for Library Records

LESLIEDIANA JONES

It is not a part of any library's routine to get requests from law enforcement officers to access user records. The legal landscape around these inquiries requires libraries to balance user privacy and complying with lawful demands. Libraries must have clear policies and procedures in place that explain how staff will handle these requests. If a library is developing the policy and procedures for the first time, consult "How to Respond to Law Enforcement Requests for Library Records and User Information—Suggested Guidelines" earlier in this chapter.

It is likely that other libraries in your state have policies and procedures in place for you to use as models. Libraries should tailor their policy based on their needs. If the library has access to appropriate legal counsel, the policy should be reviewed by them before it is finalized.

Libraries should also use local laws for guidance in creating policies and procedures. Forty-eight states and the District of Columbia have laws that protect library records from disclosure. Kentucky and Hawaii rely on the state attorney general's opinions to protect library users' privacy.[1] These state laws protect library records by keeping them private or exempting them from public record disclosure if the records show who the user is or their library use. All the statutes require libraries to release records when a court issues an order.[2]

For criminal investigations, law enforcement is seeking to secure documentary evidence. This may include various types of user records such as:

- circulation;
- computer usage;
- program attendance; or
- reference records.

To secure these records, a library may receive a search warrant for items of evidentiary value.[3] The First Amendment does not automatically protect against search warrants. Some courts use state laws to address the situation. In *Tattered Cover, Inc. v. City of Thornton,* the Colorado Supreme Court looked at the privacy clause in the state's constitution. The court ruled that a warrant served on a bookstore was not enforceable. The court said the warrant must show a compelling need that outweighs the potential harm that could be caused and that the warrant cannot be overly broad.[4]

A search warrant is a type of court order that authorizes law enforcement to immediately search for and seize any item, record, or property listed in the order. It must be signed by a judge after a "probable cause" hearing. That means the judge thinks the search will produce evidence of a crime. Search warrants can be served at any time, and the library must immediately provide the items or permit the officer to search.

A library may be served with a subpoena, which is different from a warrant. Rather than seeking seizure of materials, subpoenas are legal documents, issued by a court, that compel the production of documents or other tangible goods.[5] It is broader than a search warrant because it is used to gather any information that is relevant.

Sometimes, law enforcement can search without a warrant. These exceptions rely on the authority of "exigent circumstances." Exigent circumstances means "circumstances that would cause a reasonable person to believe that entry (or other relevant prompt action) was necessary to prevent ... the destruction of relevant evidence, ... improperly frustrating legitimate law enforcement efforts."[6]

However, even in this situation, a library can agree, in writing, to preserve the records until a warrant is issued. This written agreement may remove the urgency that would otherwise justify immediate action. If an exigent exception led to a seizure of records, subsequent searches without a warrant are not valid under the same exception.[7]

Law enforcement may make verbal requests without having any court-ordered warrants or subpoenas.[8] It is not against the law for officers to make these requests, but libraries must consider the rights of users. They must ensure they are not disclosing users' information if they choose to respond. Additionally, disclosure could violate state-specific privacy laws.

It is difficult for most library workers to interpret what to do when faced with a court order. To help staff, all libraries must have clear and explicit policies on how to handle formal or informal requests for access to library records. The policy must have specific people—senior personnel and legal counsel—as the official recipients of court orders.

Things to include in policies and procedures:

- Always ask for identification.
- Refer the officer to the library's senior leadership, legal counsel, or other staff responsible for responding to records requests. Even non-confidential information requests should be referred to senior management. Indicate in the policy who the contact person is.
- Do not disclose any library records or user information without permission from designated staff.
- No library worker is authorized to release library information based on oral requests by law enforcement officers.
- Know how to respond in an emergency when the designated person is unavailable or when law enforcement insists on taking records without a proper order.

Staff should be aware of and trained in implementing the policies and procedures so that a request from law enforcement can go as smoothly as possible. It is the duty of library management, with the help of legal counsel, to ensure that the library's policies and procedures are current and based on applicable laws.

Types of Court Orders and Requests

Subpoena—A legal document issued by a court or grand jury. It orders the library to provide evidence, such as documents or records. It tells a library to provide the information at a certain date, time, and place. Library counsel should examine the subpoena to ensure it was issued correctly with the required signatures, information, and notices. If counsel believes the subpoena is unjustified or will chill the exercise of First Amendment rights, they can file a motion with the court to quash it.

Search Warrant—A type of court order that lists specific items law enforcement officers can search for and seize immediately. Officers can present the warrant to the library at any time. The library must promptly provide access to or hand over the listed records or items.

FISA Order—A type of court order authorized by the Foreign Intelligence Surveillance Act (FISA). These orders allow FBI agents to seize "any tangible thing." This includes:

- documents;
- records;
- hard drives; or
- any other physical object.

The FBI agent must allege that the item is relevant to an ongoing investigation into terrorism or foreign espionage. Libraries served with a FISA order are under an automatic nondisclosure or "gag" order. This forbids the library from disclosing that it received the order or that records have been turned over to the FBI. The library must comply with a valid FISA warrant. However, staff can speak to legal counsel about the warrant at the time it is received. The gag order does not remove the library's right to consult with legal counsel or to inform the staff needed to produce the information.

National Security Letter (NSL)—Libraries are now exempt from NSLs as of the 2024 amendment to FISA.

Voluntary or Informal Requests—Law enforcement officers, truant officers, or immigration agents may ask a library worker to tell them if a person is in the library or to call the police when that person arrives. Library workers should not disclose this information unless a crime has been committed, and they have personal knowledge about the crime. No law requires libraries to reveal that a person is in the library. Some states actually forbid revealing any information that identifies a person as having used the library's resources or facilities. Any person asking if someone is in the library should be told they can come visit when the facility is open. This applies to requests by parents, spouses, or other relatives.

Key Things to Remember When Responding to a Request from Law Enforcement

1. Always ask for identification.
2. Refer the officer to the library director, legal counsel, or assigned designee.
3. Do not give any records or information about a library user without first getting permission from the director, legal counsel, or assigned designee.
4. Know how to respond in an emergency when the director or legal counsel cannot be reached or is unavailable.
5. Know the steps to take when an officer insists on taking records or other items without a proper order.
6. Understand the steps for responding to different types of requests for library records or information.

NOTES

1. "State Privacy Laws Regarding Library Records," American Library Association, Advocacy, Legislation & Issues, May 29, 2007, ala.org/advocacy/privacy/statelaws.
2. Kathryn Martin, "The USA Patriot Act's Application to Library Patron Records," *Journal of Legislation* 29 (2003): 283.
3. *Warden v. Hayden,* 87 Sp. Ct. 1642 (1967).
4. *Tattered Cover, Inc. v. The City of Thornton,* 44 P.3d 1044 (2002).
5. University of California at Berkeley, Office of the Chancellor, "Frequently Asked Questions – Subpoena FAQs," https://chancellor.berkeley.edu/about/offices/legal-affairs/FAQs.
6. *United States v. McConney,* 728 F. 2d 1195, 1199 (9th Cir. 1984) (en banc).
7. *United States v. David,* 756 F. Supp. 1385 (D. Nev. 1991).
8. Eric Lichtblau, "U.S. Demanded Data from Libraries, Study Finds," *New York Times,* June 21, 2005, nytimes.com/2005/06/21/world/americas/us-demanded-data-from-libraries-study-finds.html.

Part III
Advocacy and Assistance

CHAPTER 13
Advocating and Lobbying for Intellectual Freedom

Advocating for Intellectual Freedom

MEGAN MURRAY CUSICK

Access, intellectual freedom, and the freedom to seek knowledge are core values of librarianship. Because of this, advocating for these values is part of a library worker's entire career. Sometimes, people will have honest questions about a library's collection, program, display, or service. Library workers must be ready to respond to those questions. They must also protect the constitutional rights of users who rely on the library for information and opportunity. Today, as the nation faces another surge of threats to library materials and services, it is essential that all library workers are prepared to defend intellectual freedom and user privacy.

Before an Issue Arises

Preparing for a threat to intellectual freedom can mean the difference between resolution and escalation. Some common threats include:

- a book challenge;
- a First Amendment audit;
- a meeting room dispute;
- adverse legislation; or
- a challenge to library services.

In addition to clear policies and procedures, it is essential to build an advocacy foundation that positions you and your library to effectively navigate whatever threats may arise.

The good news is that library workers start from a position of strength. The vast majority of Americans oppose book bans and have high regard for the library profession.[1] How can library workers leverage that to advocate for the rights of all library stakeholders?

First, build capacity within your library. Ensure that the staff, board, and volunteers understand both how and why the library defends privacy and intellectual freedom. The "how" comes from policies and procedures; the "why" comes from our core values. Not everyone needs to be an expert, but everyone should feel a shared sense of ownership. They should also have basic talking points they can use—whether at the circulation desk or in the grocery store. Strengthen this understanding by collecting and sharing user stories. These stories show the value of a well-resourced library that reflects a wide variety of perspectives, experiences, and backgrounds.

Internally, establish and share clear structures for ongoing and crisis communications. Establish a team that can serve in an advisory capacity as needed. Provide training for front-line staff so that they feel prepared to respond when an incident arises and to elevate the process to a colleague or supervisor if needed. Identify your spokespeople—often the board president or library director—and provide them with media training.

Keep your intellectual freedom messaging simple, direct, and focused on community benefits. For example: "By increasing the diversity of our teen collection, we now welcome twice as many teens during after school hours as we did two years ago."

Make sure that your messaging reaches all stakeholders, including those without digital access or who speak languages other than English. Common communication channels include:

- library board meetings;
- newsletters;
- social media; and
- local news outlets.

There are also many ways to engage your community to build support for intellectual freedom. Libraries can:

- host programs with guest speakers;
- lead book discussions;
- celebrate events like National Library Week, Banned Books Week, or Constitution Day;
- share updates outside the library;
- attend community events; or
- partner with other organizations to speak with a united voice in support of intellectual freedom.

Build relationships with community stakeholders, such as:

- users (and parents, if a school library);
- community partners;
- local authors;
- educational institutions;

- faith groups;
- civic organizations;
- business leaders;
- local news outlets; and
- elected officials.

Learn what your stakeholders care about and let them know how the library supports their priorities. Keep these relationships professional, transparent, and rooted in trust. You don't need to agree on every issue, but you do need to build credibility and rapport with a wide range of stakeholders.

When an Issue Arises

Even with the best preparation, some intellectual freedom issues will not resolve themselves seamlessly. When that happens, you'll need to stand firm on the foundation you've built and boost your advocacy efforts.

Assess the situation with your designated team and map a strategy that can be changed as things develop. Do not be afraid to ask for support. The American Library Association's Office for Intellectual Freedom provides confidential, expert assistance; your state association may offer support, too.

Analyze the situation and how it could affect the library and its users. Identify the desired remedy, what might help or get in the way, and who in your library will be making decisions. Figure out what resources or support are needed to follow policies, resolve the issue, maintain community trust, and protect the library and staff.

Know whether you are dealing with an individual or an organized group, a genuine concern or a copycat action. Consider the context of the situation and what tactics are best suited for that context.

Understand the political and social dynamics of your community. Most libraries enjoy support from across the political spectrum, but political actors are weighing multiple issues at any given moment. Whenever possible, do not place impossible demands on an ally or decision-maker, and never break their trust. Not only might you lose their support in this situation, but they may be less likely to support you or your library in the future.

Some of the greatest success stories of defending intellectual freedom are those that are never widely told. For example, a bill that would restrict access to library materials in schools that was held in committee by a long-standing ally in a state legislature; or the meeting room dispute that was resolved with the help of a community partner. These and other unknown stories reflect a vast amount of foundation-building and a powerful form of advocacy. In other cases, however, the situation unfolds in the public view.

No matter how your situation develops, effective communication is your most valuable tool in successfully navigating a threat to intellectual freedom. Consider your stakeholders and the best ways to communicate with them. Decide whether a broad and visible campaign that engages with the entire community is required, or if your situation requires a more focused and restrained communications plan. Either way, make sure that the staff, board members, and key partners are informed and updated regularly. Develop talking points and prepare your spokespeople to deliver them, using these tips:

- Keep talking points focused and concise.
- Use brief stories to illustrate the talking points; spokespeople should practice the stories before public speaking or interviews.
- Focus on a tangible outcome and show how the library's role in providing access to information benefits the community.
- Avoid jargon, including the term "intellectual freedom," which is primarily used within the profession.
- Never repeat falsehoods, even to dispel them.
- Acknowledge concerns and speak without attack or judgment.
- Know when *not* to respond. Focus on the library's messaging, and do not respond to every comment lobbed on social media or during heated public meetings.

Activate your communications channels and know the strengths and limits of each type of channel. Social media can be a fantastic tool for reinforcing key messages and sharing real-time updates, but face-to-face conversations are better for real dialogue. Traditional media can also be a powerful ally. Even if an issue is all-consuming for you and your staff, the public may not know what's happening. Reach out to local editors or reporters at radio stations, television stations, and newspapers. Ask a board member or other prominent supporter to write a letter to the editor or an opinion piece.

Handling Negative Publicity

If negative publicity is severe or extends beyond the initial incident, activate your crisis communications plan. Give your spokespeople extra training so they're ready to answer tough questions and pivot the conversation when needed. Know when to correct misinformation—like a wrong fact in a news story—and when not to engage—like in a heated social media thread. Keep your staff and volunteers informed and make sure they know who to contact with any questions and concerns they might have. Think about whether you need more communication channels and who is best positioned to take the lead with them.

Seek support from your stakeholders, especially those allies that you have cultivated over time. Look to Friends groups, foundations, library users, community partners, civic organizations, and faith groups to help organize supporters. It is important to note that grassroots advocates do not speak for the library;

they speak as stakeholders. Still, they can provide a powerful signal of broad support for the library. ALA's Unite Against Book Bans campaign offers a toolkit for grassroots advocacy.[2]

You may also want to engage your "grasstops" advocates. These are people who have a direct connection to decision-makers or who are influential in your community. They are smaller in number but can help to shore up your support with key audiences, like elected officials. Grasstops advocates may be found on your library board or among stakeholders that you know and who know the library.

If the issue persists over a long period of time, try to provide spokespeople, leaders, and front-line staff with breaks and reinforcements to help prevent burnout. Refresh your talking points as needed and turn to additional supporters for assistance. Advocacy is a team sport.

Advocacy is a long-term effort to build lasting support for the library. While you need to be nimble when responding to immediate issues, every interaction with stakeholders can either strengthen or weaken your future efforts. Be sure to thank library supporters and stay engaged with those who may not support you yet. Keep talking with stakeholders about the value of providing access to all members of the community. Build your professional network so you have strong support when an issue arises.

And when it does, the few small steps listed here will go a long way to preparing yourself and supporting your colleagues:

- *Read up.* Keep yourself informed, including through ALA's weekly intellectual freedom newsletter, at oif.ala.org.
- *Gear up.* Use the Unite Against Book Bans toolkit to prepare and practice your elevator speech about intellectual freedom.
- *Show up.* When an issue arises in your community or your state, show up for your colleagues and for the rights of library users everywhere.

We are stronger together. Collectively, we carry forward a proud tradition of defending access to ideas, information, and the free exchange of ideas that form the cornerstone of American democracy.

NOTES

1. "Voters Oppose Book Bans in Libraries," American Library Association, ala.org/advocacy/voters-oppose-book-bans-libraries.
2. Unite Against Book Bans, "Action Toolkit," uniteagainstbookbans.org/toolkit/.

Intellectual Freedom Advocacy and Education

Adopted June 25, 2019, by the ALA Council.

As members of the American Library Association, we recognize intellectual freedom as a universal human right.[i] This right ensures free access to seek and receive information and expression of ideas from all points of view without restriction for every individual of any age, ability, socioeconomic status, religious affiliation, race, ethnicity, sexual orientation, gender identity, or other form of identity or status. The *Library Bill of Rights* and *Code of Ethics of the American Library Association* express core values of our profession and affirm the primacy of intellectual freedom for full participation in a just, equitable, and informed society. We acknowledge our professional obligation to actively defend intellectual freedom rights and to protect the privacy and confidentiality of library users. We advocate for intellectual freedom and strive to educate ourselves, library users, the community we serve, and the broader society about intellectual freedom and related topics, including privacy, information literacy, and inclusion.

NOTE

i. "The Universal Right to Free Expression: An Interpretation of the *Library Bill of Rights*," adopted January 16, 1991, by the ALA Council; amended on July 1, 2014; and May 29, 2025.

PERSONAL STORY

Ground Zero for Public Libraries: Fighting Censorship in Llano, Texas

LEILA GREEN LITTLE

My mom always told me I could read whatever I wanted, and this is a family heirloom I've passed down to my own children. My local public libraries were where I connected with other moms and created strong friendships, where my son carried towering stacks of books to the car as a toddler, and where I staved off the exhausted monotony with my newborn daughter in tow. I began advocating for the freedom to read because I saw an organized group of citizens speaking in favor of the hasty removal of books at a public commissioners' court meeting. I certainly support the right of all citizens to petition their government (thank you again, First Amendment), and I felt the commissioners needed to hear a contrasting opinion. What began as reading aloud a public comment culminated in my banding together with six others to file a federal lawsuit against my county, elected officials, and government employees. We have prevailed so far at each stage in this judicial process, and are currently awaiting a ruling from the Fifth Circuit en banc panel.

I write this from my home in Texas, in the aftermath of the 2024 presidential election, with an enduring hope in the fidelity of our judicial system, and fear for my GOP-controlled state and federal government. There's good reason to be wary of what the next four years may hold for our public and school libraries. We are seeing some good, as other states enact their own freedom to read legislation, but that won't be happening in Texas anytime soon. On the contrary: Texas's attorney general (and seventeen others) filed an amicus brief in opposition to our case. Their brief and oral arguments in New Orleans proposed a truly horrific legal premise: that the selection of library books is government speech, and is therefore not subject to First Amendment protections. If successful, this gambit would turn public libraries into propaganda centers, beholden to the whims of the local elected officials.

The wholesale destruction of our libraries as we know them is on the line. When book banners attempt to justify their actions, we must not acquiesce, nor believe that these requested limitations on our reading will be restricted to one arena. My court case is about a public library, though we've seen efforts to ban (and yes, I do mean ban) books in retail stores, Little Free Libraries, college campuses, and K–12 school libraries. The word "unconstitutional" seems to be devoid of meaning for those who wish to censor books.

Why, despite seeing book bans spreading across the country and enduring hardships that accompany this advocacy work, do we keep fighting for the right to read? For the same reason that we do not cheer for Darth Vader and the Empire, nor wish for Reverend Shaw Moore to prevail in *Footloose*. We fight because we are right, and we must: Our public libraries, and our very democracy, depend on it. I am simply unable to stand idly by while legislators or other local elected officials steer us into purely sanitized reading choices, or politicized library boards, or the closing of libraries. I hope you join me. There's a great deal of work to do, and I need your help.

> Since this chapter was written, the Fifth Circuit has issued its en banc ruling. See part I, chapter 3, "Intellectual Freedom: The Law in Flux" for more on this ruling and its impact on the freedom to read.

A DEEPER LOOK

Lobbying and Working with Public Officials

MAX PRIME

Whether fighting to protect intellectual freedom or campaigning for local or state initiatives, gaining the support of key elected officials is essential for success. To reach your goals, it's important to develop lobbying efforts that can influence those in power. This chapter explores the basics of lobbying and highlights the skills and information that are most useful for new library advocates working at the local, state, and federal levels.

Introduction to Lobbying

Lobbying is a specialized form of advocacy that focuses on influencing the actions of legislators and other public officials. While general advocacy supports a cause in broad ways, it becomes *lobbying* when the goal is to affect specific policy decisions made by those in power. Convincing a public official to act on your requests can feel intimidating. However, new advocates can take three key steps to prepare for success.

1. **Find out how local, state, and federal governments influence library operations in your community.**
   - Research which levels of government fund, regulate, and make laws about library operations in your area. This will ensure that your lobbying efforts reach the right decision-makers.
   - If your goal is to secure statewide legislation that protects intellectual freedom in libraries, focus on the state's legislators and governor. If you want to stop the removal of challenged books from a local library, focus on that library's board of trustees instead.
2. **Understand the legislative and regulatory processes of your local, state, and federal governments.**
   - Advocates need to understand how laws are proposed and approved—known as the legislative process—before they can effectively lobby officials.
   - Understanding the legislative process gives you a full picture of what actions are needed for legislation to become law. It also helps you track bills and spot the best times for your lobbying to have the greatest impact.

3. **Research which public officials at the local, state, and federal levels have jurisdiction in your community.**
   - Success in lobbying depends on knowing who needs to support your priorities for them to advance. You should know who is in office, what roles they play, and what opinions they hold.

For each step, there are many online resources to support your learning. Government websites usually include information about their officials, structures, and recent actions. For example, the U.S. House of Representatives' website (house.gov) has menu options entitled "Leadership," "Committees," and "Legislative Activity." It also has a tool to find your representative by zip code. A page called "The House Explained" covers the rules of the chamber and its legislative process.

Legislative tracking tools like legiscan.com and www.govtrack.us have free versions that can help amateur lobbyists follow legislation related to their priorities. Both sites also let users review what bills elected officials currently sponsor and their voting records on past library-related proposals.

Lobbying and Advocacy in Practice

Knowing which governments, processes, and people make public policy decisions in your community gives you the context needed to develop and launch effective lobbying strategies. The following tips will help you as you begin your lobbying journey.

1. **Set clear objectives.**
   - *Decide what you want to accomplish and use that information to plan your activities.* Clear objectives keep your lobbying intentional and purpose-driven. Poorly defined objectives can lead to directionless and inefficient endeavors.
   - *Check for existing initiatives.* New advocates can find opportunities to take action through the American Library Association (ala.org/advocacy), their state library association (e.g., nyla.org/advocacy), and other organizations with shared interests. This helps ensure that your lobbying is coordinated with others and reduces the risk of:
     » inconsistent messaging;
     » accidentally working at cross purposes; or
     » distracting from campaigns that are currently gaining traction.
2. **Select lobbying targets with strategic significance for the objectives you set.**
   - *Prioritize building relationships with the people who represent you directly.* These include local elected officials, state legislators for the districts you live in, and members of the U.S. Congress. Because they have a personal stake in your community, they are often natural champions for your library's initiatives.

   - *Explore which officials hold appointments that are important for reaching your goals.* For example, a city council or state legislature may have specific committees that review library-related bills before the full chamber votes on them. In that case, gaining the support of the committee's chairperson is essential to move your priorities forward and stop bills you oppose from passing.

3. **Establish direct connections with the offices and officials you identify as lobbying targets.**
   - *Schedule meetings using each office's preferred method.* When requesting a meeting with an official for the first time, visit the office's website to see if it lists a preferred method for submitting meeting requests or event invitations. Many offices use webforms to make sure that all the required information is included in the request. If no method is listed, you can call or email the office to make your request and ask what method they prefer in the future. Using their preferred method helps make a good first impression with the staff who decide which groups get access to their boss.
   - *When possible, prioritize in-person meetings over remote ones.* While videoconferencing and phone calls are convenient, face-to-face meetings are still the best way to hold someone's attention and build lasting connections. Even so, virtual meetings are still valuable and can help make lobbying accessible for all library advocates.
   - *Take meetings with staff just as seriously as meetings with their bosses.* Depending on the office, staff can play a significant role in shaping the policy decisions of the officials they work for. Winning them over can earn you important, lasting allies as they rise in seniority and are hired for more powerful positions.

4. **Prepare clear, concise talking points and use them to guide your meetings with lobbying targets.**
   - *Don't wing it.* Even veteran lobbyists struggle to stay on message without thorough preparation. Talking points are outlines of the key ideas and arguments you intend to present in a meeting. Their creation keeps your messaging consistent and ensures that conversations with officials stay focused on the information you want them to remember after the meetings are over. You can find examples of talking points for specific issues from the American Library Association (ALA) and your state library association.
   - *Be efficient with your communication and balance being memorable with being succinct.* Meetings with public officials are typically brief, often only 20 or 30 minutes. To make the most of that time, your talking points should highlight the top issues you are there to discuss, why those issues matter, and the policy actions you are asking the official to take. You can leave handouts containing key information in case you run short on time.

- *Use personal stories and data to make abstract ideas real.* Officials care most about issues that directly affect their constituents. Stories and statistics can show the human impact of issues like intellectual freedom and library funding in their region. To encourage action, use this approach to:
   » build an emotional connection;
   » show real concern for the well-being of community members; and
   » highlight practical concerns like constituent satisfaction.

- *End meetings by restating your requests and thanking the office.* If you oppose a bill and want officials to vote against it, make sure they leave the meeting knowing the bill number and that you're asking them to vote nay. If you are building support for a bill, clearly state that you want them to co-sponsor it. If a bill is unfavorable but sponsored by someone strategically important—like a committee chair or leader—ask them to amend the bill. Give them specific language you've written to help guide the change.

5. **Stay connected with lobbying targets after and between meetings.**
   - *Approach advocacy as a continuous and dynamic endeavor.* The requests you make of public officials will evolve over time, but the need to build and maintain relationships with those officials is constant.
   - *Request contact information from all staff involved in arranging and facilitating meetings.* Use staff contacts to follow up with officials once you've met to reinforce key asks. Offer to answer any questions those staff members might have about proposals you've presented or library issues in their districts.
   - *Invite officials to your library and community events you organize.* With each interaction, officials are more likely to remember you, your role, and your place in their community. The more familiar they are with you, the more likely they'll be to consider you a trusted contact and an expert in your field. Also consider inviting officials you haven't connected with yet. That way, when you ask for their support later, you won't be a stranger.
   - *Follow officials you meet on social media and engage them.* Post pictures of your interactions with them and tag relevant accounts. This expands your reach to their audiences and shows your value as a trusted community institution. Posts about which local events they plan to attend also give you more chances to connec
   - *Use events and informal interactions throughout the year to raise key library issues.* When an official visits your library, mention how book challenges are impacting your library's users and staff. If you see them at a school fundraiser, talk about how the federal E-rate program and state-funded initiatives have expanded broadband access

for local students. Each interaction is a chance to introduce a priority tied to a policy proposal that you may ask them to support later.

6. **Cultivate a grassroots network of support to amplify your efforts.**
   - *Spread the word.* Grassroots lobbying means mobilizing others to influence public officials' policy decisions. Communicate with:
     » Friends of the Library groups;
     » library professionals;
     » users;
     » community leaders; and
     » other supporters.
   - Keep them informed about library laws, funding, policy fights, and attempted book bans. Let them know where their voices are needed most. Use both new and traditional media—like social media, email campaigns, letters to the editor, and discussion lists—to reach new audiences. Sharing clear, unified messaging helps ensure that all advocates will speak with one voice.
   - *Local action matters.* Decisions made at the local level often have a big impact on people's daily lives. Grassroots lobbying can alert your supporters about important municipal or school board meetings. Packing rooms with library supporters and filling public comment periods with advocates can stop harmful proposals. It's sometimes hard to see the impact of your lobbying at the state and federal levels. But in local government each voice matters and can be the difference between success and failure.

Considerations for Future Lobbying

Lobbying and advocacy take time. You may not see results right away, but remember that you're not alone. Around the world, people just like you are working to support the core mission of libraries in their communities.

As you grow as an advocate, look to resources like the ALA's Chapter Advocacy Exchange webinar series (ala.org/advocacy/chapter-advocacy-exchange) and training from your state library association to keep learning. With persistence at every level of government, we can—and will—protect intellectual freedom today and help libraries keep offering the collections and services their users deserve.

PERSONAL STORY

Empowering Library Boards: Advocating for Intellectual Freedom

SAM HELMICK AND ANNE MANGANO

Need an advocate? Look to your library's board of trustees. They are passionate individuals who know the power and value of libraries. At the Iowa City Public Library, we knew we would face laws restricting access to library materials when the Iowa state legislature convened in 2022. Legislation would move fast, and our board would be our advocate.

Restrictive legislation was fresh territory for our board. Historically, Iowa's public libraries had strong civic support. User access and privacy are protected in the Iowa Code, and communities are required to fund public library services. The American Library Association's *Library Bill of Rights,* written by an Iowan in 1938, reflects our state's tradition of protecting personal liberty. As the year progressed, however, we watched Iowa libraries face challenges to their materials and services. We also saw our colleagues in other states face restrictive library legislation. Even before the legislature met in January, it was important to prepare our board.

We first gave them the lay of the land. During the summer, Sam Helmick traveled around the state and spoke at public meetings of schools and libraries that were facing book challenges. Representing the Iowa Library Association (ILA)'s Intellectual Freedom Committee, Sam emphasized the importance of providing access to titles like *All Boys Aren't Blue* and *Gender Queer*. After these meetings, Sam presented this work to the board and encouraged them to voice their support for intellectual freedom.

It would start as a public statement. To prepare, the board reviewed the Iowa City Public Library's key policies and our process for handling complaints about the collection. They discussed the ILA's intellectual freedom statement and examples from other libraries. The board convened a subcommittee to craft language. Adopted at the board's February 2022 meeting, the statement affirmed intellectual freedom as a core library value and its solidarity with libraries and library workers facing challenges and censorship.

And then it happened. Iowa legislators introduced several bills restricting access to materials. Empowered by its statement on intellectual freedom, our board built upon its words with actions. They lobbied city officials to make intellectual freedom a legislative priority and met with county and state representatives. They commented on restrictive legislation and spoke at committee hearings at the statehouse. One board member worked with Anne Mangano to create statewide training on a board's intellectual freedom responsibilities. Our board moved the needle by supporting our staff, advocating for our community, and building relationships with government officials, ready to roll up their sleeves for what came our way next.

Board documents carry weight. The *Library Bill of Rights* itself started as a board document, a declaration of the rights of the Des Moines Public Library users. It is now a national statement and a guiding commitment to our users. Collaborate with your board to show the impact of legislation on your users, your library, and your staff. Continually update and provide education to your board so they can advocate for intellectual freedom and confidently answer questions about library policies. If they are empowered, they can act.

CHAPTER 14
Where to Get Help and Get Involved

Eric Stroshane

Threats to intellectual freedom can be intimidating, disorienting, and overwhelming. They can also kindle a desire to do more in defense of the freedom to read. No matter what you're facing or feeling, you are not alone. In this chapter, you will find places to turn to if you need assistance, someone to talk to, or positive ways to direct your energy.

The American Library Association's (ALA) Office for Intellectual Freedom (OIF) is the first place you should turn to. Established in 1967, OIF:

- maintains intellectual freedom-related services, programs, publications, and online resources;
- provides confidential support during challenges;
- oversees ALA's intellectual freedom groups;
- educates library workers and the public about the nature and importance of intellectual freedom in libraries; and
- maintains collaborative relationships with other entities concerned about intellectual freedom.

CHALLENGE SUPPORT AND INFORMATION

Office for Intellectual Freedom

ala.org/tools/challengesupport
(312) 280-4221, oif@ala.org
OIF staff are available to provide support whenever library resources or services are challenged. As needed, OIF staff provide:

- book résumés for challenged resources;
- information on applicable ALA policies;
- advice on implementing reconsideration policies;

- written position statements defending the principles of intellectual freedom in libraries;
- connections to state intellectual freedom committees and other experts who can provide local assistance or offer testimony before library boards and governing bodies;
- access to legal assistance through Lawyers for Librarians (L4L) and the Freedom to Read Foundation (FTRF); and
- counseling tailored to your situation.

When facing a challenge, library workers should review the resources available on the ALA's website at ala.org/tools/challengesupport, or contact OIF directly for assistance. Help is available to all, regardless of ALA membership. Reports can be submitted to OIF confidentially and anonymously. Identifying information is kept confidential.

Since 1990, OIF has maintained a database of challenges to library resources and services across the country. All challenges and censorship incidents should be reported to OIF, even if support is not needed. OIF estimates that 67 to 94 percent of all challenges remain unreported. The data helps us:

- identify censorship trends;
- assist those facing challenges;
- raise awareness of the harms caused by censorship;
- compile the annual 10 Most Challenged Books list; and
- amplify Banned Books Week messaging.

STATE LIBRARY ASSOCIATION INTELLECTUAL FREEDOM COMMITTEES

State library association chapters' intellectual freedom committees are excellent places to turn for local support. Committee information can usually be found on your state library association's website. Reach out to OIF with information on intellectual freedom issues in your state, including your concerns with legislation, administrative rules, pressure groups, and litigation.

PROGRAMMING AND CONTINUING EDUCATION

Office for Intellectual Freedom

OIF offers free and low-cost webinars on emerging intellectual freedom issues and the ways library workers can oppose censorship. It can offer suggestions on speakers and topics to fit any intellectual freedom program. Contact OIF for more information.

ALA Conferences

ALA conferences include programs on all topics and trends of librarianship. Attendees are invited to membership meetings of the Intellectual Freedom Committee (IFC) and its Privacy Subcommittee, the Committee on Professional Ethics (COPE), and the Freedom to Read Foundation.

Banned Books Week

ALA is one of the sponsors and founders of Banned Books Week, an annual celebration of the freedom to read. Launched in 1982, Banned Books Week highlights the benefits of unrestricted reading and draws attention to the harms of censorship.

- Themed materials on banned and challenged books can be purchased from the ALA Store at ala.org/advocacy/bbooks/shop.
- Challenged book lists, program and display ideas, and promotional materials can be found at ala.org/bbooks.
- Publicize and discover events at bannedbooksweek.org.

ONLINE RESOURCES AND PUBLICATIONS

ALA, and the organizations it works in coalition with, have created many online resources to help explain, promote, and defend intellectual freedom.

ALA Intellectual Freedom Websites

ala.org/oif
ala.org/advocacy/intfreedom
These two websites provide information about initiatives and projects, educational programs, and intellectual freedom groups. They include links to documents, guidelines, publications, and toolkits.

Book Résumés

bookresumes.uniteagainstbookbans.org
The hundreds of book résumés on United Against Book Bans' "Book Résumés" resource can be used to help defend books from censorship. Each résumé details:

- a title's significance;
- educational value; and
- literary merit.

The résumés show how a title aligns with library selection criteria.

The website's book résumés are easy to find and share with administrators, book review committees, elected officials, board members, and journalists. New résumés created by publishers, librarians, and education professionals are regularly added.

Intellectual Freedom Blog

oif.ala.org

This blog raises awareness about intellectual freedom and professional ethics issues impacting library workers. It features:

- a weekly roundup of news articles compiled by OIF;
- opinion pieces; and
- information on award, grant, and e-learning opportunities.

Unite Against Book Bans

uniteagainstbookbans.org

Unite Against Book Bans empowers people everywhere to stand together in the fight against censorship. Unite has more than 200 partner organizations and tens of thousands of individual supporters. They connect, equip, and mobilize the public to advocate for the right to read in their communities. Toolkits, research, and other resources are available on their website.

Comic Book Legal Defense Fund (CBLDF)

cbldf.org

CBLDF is a nonprofit organization dedicated to the protection of First Amendment rights of the comics art form and its community.

Cooperative Children's Book Center (CCBC)

ccbc.education.wisc.edu

CCBC creates research, resources, and infographics about children's and young adult literature and supports intellectual freedom.

Get Ready Stay Ready

getreadystayready.info/home

This is a toolkit compiled by parents and librarians to inform collective pushback against those seeking to censor library materials.

PEN America

pen.org
PEN America champions free expression and publishes research on censorship in schools and school libraries.

Social Media

OIF provides news, videos, educational programs, and event coverage through a variety of social media, including:

- Bluesky:
  - Banned Books Week: @BannedBooksWeek
  - OIF: @OIF
  - Unite Against Book Bans: @UABookBans
- Facebook:
  - Banned Books Week: @BannedBooksWeek
  - Intellectual Freedom Round Table: @IFRTALA
  - OIF: @ALAOIF
  - Unite Against Book Bans: @UniteAgainstBookBans
- Instagram:
  - Banned Books Week: @banned_books_week
  - IFRT: @intellectualfreedomroundtable
  - Unite Against Book Bans: @UniteAgainstBookBans
- X:
  - Banned Books Week: @BannedBooksWeek
  - IFRT: @IFRT_ALA
  - OIF: @OIF
  - Unite Against Book Bans: @UABookBans
- YouTube:
  - Banned Books Week: @BannedBooksWeek
  - FTRF: @FTRFOrg

MONOGRAPHS, JOURNALS, AND OTHER PUBLICATIONS

ALA Store

alastore.ala.org
ALA Editions publishes many books on intellectual freedom topics. These are available for purchase at the ALA Store.

Journal of Intellectual Freedom and Privacy (JIFP)

ala.org/aboutala/offices/oif/JIFP
(800) 545-2433, ext. 4221
JIFP is a quarterly publication on intellectual freedom and privacy in libraries, archives, and educational institutions. It is the periodical of record documenting censorship at public institutions in the United States.

JIFP is an expansion of the retired *Newsletter on Intellectual Freedom,* which started in 1952. OIF staff have edited and produced it since 1970. The journal includes:

- coverage of book bans;
- court rulings;
- legal controversies;
- peer-reviewed articles; and
- opinion pieces.

Submissions of peer-reviewed research, personal accounts of censorship, and book reviews are welcome. New writers can pitch content at: journals.ala.org/index.php/jifp/about/submissions#onlineSubmissions.

ALA POLICY-MAKING AND NETWORKING GROUPS

Intellectual Freedom Committee (IFC)

ala.org/groups/committees/ala/ala-if
The Intellectual Freedom Committee is a standing committee of the ALA Council. The committee works with OIF and other ALA units and officers on intellectual freedom matters. It was created to recommend steps to safeguard the rights of libraries, library users, and library workers in line with the First Amendment and the *Library Bill of Rights.*

IFC recommends intellectual freedom policies to the ALA Council. Council-approved policies establish the professional standards that ALA is committed to defending. They also provide administrators with policies and model language to adopt in their libraries.

IFC also writes guidelines and organizes conference programs to assist library workers in promoting and defending intellectual freedom.

Committee members must be members of ALA and are appointed by ALA's president-elect. To volunteer, fill out the Committee Volunteer Form at ala.org/aboutala/committees.

Committee on Professional Ethics (COPE)

ala.org/groups/committees/ala/ala-profethic
The Committee on Professional Ethics is another standing committee of the ALA Council. It is charged with maintaining, revising, and augmenting the ALA *Code of Ethics*. COPE does this by regularly reviewing the Code and developing interpretations and statements.

COPE meets at ALA conferences and develops educational programs on ethical issues for the library profession. COPE documents are available at ala.org/tools/ethics.

Committee members must be members of ALA and are appointed by the ALA's president-elect. To volunteer, fill out the Committee Volunteer Form at ala.org/aboutala/committees.

Intellectual Freedom Round Table (IFRT)

ala.org/ifrt
The Intellectual Freedom Round Table was established in 1974 to provide a forum to discuss intellectual freedom. It provides ALA members with a greater opportunity to get involved in the defense of intellectual freedom. IFRT enables ALA members to maintain close contact with and assist OIF, IFC, and FTRF.

IFRT sponsors intellectual freedom programs at ALA conferences and gives three awards. Go to the "Intellectual Freedom Awards" section later in this chapter for more information.

IFRT is a great place to enter ALA's intellectual freedom network. Every ALA member is welcome to join.

Information and Advocacy on State and Federal Legislation

ala.org/advocacy/addressing-adverse-legislation
Legislation limiting intellectual freedom restricts library workers from providing service that follows the First Amendment, their state constitutions, and the principles of the *Library Bill of Rights.*

ALA's Public Policy and Advocacy Office (PPA) raises awareness about pending legislation in the U.S. Congress that would impact libraries. OIF works with PPA, the ALA Committee on Legislation, IFC, and FTRF to monitor and address federal legislation.

OIF also works with PPA, its Chapter Relations Office, and its deputy director of state and local advocacy to develop strategies to defeat state legislation aimed at restricting access to information. OIF works with the Media Coalition to track state-level legislation related to intellectual freedom.

When requested, ALA—through IFC, OIF, and FTRF—supplies testimony informing lawmakers of the effects that legislation limiting intellectual freedom would have on library service. With the assistance of legal counsel, OIF provides analyses of proposed state or local statutes affecting intellectual freedom.

LEGAL DEFENSE OF INTELLECTUAL FREEDOM AND HUMANITARIAN AID FOR LIBRARY WORKERS

Freedom to Read Foundation (FTRF)

ftrf.org
(800) 545-2433, ext. 4221
ftrf@ala.org
The Freedom to Read Foundation was incorporated by ALA in 1969 as a separate organization. It acts as ALA's legal defense arm for intellectual freedom in libraries. The purposes of FTRF are to:

- promote and protect the freedom of speech and of the press;
- protect the public's right to access information and materials in libraries;
- safeguard libraries' right to collect and make available any creative work they may legally acquire; and
- support libraries, library workers, authors, publishers, and booksellers in their defense of First Amendment rights by supplying legal counsel or the means to secure it.

FTRF engages in three primary activities. It:

- provides grants to individuals and groups primarily to aid them in litigation;
- participates in litigation dealing with freedom of speech and of the press; and
- educates and advocates about the importance of library workers and the First Amendment to our democracy.

FTRF's litigation work focuses mainly on issues impacting the freedom to read or access materials and information in libraries. The foundation also joins other organizations in litigating broader free-speech issues in the courts.

Among those who should contact FTRF are:

- library workers affected by legislation or official actions that are adversely affecting intellectual freedom;
- those whose professional positions and personal well-being are endangered by their defense of intellectual freedom; and
- library boards and library workers that are threatened with legal action on such grounds.

FTRF also provides statements to assist library workers opposing censorship. These are general discussions rather than opinion letters. Statements are posted on FTRF's website to help library workers understand the legal implications of issues impacting their work.

FTRF is supported through donations and membership. A timeline of FTRF activities and a list of member benefits can be found on their website.

Lawyers for Libraries and Law for Librarians

lawyersforlibraries.org
In 2024, OIF expanded its legal initiatives to offer more support to library workers facing censorship and legislative attacks on intellectual freedom.

Lawyers for Libraries is a network of attorneys committed to defending the freedom to read. They help apply the law to library policies, principles, and problems.

Law for Librarians provides training on the legal foundations of intellectual freedom. These sessions are for both legal and library professionals and help them respond to censorship attempts with confidence and expertise.

To schedule a training session with a Law for Librarians representative from your state—or on a related topic—email oif@ala.org.

LeRoy C. Merritt Humanitarian Fund

merrittfund.org
(312) 280-4221
merrittfund@ala.org
Library workers requiring immediate financial aid should contact the LeRoy C. Merritt Humanitarian Fund.

Established in 1970 as a special trust in memory of Dr. LeRoy C. Merritt, the Merritt Fund is devoted to the support, maintenance, medical care, and welfare of library workers who, in the trustees' opinion, are:

- denied employment rights or discriminated against on the basis of gender, sexual orientation, race, color, creed, age, disability, or place of national origin; or
- denied employment rights because of their defense of intellectual freedom, including promotion of freedom of the press, freedom of speech, and the freedom of library workers to select items for their collections.

The Merritt Fund is supported solely by donations. For information about making a donation to support the Merritt Fund, visit merrittfund.org.

Building Intellectual Freedom Coalitions

OIF works with national, state, and regional organizations to support intellectual freedom. This often happens through coalitions like the National Coalition Against Censorship's Free Expression Network. ALA members are also encouraged to help build and strengthen coalitions.

We can defend intellectual freedom more effectively by joining with others who share First Amendment concerns. By forming coalitions, individuals and organizations can:

- identify allies before an intellectual freedom crisis occurs;
- focus limited resources where they are most needed; and
- reach wider audiences.

Coalitions can also:

- support intellectual freedom legislation;
- help defeat harmful legislation that would negatively affect libraries; and
- work to overturn decisions that censor library resources or services.

OIF is available to advise individuals and organizations that are interested in starting or joining local or national coalitions. OIF also offers guidance on organizing and managing new coalitions. Contact OIF at (800) 545-2433, ext. 4221, or at oif@ala.org.

Unite Against Book Bans

uniteagainstbookbans.org
Unite Against Book Bans empowers people everywhere to stand together in the fight against censorship. Unite is a coalition of:

- readers;
- parents;
- students;
- educators;
- library workers;
- authors;
- publishers;
- community and advocacy organizations;
- businesses;
- faith groups;
- elected officials;
- civic leaders; and
- other concerned people who stand ready to oppose censorship.

Talking points, toolkits, and other resources are available on their website.

State Intellectual Freedom Network (SIFnet)

ala.org/aboutala/offices/oif/sifnet
SIFnet is a coalition of OIF and state and regional library associations' intellectual freedom committees. Their goal is to empower committee volunteers with resources and a network of people to help engage their state membership in intellectual freedom advocacy. They meet regularly to assist each other and raise awareness of emerging intellectual freedom issues.

Authors Against Book Bans

authorsagainstbookbans.com
This coalition of book creators was formed to support educators, library workers, parents, students, and authors who are impacted by unconstitutional efforts to limit the freedom to read.

INTELLECTUAL FREEDOM AWARDS

Several ALA units offer awards related to intellectual freedom. Check with the various divisions of ALA to learn about additional awards that may be available.

Freedom to Read Foundation

- *The Judith Krug Fund Banned Books Week Event Grants* are awarded to nonprofit organizations to support programming and displays during Banned Books Week.
- *The Freedom to Read Foundation Roll of Honor* recognizes individuals who have contributed substantially to FTRF by following its principles or by substantial monetary support.
- *The Gordon M. Conable Conference Scholarship* is an annual scholarship for library school students and new professionals to attend ALA's annual conference. The goal of the scholarship is to advance two principles that Conable held dear: intellectual freedom and mentoring.
- *The Robert P. Holley Fund* is a free, one-year FTRF membership for any current LIS student in a graduate-level program. The fund was established by the retired library science educator Robert Holley and his spouse, Martha Spear, to support FTRF's litigation efforts and to encourage library student membership in the foundation.

Intellectual Freedom Round Table

- *The John Phillip Immroth Memorial Award* is annually bestowed for extraordinary personal courage in defense of intellectual freedom.
- *The Gerald Hodges Intellectual Freedom Chapter Relations Award* annually recognizes an organization that is focused on intellectual freedom. Selected organizations have developed a strong and ongoing multiyear program or a one-year project showing support for intellectual freedom or library user confidentiality.
- *The Eli M. Oboler Memorial Award* honors the best literary work in the area of intellectual freedom. The work must have been published in the two calendar years prior to the presentation of the award.
- The Office for Intellectual Freedom wishes to acknowledge and thank Don Wood, Angela Maycock, Nanette Perez, and Eleanor Diaz, former program officers of OIF, and Trina Magi, whose previous work forms the basis for parts of this chapter.

Take Action

Protecting intellectual freedom is a critical part of every library worker's role. Here are ways you can take action:

- Make intellectual freedom a key part of your library's mission. Adopt the *Library Bill of Rights* as part of your formal policies.
- Educate others about the importance of intellectual freedom. Discuss how the current political environment makes the need for intellectual freedom in libraries even more critical. Volunteer as a speaker for local civic groups and write a letter to the editor for your local press.
- Advocate for the library's role in preserving intellectual freedom. Talk to local library and school boards, the media, and elected officials.
- Monitor the news and your community for censorship incidents. Report them to ALA's Office for Intellectual Freedom.
- Lend your support to others who face censorship challenges. Donate to the LeRoy C. Merritt Humanitarian Fund to give financial support to library workers who are experiencing hardship for defending intellectual freedom: ala.org/aboutala/affiliates/relatedgroups/merrittfund/merritthumanitarian.
- Foster voter turnout and year-round civic engagement at your library: ala.org/advocacy/reader-voter-ready.
- Make intellectual freedom a part of your ongoing programming. Participate in events like Banned Books Week, but don't let this be the only time you talk about the right to read with library users. Some suggestions:
  - Many of the program ideas for Banned Books Week can be done any time of year: read-outs, trivia, scavenger hunts, arts and crafts activities, etc.
  - Include books targeted for censorship in book clubs and displays.
  - Add a brief discussion of censorship to existing programs.
  - Spotlight the role free expression played in civil rights campaigns as part of your holiday and heritage month observations.
  - Display the First Amendment, the *Library Bill of Rights*, and the *Freedom to Read* statement year-round.
- Stay up-to-date on legislation and court cases that could affect intellectual freedom in libraries.
- Be a leader. Start a local group dedicated to protecting intellectual freedom in libraries. When local libraries are under attack, a well-organized group is a huge help.
- Join ALA and your state library association. Our profession is stronger and more resilient when we stand together. If you're already a member, join a committee devoted to intellectual freedom or advocacy.

Appendix 1: Glossary of Terms

arbitrary distinctions: Unfair rules that group people, behaviors, or things in ways that don't make sense for the rule's purpose. For example, a policy about how long someone can borrow a library item shouldn't be based on something unrelated, like the person's age or housing status.

ban: The removal of materials from a library's collection based on the objections of a person or group.

behavioral data surveillance: The collection of data about how a person uses the library that can be used on its own or with other information to identify them. This data may be used to monitor, track, or create a profile of someone's library use beyond what's needed for normal library operations. These practices often harm minority and marginalized groups, who are more likely to be unfairly identified or misidentified. *See also* **privacy audit.**

censorship: The limiting or removing of access to words, images, or ideas. The decision to restrict or deny access is made by a governing authority. This could be a person, group, or organization/business. Censorship by the government is illegal.

challenge: An attempt to have a library resource removed, or access to it restricted, based on the objections of a person or group.

child sexual abuse material (CSAM): Images and videos that show a child engaged in sexual activity or appearing to engage in sexual activity. The First Amendment does not protect CSAM because a child cannot legally give consent. The possession of CSAM is also illegal. Computer-generated images and adults portraying minors are not considered CSAM. While "child pornography" is still used in many laws, CSAM is the preferred term.

Children's Internet Protection Act (CIPA): Enacted into law in 2000, CIPA places restrictions on public schools and libraries that use federal funding for internet access. CIPA requires funding recipients to adopt internet safety policies and use filtering software. The filtering software must block or filter access to pictures that are obscene, child sexual abuse material, or harmful to minors.

Children's Online Privacy Protection Act (COPPA): COPPA imposes requirements on commercial online content providers that collect personal information from a child under thirteen years of age. The requirements are for websites or online services directed to children or those who have actual knowledge that they are dealing with a child under thirteen years of age. COPPA requires providers to obtain verifiable parental consent before they can collect, archive, use, or resell any of the child's personal information.

collection development policy: The guidelines libraries use for the selection, purchasing, and deselection of materials. The policy assists library workers in building a collection that aligns with the library's mission and can be made public to inform users of the guidelines. It also has procedures for handling challenges.

compelling government interest: A term used by courts when assessing the burden of government regulation or action on the exercise of a fundamental right, such as freedom of speech. For a rule to withstand a constitutional challenge, the government must show more than merely an important reason for the rule. The reason must be compelling. This means it must be so important that it outweighs even the most valued and basic freedom it negatively affects. *See also* **strict scrutiny.**

confidentiality: An obligation not to share personally identifiable information (PII) without user consent or as required by law. In a library, confidentiality is when the library possesses users' PII and keeps the information private on their behalf.

content-neutral restrictions: Legal limits on speech that apply equally to all speakers and topics. These restrictions don't consider what's being said, only how, when, or where it's said. Government entities, including public libraries, must use this approach when limiting speech. Libraries can't silence speakers based on their message or the potential to cause controversy. *See also* **time, place, and manner restrictions** and **viewpoint-neutral restrictions.**

court order: A legal document issued by a court that tells a person to do or not do something. This includes search warrants and the preservation of documents orders.

Creative Commons (CC): A nonprofit organization with a mission to increase the number of creative works available for others to legally build upon and share. The organization provides a variety of free copyright licenses known as Creative Commons licenses. These licenses allow creators to explicitly grant additional uses of copyrighted materials that are not normally allowed under current copyright law.

due process: The government must follow proper legal procedures before taking away someone's life, freedom, or property. This includes giving people the right to defend themselves, have a fair hearing, and appeal decisions they disagree with. Due process is guaranteed by the Fifth and Fourteenth Amendments of the U.S. Constitution.

equitable access: Equitable access to information means recognizing and addressing the different barriers people face. It's not about treating everyone the same, it's about providing access to information, services, and materials in ways that account for those differences so that everyone has an opportunity to benefit.

E-rate: A Federal Communications Commission (FCC) program that provides schools and libraries with discounts to acquire telecommunications services, internet access, and internal connections. The discounts are based on the poverty level and location (rural/urban) of the school or library. The discounts range from 20 to 90 percent. Eligible schools and libraries may apply individually or as part of a consortium. Applicants must provide the computers, telephones, and software that are needed to use the connectivity provided by the program. The recipients of funds are subject to CIPA and must adopt an internet safety policy and use internet filtering software.

Establishment Clause: Language in the First Amendment that prohibits the government from making any law "respecting an establishment of religion." The clause forbids the government from:

- establishing an official religion;
- taking actions that unduly favor one religion over another; or
- unduly favoring religion over non-religion or vice versa.

fair use: A limitation and exception to the exclusive rights granted by copyright law to the author of a creative work. In U.S. copyright law (17 U.S.C.), fair use permits the limited use of copyrighted material without getting permission from the rights holder. Courts use a four-part test to see if a particular use of a work is "fair":

1. the purpose and character of the use;
2. the nature of the copyrighted work;
3. the amount and substantiality of the portion taken; and
4. the effect of the use upon the potential market.

Examples of fair use include:

- Commentary
- Search engines
- Criticism
- Parody
- News reporting

- Research
- Teaching
- Library archiving
- Scholarship

Family Educational Rights and Privacy Act (FERPA): FERPA controls the disclosure of a student's educational records and information. The act gives parents and students the right to inspect and correct a student's records. FERPA applies to all schools that receive funds under an applicable program of the U.S. Department of Education.

filtering software: Software that monitors and blocks access to certain kinds of online content. To be CIPA-compliant, the filtering software must block minors' access to images that are harmful to minors, obscene, or contain child sexual abuse material. Schools and libraries that accept funds through the Universal Service E-rate program and the Library Services and Technology Act (LSTA) must certify that they use filtering software. Using filtering software is only one part of complying with CIPA. *See also* **Children's Internet Protection Act (CIPA).**

First Amendment: Part of the Bill of Rights of the U.S. Constitution:

> Congress shall make no law respecting an establishment of religion, or prohibiting the free exercise thereof; or abridging the freedom of speech or of the press; or the right of the people peaceably to assemble, and to petition the government for a redress of grievances.

First Amendment audit: A form of citizen activism in which a person or group records their interactions with government workers to test whether their First Amendment rights are respected. These individuals may ask challenging questions or act in ways meant to provoke a reaction. They believe they have the right to film anywhere the public is allowed, including libraries.

Fourth Amendment: Part of the Bill of Rights of the U.S. Constitution:

> The right of the people to be secure in their persons, houses, papers, and effects, against unreasonable searches and seizures, shall not be violated, and no warrants shall issue, but upon probable cause, supported by oath or affirmation, and particularly describing the place to be searched, and the persons or things to be seized.

free expression: The right of people to share their thoughts, ideas, beliefs, or opinions without fear of punishment from the government. Free expression is protected by the First Amendment of the U.S. Constitution.

Freedom of Information Act (FOIA): A federal public records law passed in 1967 that gives people the right to access records from federal government agencies, unless the information falls under certain exemptions. Many states also have their own public records laws. Public libraries that receive government funding may be required to share records under these laws.

gender identity: How a person understands and experiences their own gender. This may be the same as or different from the sex they were assigned at birth.

harassment: Unsolicited and unwelcome speech or actions. This is usually part of a pattern of behavior that:

- demeans;
- threatens;
- annoys;
- intimidates;
- humiliates;
- causes emotional distress; or
- causes a person to fear for their safety.

harmful to minors: Sexually explicit materials that adults have a legal right to access may be considered "harmful to minors" if they lack serious literary, artistic, political, or scientific value for minors. It is illegal to knowingly distribute such materials to a minor. However, a work is not "harmful to minors" simply because it addresses sexual topics or contains sexual content. Not all states have laws defining or prohibiting material deemed harmful to minors. In some states, the law specifies that libraries and library workers may use professional judgment and the library's mission as a positive defense if prosecuted for allegedly providing such content.

hate group: An organization or group of individuals that spreads anger and fear toward specific types of people. These groups target others based on:

- race;
- culture;
- country of origin;
- religion;
- gender;
- gender identity;
- sexual orientation; or
- some other social category.

These groups may use lies, threats, or violence to push their ideas and harm others.

hate speech: Words or expressions that attack, insult, or threaten a person or group based on who they are (e.g., race, religion, sexual orientation, etc.). Hate speech often involves insulting or threatening the targeted group and promoting harmful stereotypes and discrimination against them. "Hate speech" doesn't have a legal definition under U.S. law and is protected by the First Amendment. It can only be criminalized when it directly incites imminent criminal activity or makes specific threats of violence against a person or group.

intellectual freedom: Intellectual freedom gives people the right to think for themselves. It respects individual dignity and self-rule. This freedom allows people to form their own ideas and opinions by questioning the world around them. Every person has the right to access information from all points of view, in all formats, and without restriction. Privacy is required for true intellectual freedom. The protection of this freedom ensures every person's right to form their own ideas and opinions.

intellectual property: Property that results from original creative thought. This includes works that are patented, copyrighted, or trademarked.

Library Services and Technology Act (LSTA): A federal grant program managed by the Institute of Museum and Library Services (IMLS).

marginalized groups: Communities that have been unfairly left out of access, opportunities, or decision-making because of long-standing systems of power and inequality.

Neighborhood Children's Internet Protection Act (NCIPA): A subsection of CIPA that requires an internet policy with additional requirements to qualify for E-rate discounts.

obscenity or obscene material: Sexually themed speech or expressive materials that are not protected by the First Amendment. The legal test for obscenity includes the following criteria:

1. whether the average person, applying contemporary community standards would find that the work, taken as a whole, appeals to "prurient interest";
2. whether the work depicts or describes, in a patently offensive way, sexual conduct specifically defined by the applicable state law; and
3. whether the work, taken as a whole, lacks serious literary, artistic, political, or scientific value.

Only a judge or jury can find a work legally obscene.

partisan or doctrinal disapproval: The act of disagreeing with an idea, book, or resource because it goes against someone's political beliefs (partisan) or religious or ideological beliefs (doctrinal).

personally identifiable information (PII): Information that makes it possible to identify someone. This could be one piece of information by itself, or several pieces put together. PII might include things like a person's name, address, or phone number. Additional information such as birth date, email address, or IP address may be combined to reveal someone's identity.

pornography: Written or visual materials that are designed to cause sexual excitement. Under U.S. law, "pornography" has no legal definition. Instead, courts and legislatures identify illegal sexually themed content as "obscenity," which is defined by statute in federal and state law.

prejudicial labels: Labels that are used to influence opinions or limit access to materials, which is a form of censorship. These labels often reflect personal judgments about a work's content, language, themes, or the background or beliefs of its creator. They may mark materials as inappropriate or offensive for certain groups and are used to warn, discourage, or prevent people from using the materials.

privacy: The right to keep personal information and activities to yourself. In a library (physical or virtual), users have the right to seek information without others knowing or judging what they're interested in. It's the freedom to learn about any topic without people watching. *See also* **behavioral data surveillance** and **privacy audit**.

privacy audit: A review of how an organization handles people's personal information. It looks at how information about users is collected, stored, shared, used, and destroyed. The goal is to make sure the library's promises of privacy and confidentiality are supported by its practices. *See also* **behavioral data surveillance**.

probable cause: A reasonable basis for believing that a crime has been committed or that grounds exist for a legal action.

protected speech: Speech that is protected from government censorship or regulation under the First Amendment, as interpreted by the U.S. Supreme Court. Speech is considered protected until a court decides it falls into a category of unprotected speech. The Supreme Court has identified several categories of speech that are unprotected by the First Amendment. *See also* **unprotected speech**.

public forum: A "traditional public forum" is a government-owned place where people can freely express their ideas and opinions. This is usually a place open for public use, like parks, sidewalks, streets, etc.

- A "designated or limited public forum" is a space that is designated for a specific purpose. The government may choose to open the space for public speech but can set limits on use. These limits must be fair and apply to everyone equally.

- A "nonpublic forum" is a place that isn't meant for public speech or expression. The government can set stricter limits on who can speak and what can be said there.

publicly supported libraries: Libraries created by a government entity, or that receive the majority of their financial support from government funding.

request for reconsideration: A formal, written request that a library remove or restrict access to a particular resource. It may also be called a "statement of concern."

search warrant: A court order that authorizes police or other officials to search a person or place for specific items. Search warrants are signed by a judge or magistrate who believes there is probable cause to think that evidence of a crime will be found.

strict scrutiny: A test applied to see if a restriction on speech is unconstitutional under the First Amendment. To justify a restriction on speech, the government must show that:

1. it has a compelling government interest in enforcing the restriction;
2. the restriction is narrowly tailored to achieve that compelling interest; and
3. there is no less restrictive alternative to achieving that interest.

See also compelling government interest.

subpoena: A legal order issued by a court, grand jury, legislative body, or administrative agency that tells someone they must:

1. appear at a specified time; and
2. answer questions or provide information under oath.

Compliance with a subpoena is mandatory, and failure to follow the order may result in legal consequences.

time, place, and manner restrictions: Rules that limit when, where, or how people can express themselves in public. These rules are allowed if they:

1. Serve an important government purpose
2. Apply to everyone equally
3. Don't target specific ideas or viewpoints

For example, a library might not allow loud noises in its meeting rooms. This is allowed because it:

1. Keeps the library quiet for everyone (important purpose)
2. Applies to all groups using the rooms
3. Doesn't care about what people are saying, just how loudly they're saying it

See also **viewpoint-neutral restrictions** and **content-neutral restrictions.**

unprotected speech: Speech or expressive activity that is not protected by the First Amendment. The main categories of unprotected speech identified by the U.S. Supreme Court include:

- obscenity;
- child sexual abuse material;
- defamation; and
- expression intended and likely to incite imminent lawless action (e.g., fighting words or true threats).

See also protected speech.

viewpoint-neutral restrictions: Restrictions on expression that are allowed under the U.S. Constitution. The restrictions must apply uniformly to all speech, regardless of the point of view expressed by the speaker. Public libraries, like all government agencies, may not silence speakers the government opposes or only allow those whom the government supports. Libraries also cannot silence speakers because of controversy. For example, libraries may not use filtering software to block or filter content favoring same-sex marriage while allowing access to content that opposes same-sex marriage. *See also* **content-neutral restrictions** and **time, place, and manner restrictions**.

Appendix 2: For Further Reading

Compiled by Emily Knox

PART I: INTELLECTUAL FREEDOM AND LIBRARIES

Alfino, Mark, and Laura Koltutsky, eds. *The Library Juice Press Handbook of Intellectual Freedom: Concepts, Cases and Theories*. Library Juice, 2014.

Gaffney, Loretta M. *Young Adult Literature, Libraries, and Conservative Activism*. Rowman & Littlefield, 2017.

Geller, Evelyn. *Forbidden Books in American Public Libraries, 1876–1939: A Study in Cultural Change*. Greenwood, 1984.

Knox, Emily. *Foundations of Intellectual Freedom*. American Library Association, 2023.

LaRue, James. *On Censorship: A Public Librarian Examines Cancel Culture in the US*. Fulcrum, 2023.

Latham, Joyce M. "Wheat and Chaff: Carl Roden, Abe Korman, and the Definitions of Intellectual Freedom in the Chicago Public Library." *Libraries & the Cultural Record* 44, no. 3 (2009): 279–98.

Oltmann, Shannon M. *Practicing Intellectual Freedom in Libraries*. ABC-CLIO, 2019.

Robbins, Louise S. *Censorship and the American Library: The American Library Association's Response to Threats to Intellectual Freedom, 1939–1969*. Greenwood, 1996.

Samek, Toni. *Intellectual Freedom and Social Responsibility in American Librarianship: 1967–1974*. McFarland, 2001.

Wiegand, Shirley A., and Wayne A. Wiegand. *Books on Trial: Red Scare in the Heartland*. University of Oklahoma Press, 2007.

Policies

Batch, Kristen R. *Fencing Out Knowledge: Impacts of the Children's Internet Protection Act 10 Years Later*. American Library Association, 2014.

Braman, Sandra. *Change of State: Information, Policy, and Power*. MIT Press, 2006.

Garnar, Martin, Trina J. Magi, American Library Association, and Office for Intellectual Freedom, eds. *A History of ALA Policy on Intellectual Freedom: A Supplement to the* Intellectual Freedom Manual. Tenth Edition. American Library Association, 2021.

Jaeger, Paul T., and Natalie Greene Taylor. *Foundations of Information Policy*. American Library Association, 2019.

Nelson, Sandra S., June Garcia, and Public Library Association. *Creating Policies for Results: From Chaos to Clarity*. American Library Association, 2003.

PART II: INTELLECTUAL FREEDOM TOPICS AND BEST PRACTICES

Access to Library Resources and Services

Asheim, Lester. "Not Censorship but Selection." *Wilson Library Bulletin* 28, no. 1 (1953): 63–67.

Austin, Jeanie. *Library Services and Incarceration: Recognizing Barriers, Strengthening Access*. American Library Association, 2022.

Belarde-Lewis, Miranda H., and Sarah R. Kostelecky. "Tribal Critical Race Theory in Zuni Pueblo: Information Access in a Cautious Community." In *Knowledge Justice: Disrupting Library and Information Studies Through Critical Race Theory,* edited by Sofia Y. Leung and Jorge R. López-McKnight. MIT Press, 2021.

Cooke, Nicole A. *Information Services to Diverse Populations: Developing Culturally Competent Library Professionals*. Second Edition. American Library Association, forthcoming.

Farkas, Meredith. "When Values Collide: Reconciling Our Commitments When Hate Speech Is Involved." *American Libraries* 49, no. 11/12 (2018): 54–54.

Hofstadter, Richard. *Anti-Intellectualism in American Life*. Vintage Books, 1963.

Laskin, Kodi, ed. *Serving Patrons with Disabilities: Perspectives and Insights from People with Disabilities*. American Library Association, 2023.

Mann, Jesie D. "Intellectual Freedom, Academic Freedom, and the Academic Librarian | AAUP." *Journal of Academic Freedom* 8 (2017). aaup.org/JAF8/intellectual-freedom-academic-freedom-and-academic-librarian.

Mathiesen, Kay. "Access to Information as a Human Right." SSRN Scholarly Paper No. 1264666. Social Science Research Network, September 7, 2008. doi.org/10.2139/ssrn.1264666.

Noble, Safiya Umoja. *Algorithms of Oppression: How Search Engines Reinforce Racism*. New York University Press, 2018.

Oltmann, Shannon M., Vanessa Kitzie, and Sarah Barriage. "'For Me, It Is an Intellectual Freedom Issue': Drag Storytimes, Neutrality, and ALA Core Values." *Journal of Librarianship and Information Science* 55, no. 3 (2022): 734–43. doi.org/10.1177/09610006221100853.

Smith, Catherine. "Automating Intellectual Freedom: Artificial Intelligence, Bias, and the Information Landscape." *IFLA Journal* 48, no. 3 (2022): 422–31. doi.org/10.1177/03400352211057145.

Censorship, Challenged Resources, and Internet Filtering

American Booksellers Association. *The ABA Right to Read Handbook: A Reader's Guide to Fighting Book Bans*. American Booksellers Association, 2024.

Caldwell-Stone, Deborah. "Filtering and the First Amendment." *American Libraries* 44, no. 3/4 (2013): 58–61.

Calzada, Becky, Val Edwards, Maegan Coffin Heindel, and Steven D. Yates. *Prepared Libraries, Empowered Teams: A Workbook for Navigating Intellectual Freedom Challenges Together*. American Library Association, 2024.

Doyle, Robert P. *Banned Books: Defending Our Freedom to Read*. American Library Association, 2017.

Jones, Amanda. *That Librarian: The Fight Against Book Banning in America*. Bloomsbury, 2024.

Knox, Emily J. M. *Book Banning in 21st-Century America*. Bloomsbury Libraries Unlimited, 2025.

Knox, Emily J. M. "Silencing Stories: Challenges to Diverse Books." *The International Journal of Information, Diversity, & Inclusion (IJIDI)* 3, no. 2 (2019).

LaRue, James. *The New Inquisition: Understanding and Managing Intellectual Freedom Challenges*. Libraries Unlimited, 2007.

Nye, Valerie, ed. *Intellectual Freedom Stories from a Shifting Landscape*. American Library Association, 2020.

Oltmann, Shannon M., ed. *The Fight Against Book Bans: Perspectives from the Field*. Bloomsbury Libraries Unlimited, 2023.

Peterson, Chris, Shannon M. Oltmann, and Emily J. M. Knox. "The Inconsistent Work of Web Filters: Mapping Information Access in Alabama Public Schools and Libraries." *International Journal of Communication* 11, no. 0 (2017): 27. ijoc.org/index.php/ijoc/article/view/6944.

Children and Youth

Dawkins, April M., ed. *Intellectual Freedom Issues in School Libraries*. Libraries Unlimited, 2021.

Heins, Marjorie. *Not in Front of the Children: "Indecency," Censorship, and the Innocence of Youth*. 2nd edition. Hill and Wang, 2007.

Kent, Chelsea Rae, and Jillian M. Kneeland. "'Dear George, with Love': Reading All Boys Aren't Blue Through a Lens of Critical Love Amidst Rampant Book Bans." *Research on Diversity in Youth Literature* 6, no. 1 (2024): 1. doi.org/10.21900/j.rydl.v6i1.1359.

Knox, Emily J. M. "Indoctrination and Common Sense Interpretation of Texts: The Tucson Unified School District Book Banning." *Journal of Intellectual Freedom & Privacy* 2, no. 2 (2017): 11–22. doi.org/10.5860/jifp.v2i2.6246.

Kobabe, Maia. "Opinion | Schools Are Banning My Book. But Queer Kids Need Queer Stories." *Washington Post*, October 29, 2021. washingtonpost.com/opinions/2021/10/29/schools-are-banning-my-book-queer-kids-need-queer-stories/.

McNicol, Sarah. "Freedom to Teach: Implications of the Removal of Persepolis from Chicago Schools." *Journal of Graphic Novels and Comics* (September 2014): 1–11. doi.org/10.1080/21504857.2014.943409.

Pappano, Laura. *School Moms: Parent Activism, Partisan Politics, and the Battle for Public Education*. Beacon, 2024.

Price, Richard S. "Contesting Obscenity: Book Challengers and Criminalizing Literature." *Journal of Intellectual Freedom & Privacy* 7, no. 4 (2022): 4. doi.org/10.5860/jifp.v7i4.7747.

Robinson, Kerry H. *Innocence, Knowledge, and the Construction of Childhood: The Contradictory Nature of Sexuality and Censorship in Children's Contemporary Lives*. Routledge, 2013.

Rodriguez, Sanjuana, and Sandra Osorio. "Censorship in Early Childhood: A Critical Content Analysis of Banned and Challenged Latine Picture Books." *Research on Diversity in Youth Literature* 6, no. 1 (2024): 1. doi.org/10.21900/j.rydl.v6i1.1400.

Ross, Catherine J. *Lessons in Censorship: How Schools and Courts Subvert Students' First Amendment Rights*. Harvard University Press, 2015.

Scales, Pat R. *Scales on Censorship: Real Life Lessons from School Library Journal*. Edited by Rebecca T. Miller and Barbara A. Genco. Rowman & Littlefield, 2015.

Scales, Pat R. *Teaching Banned Books: 32 Guides for Children and Teens*. American Library Association, 2020.

Collection Development and Management

Adler, Melissa. *Cruising the Library: Perversities in the Organization of Knowledge*. Fordham University Press, 2017.

Jensen, Kelly. "What Updates Should Library Collection Policies Include? Book Censorship News, February 23, 2024." Book Riot, February 23, 2024. bookriot.com/what-updates-should-library-collection-policies-include/.

Johnson, Peggy, and Mary Beth Weber. *Fundamentals of Collection Development and Management*. 5th edition. American Library Association, 2025.

Schrader, Alvin M. "Why You Can't 'Censorproof' Your Public Library." *Public Library Quarterly* 16, no. 1 (1997): 3–30. doi.org/10.1300/J118v16n01_02.

Copyright

Benson, Sara. *Compact Copyright: Quick Answers to Common Questions.* American Library Association, 2021.

Crews, Kenneth D. *Copyright Law for Librarians and Educators: Creative Strategies and Practical Solutions.* American Library Association, 2020.

Dews, Fred. "Why Copyright Law Allows You to Borrow a Book, But Not Share a Digital Song." Brookings, November 30, 2014. brookings.edu/blog/brookings-now/2014/06/09/why-copyright-law-allows-you-to-borrow-a-book-but-not-share-a-digital-song/.

Heller, Michael A., and James Salzman. *Mine! How the Hidden Rules of Ownership Control Our Lives.* Knopf Doubleday, 2021.

Simpson, Carol, and Sara E. Wolf. *Copyright for Schools: A Practical Guide.* Libraries Unlimited, 2021.

Suber, Peter. *Open Access.* MIT Press, 2012.

Meeting Rooms, Exhibit Spaces, and Programming

Atkins, Robert, Svetlana Mintcheva, and National Coalition against Censorship (U.S.), eds. *Censoring Culture: Contemporary Threats to Free Expression.* New Press, 2006.

Kelly, Spencer D., and Yukari Hirata. "Preparing the Campus for a Controversial Speaker." Inside Higher Ed, May 31, 2023. insidehighered.com/opinion/views/2023/05/31/preparing-campus-controversial-speaker-opinion.

Pekoll, Kristin. *Beyond Banned Books: Defending Intellectual Freedom Throughout Your Library.* American Library Association, 2019.

Politics, Religion, and Free Expression

American Booksellers Association. *The ABA Right to Read Handbook: A Reader's Guide to Fighting Book Bans.* American Booksellers Association, 2024.

Asato, Noriko. "Librarians' Free Speech: The Challenge of Librarians' Own Intellectual Freedom to the American Library Association, 1946–2007." *Library Trends* 63, no. 1 (2014): 75–105. doi.org/10.1353/lib.2014.0025.

Matsuda, Mari J., Charles B. Lawrence, Richard Delgado, and Kimberle Williams Crenshaw. *Words That Wound: Critical Race Theory, Assaultive Speech, and the First Amendment.* Westview, 1993.

Mchangama, Jacob. *Free Speech: A History from Socrates to Social Media.* Basic Books, 2022.

Strossen, Nadine. *Free Speech: What Everyone Needs to Know.* Oxford University Press, 2024.

Tushnet, Mark V., Alan K. Chen, and Joseph Blocher. *Free Speech Beyond Words: The Surprising Reach of the First Amendment.* NYU Press, 2017.

Privacy and Confidentiality

Berman, Erin, and Bonnie Tijerina. *The Ultimate Privacy Field Guide: A Workbook of Best Practices.* American Library Association, 2022.

Briney, Kristin, and Becky Yoose. *Managing Data for Patron Privacy: Comprehensive Strategies for Libraries.* American Library Association, 2022.

Chin, Chieh-Li, Tian Wang, Erh-Hsuan Wang, and Masooda Bashir. "Patron Privacy Protections in Public Libraries: IT Professionals' Points of View." *Journal of Intellectual Freedom & Privacy* 8, no. 3 (2024): 3. doi.org/10.5860/jifp.v8i3.7965.

Fiscus, Moira. "Knowledge Held Hostage: What the British Library Ransomware Attack Can Teach Us." *College & Research Libraries* 85, no. 5 (2024): 5. doi.org/10.5860/crl.85.5.628.

Hartman-Caverly, Sarah, and Alexandria Chisholm, eds. *Practicing Privacy Literacy in Academic Libraries: Theories, Methods, and Cases.* Association of College & Research Libraries, 2023.

Keen, Caroline. "Apathy, Convenience or Irrelevance? Identifying Conceptual Barriers to Safeguarding Children's Data Privacy." *New Media & Society* 24, no. 1 (2022): 50–69. doi.org/10.1177/1461444820960068.

Lamdan, Sarah. *Data Cartels: The Companies That Control and Monopolize Our Information.* Stanford University Press, 2022.

Nissenbaum, Helen. *Privacy in Context: Technology, Policy, and the Integrity of Social Life.* Stanford University Press, 2009.

Pedley, Paul. *A Practical Guide to Privacy in Libraries*. Facet, 2020.

Solove, Daniel J. *Nothing to Hide: The False Tradeoff Between Privacy and Security*. Yale University Press, 2011.

Visits and Requests from Law Enforcement

Albrecht, Steve. *The Safe Library: Keeping Users, Staff, and Collections Secure*. Rowman & Littlefield, 2023.

Ceccato, Vania, Emrah Ercin, Julia Hazanov, Sara Elfström, and Adriana Sampaio. "Safety in a Public Library: The Perspective of Visitors and Staff." *Library Management* 44, nos. 3–4 (2023): 229–45. doi.org/10.1108/LM-12-2022-0127.

Dapier, Jarrett, and Emily Knox. "When Not to Call the Cops." *American Libraries*, July 8, 2020. americanlibrariesmagazine.org/2020/07/08/rethinking-when-to-call-the-cops/.

PART III: ADVOCACY AND ASSISTANCE

Breeding, Marshall. "Patron Engagement and Marketing Products and Services for Public Libraries." *Library Technology Reports* 58, no. 2 (2022): 2. doi.org/10.5860/ltr.58n2.

Chrastka, John, and Patrick "PC" Sweeney. *Winning Elections and Influencing Politicians for Library Funding*. American Library Association, 2017.

Diaz, Stephanie, Eva Murray, and Mary Lubbers. "Idea Lab: Engaging with the Public During Times of Increased Book Challenges." *Journal of Library Outreach and Engagement* 2, no. 1 (2022): 1. doi.org/10.21900/j.jloe.v2i1.965.

Get Ready Stay Ready Community Action Toolkit. getreadystayready.info.

Hand, Dorcas, Sara Kelly Johns, Michelle Robertson, and Eryn Duffee. *Strengthening Library Ecosystems: Collaborate for Advocacy and Impact*. American Library Association, 2024.

Hirsh, Sandra, ed. *Library 2035: Imagining the Next Generation of Libraries*. Rowman & Littlefield, 2024.

Jensen, Kelly. "56 Small Tasks to Be Proactive Against Book Censorship in 2025 and Beyond: Book Censorship News, January 3, 2025." Book Riot, January 3, 2025. bookriot.com/56-small-tasks-to-be-proactive-against-book-censorship-2025/.

Jensen, Kelly. "How to Explain Book Bans to Those Who Want to Understand: Book Censorship News, August." Book Riot, August 9, 2024. bookriot.com/how-to-explain-book-bans/.

McDowell, Kate. *Critical Data Storytelling for Libraries: Crafting Ethical Narratives for Advocacy and Impact.* American Library Association, 2025.

Pearson, Peter D. "Sustaining Local Library Advocacy in Today's Political Environment." *The Political Librarian* 6, no. 2 (2023): 2. doi.org/10.7936/pollib.8851.

About the Contributors

STEPHANIE "COLE" ADAMS is an attorney who represents libraries, educators, students, and creative professionals. Cole's law firm, the Law Office of Stephanie Adams, provides the Ask the Lawyer service that New York State's nine library resource councils provide to each library in the state. Cole is a member of the First Amendment Lawyers Association and the ALA Lawyers for Libraries faculty. She is a board member of the Freedom to Read Foundation, is a graduate of SUNY Buffalo School of Law, and interned at the Comic Book Legal Defense Fund during her undergraduate studies at Hampshire College.

STACY LYN BURNETT is a thought leader, keynote speaker, and justice advocate advancing ITHAKA S + R's mission to democratize access to knowledge. As the senior product manager of JSTOR Access in Prison, she leads a groundbreaking initiative that reaches over one million incarcerated people across four continents. Under her leadership, JSTOR has received honors from the Association of Learned and Professional Society Publishers and the Society for Scholarly Publishing for its work expanding access to academic resources in prisons and jails. Burnett began her education while incarcerated through the Bard Prison Initiative and earned an MBA in sustainability from Bard Graduate School after her release. Her work bridges education, policy, and technology to create more equitable futures for justice-impacted communities.

DEBORAH CALDWELL-STONE is the former director of ALA's Office for Intellectual Freedom and a former appellate litigator who worked with librarians, trustees, and educators on a wide range of intellectual freedom issues, including materials censorship, internet filtering, and privacy. She contributed to the current and previous editions of the *Intellectual Freedom Manual* and the 3rd edition of *Information Services Today.*

BECKY CALZADA is a district library coordinator in Leander, Texas, and a cofounding member of Texas #FReadom Fighters. She was the 2024–2025 president of the American Association of School Librarians, has served on the ALA Intellectual Freedom Committee, and is a member of the ALA Policy Corps' Unite Against Book Bans Cadre and the Legislative Advocacy Committee for the Texas Library Association. She is the recipient of several intellectual freedom awards and is the coauthor of *Prepared Libraries, Empowered Teams: A Workbook for Navigating Intellectual Freedom Challenges Together*, published in 2024 by ALA Editions.

ADAM CHANDLER is a librarian at Cornell University, where he has worked for the past twenty-five years. His current research focus is data governance in academic libraries and higher education broadly. He is the cofounder of Cornell Library's Privacy Services Advisory Council and is a certified information privacy technologist (International Association of Privacy Professionals).

MEGAN MURRAY CUSICK is a consultant with more than two decades of experience as a library practitioner and advocate. A former staff member in ALA's Public Policy Office, she co-led the launch of ALA's Unite Against Book Bans campaign and its Ecosystem Initiative. Cusick presents and publishes about intellectual freedom, library advocacy, and civic engagement. She is a proud member of ALA and the Freedom to Read Foundation.

CATHI FUHRMAN recently retired from the State College Area High School after thirty-one years as a school librarian and supervisor in Pennsylvania and now adjuncts at Antioch University Seattle. A past president of the Pennsylvania School Librarians Association (PSLA), she co-chairs its Intellectual Freedom Task Group, which won the 2024 ALA Gerald Hodges Intellectual Freedom Award. She also received the 2024 AASL Intellectual Freedom Award for fighting censorship and creating a rapid response team to support school librarians, students, and communities in Pennsylvania. She continues this work as project director for the PSLA Helpline for Intellectual Freedom grants.

SAM HELMICK is the community and access services coordinator at the Iowa City Public Library. They have been active in national leadership roles, including as an ALA Executive Board member, ALA Intellectual Freedom Round Table chair-elect, Iowa Library Association (ILA) president, ILA Intellectual Freedom Committee chair, and chair of the Iowa Governor's Commission of Libraries. A frequent speaker and trainer, Helmick focuses on intellectual freedom, advocacy through storytelling, and community-centered librarianship. They served as president of the American Library Association for 2025–2026.

NICK HIGGINS is the chief librarian of the Brooklyn Public Library (BPL). Higgins began his career at BPL as a librarian trainee and also held the position of jail and prison librarian at the New York Public Library, building library services on Rikers Island. Higgins and his team were recently recognized as "Librarian of the Year" from *Library Journal* for their work on Books Unbanned, a freedom to read initiative that provides free access to the BPL's entire digital library collection for teens anywhere in the United States facing book bans. Higgins received an MLIS from the Pratt Institute and a BA in British literature from Hunter College.

ELDON RAY JAMES is a formerly incarcerated man who completed library school after prison. He is a retired researcher who helped to write the *Prisoners' Right to Read* as well as both international and ALA standards for library services for the incarcerated and detained. He received the 2022 Freedom to Read Foundation's Roll of Honor award.

LESLIEDIANA JONES is the associate director for public services at the Harvard Law School Library. She is the president of the Freedom to Read Foundation (2025–2026), served as its vice-president (2024–2025), and chaired ALA's Intellectual Freedom Committee (2022–2024). As a steadfast proponent of the right to read and First Amendment rights for all persons, she speaks on these topics to both U.S. and international audiences, including LIBER Journées.

EMILY KNOX is a professor in the School of Information Sciences at the University of Illinois at Urbana-Champaign. Her book *Foundations of Intellectual Freedom* won the 2023 Eli M. Oboler Prize for best published work in intellectual freedom. The second edition of her previous book, *Book Banning in 21st Century America*, will be published in 2026. She has been interviewed by numerous media outlets and also testified before the U.S. Senate Judiciary Committee on book banning. Knox received her PhD from the doctoral program at the Rutgers University School of Communication & Information.

SARAH R. KOSTELECKY is currently serving in a term position as the Indigenous program specialist at the Library of Congress. She is on leave from the University of New Mexico Libraries where she is an associate professor. Kostelecky is a coauthor of *Cultural Humility: A Special Report* and a coeditor of *Hopeful Visions, Practical Actions: Cultural Humility in Library Work*. Her research interests include Indigenous representation in library collections and outreach efforts to Indigenous communities. She is an enrolled member of the Zuni Pueblo tribe of New Mexico.

SARAH LAMDAN is the deputy director at ALA's Office for Intellectual Freedom. She is an attorney and librarian. Before joining ALA, Lamdan was a professor of law at the CUNY School of Law, specializing in administrative law, data privacy, and information law. She has also served as a librarian in various academic and private law libraries. Her work has been featured in *Library Quarterly*, the *Georgetown Law Technology Review*, and NYU's *Review of Law & Social Change*. Her book *Data Cartels* was published in 2022.

ROBIN LESTER-KENTON is a champion of intellectual freedom and played a key role in launching and promoting the Brooklyn Public Library's (BPL) groundbreaking *Books Unbanned* program, which provides free access to banned and challenged books for young people nationwide. As the BPL's executive vice president for external affairs, she leads communications and advocacy efforts that amplify that library's mission to defend the right to read and fight censorship. Her work has positioned the BPL at the forefront of the national conversation on access to information and free expression.

LEILA GREEN LITTLE is a rural mom and intellectual freedom advocate. She has been fighting against censorship in public libraries and public school libraries since 2021. In 2022, she and six others sued their county (*Leila Green Little, et al. v. Llano County, et al.*) for banning books. This case was appealed to the Supreme Court of the United States. Little was galvanized to learn more about librarianship, and earned an MLIS degree from the University of North Texas in 2024.

ANNE MANGANO is the coordinator of the Collection Services Department at the Iowa City Public Library. Serving in this position since 2013, she oversees the development, maintenance, and organization of the library's collection.

MAX PRIME is the director of government relations and advocacy at the New York Library Association (NYLA). He leads NYLA's statewide advocacy efforts in pursuit of increased state aid for libraries, as well as legislative initiatives intended to protect and empower New York's library community. Prior to his time at the NYLA, Prime worked in the district offices of several members of the U.S. House of Representatives and earned an MA degree in teaching from Union Graduate College.

KATHERINE ROTH is the copyright librarian at Chapman University in Orange, California. She is especially interested in how copyright shows up in everyday teaching, publishing, and creative work. Her goal is to make intellectual property issues easier to understand and more approachable in both academic and everyday life.

ERIC STROSHANE worked in public, special, and academic libraries for twenty years before joining ALA's Office for Intellectual Freedom (OIF). As OIF's assistant director for member services, he provides education, advocacy, and confidential support for defending the freedom to read. He maintains the Book Résumés website, curates a weekly news compilation for ALA's Intellectual Freedom blog, and writes ALA's annual publication *The Book Report: Titles Targeted for Censorship*. Stroshane is a former president of the Mountain Plains Library Association, and a former news editor of the *Journal of Intellectual Freedom and Privacy*. He presents nationwide on intellectual freedom and the dangers of censorship.

SANTANA TAPIA is the director of programs for the Drag Story Hour Bay Area, where she champions literacy, inclusivity, and joy through innovative programming that brings drag artists into libraries, schools, and community spaces. A dynamic cultural worker and storyteller, she has dedicated her career to uplifting trans and queer voices and creating transformative spaces for children and families. Tapia's leadership has positioned her as a vital advocate for equity in literacy and the arts.

MARCELLUS TURNER is an active librarian and industry veteran with over fifteen years of experience as a CEO and executive director at libraries across the country, including the Charlotte Mecklenburg Library and the Seattle Public Library. His leadership has included experiences focused on intellectual freedom and equity of access.

REBECCA WEBER has held different roles at Oklahoma State University since 2015, including professor and librarian. Her research interests include the intersection of disability and children's or young adult literature and the impact of librarianship on the student experience.

Index

INDEX

J

K

L